Hayward Gallery
on the South Bank · London

Be inspired
Join the Hayward

By becoming a Hayward member, you form a closer relationship with what *The Guardian* **calls '...***one of the country's most inspiring public art galleries***'.**

You also receive a year of special benefits, including:

- free unlimited entry to Hayward exhibitions
- invitations to private views
- discounts at the Hayward Gallery Shop, Books etc. and Aroma Cafe
- regular information on forthcoming exhibitions and much more.

There are three levels of membership from which to choose:

Hayward *Independent* £20
(for people 25 years old and under and concessions)

Hayward *Explorer* £40

Hayward *Pioneer* £95

Join now and see the following Hayward exhibitions for **free**:

Objects of Desire:
The Modern Still Life
until 4 January 1998

Francis Bacon:
The Human Body

Henri Cartier-Bresson:
Europeans
5 February - 5 April 1998

Anish Kapoor
30 April - 14 June 1998

Bruce Nauman
16 July - 6 September 1998

For full details of the many benefits available to Hayward members, telephone **0171 450 2009**

sbc

ENO

Mozart

THE MAGIC FLUTE

'A joy every inch of the way'
Daily Express

November 22 | 25 | 29
December 4 | 6
January 14 | 16 | 21
23 | 27 | 31
February 5 | 12 at 7.30pm
November 29 and
December 6 at 2.30pm

Tickets from £5

Over 50% of all seats
are £25 or less

English National Opera
at the London Coliseum
St Martin's Lane, WC2

Box Office
0171 632 8300
24 hours

Photo by Bert Loewenherz | Registered Charity No. 257210

Funded by
THE
ARTS
COUNCIL
OF ENGLAND

EN O

English National Opera

Winter–Spring 97|98

Eugene Onegin
Tchaikovsky

The Magic Flute
Mozart

The Elixir of Love*
Donizetti

Xerxes
Handel

The Tales of Hoffmann*
Offenbach

La bohème
Puccini

Sung in English
*New Production

Rosa Mannion as Giulietta in The Tales of Hoffmann
Image by Andy Wraile | Registered Charity No. 257210

Tickets from £5

English National Opera
at the London Coliseum
St Martin's Lane, WC2

For a copy of our free
season brochure call
the Box Office on
0171 632 8300

GRANTA 60, WINTER 1997

EDITOR Ian Jack
DEPUTY EDITOR Robert Winder
MANAGING EDITOR Karen Whitfield
EDITORIAL ASSISTANT Sophie Harrison

CONTRIBUTING EDITORS Neil Belton, Pete de Bolla, Frances Coady,
Ursula Doyle, Will Hobson, Liz Jobey, Blake Morrison, Andrew O'Hagan

Granta, 2–3 Hanover Yard, Noel Road, London N1 8BE
TEL (0171) 704 9776, FAX (0171) 704 0474
SUBSCRIPTIONS (0171) 704 0470

FINANCE Geoffrey Gordon
ASSOCIATE PUBLISHER Sally Lewis
SALES David Hooper
PUBLICITY Gail Lynch, Rebecca Linsley
SUBSCRIPTIONS John Kirkby, Mark Williams
PUBLISHING ASSISTANT Jack Arthurs
TO ADVERTISE CONTACT Jenny Shramenko 0171 704 9776

Granta US, 1755 Broadway, 5th Floor, New York, NY 10019-3780, USA

PUBLISHER Rea S. Hederman

SUBSCRIPTION DETAILS: a one-year subscription (four issues) costs £24.95 (UK),
£32.95 (rest of Europe) and £39.95 (rest of the world).

Granta is printed in the United States of America. The paper used in this publication
meets the minimum requirements of American National Standard for Information
Sciences—Permanence of Paper for Printed Library Materials, ANSI Z39.48-1984. ∞

Cover design by The Senate
Cover photographs: Science Photo Library and Getty Images

ISBN 0 903141 14 0

COLM TÓIBÍN
The STORY of the NIGHT
'A beautiful, fascinating novel. It is a thriller, a love story and much more ... his best book yet' Roddy Doyle
Now in paperback PICADOR

"This magazine is flush with tight smart writing"

Literary Review, edited by Auberon Waugh, is packed with witty and informative articles and is indispensible reading for those who wish to keep up with what is happening in the world of letters, especially for those with insufficient time to read everything. Its contributors include well-known writers and journalists such as A S Byatt, Julian Barnes, Beryl Bainbridge, Antonia Fraser, Dava Sobel, Hugh Trevor-Roper, Jan Morris and Christopher Hitchens.

"Literary Review is extremely informative, wonderfully well written and altogether enjoyable. It is my favourite monthly magazine." MURIEL SPARK

"A delightful magazine that manages to capture the extraordinary character of the editor, Auberon Waugh." JOHN WELLS

15 BRILLIANT ISSUES DELIVERED TO YOUR DOOR LONG BEFORE ANY APPEAR IN THE NEWSAGENTS

SUBSCRIBE NOW AND GET 15 ISSUES FOR THE PRICE OF TWELVE

❏ UK £26   ❏ EUROPE AIR £32   ❏ USA & CANADA AIRSPEED US$60/£36   ❏ ELSEWHERE AIR £50

Please start my special rate 15-month subscription to *Literary Review* with the next published issue.

❏ I enclose a cheque for $/£ _____ (payable to *Literary Review*)

❏ Please debit my VISA/MASTERCARD/AMEX/SWITCH/DELTA card £ _____ (billed in sterling)

Card no ☐☐☐☐☐☐☐☐☐☐☐☐☐☐☐☐☐☐☐☐ Expiry date: ☐☐/☐☐ Issue no. (Switch only) ☐☐

Card holder's name: _____ Signature: _____ Date: _____

Recipients name: _____ Tel: _____

Address: _____

_____

_____ Postcode: _____ Country: _____

(If the card holder's address is different from above, please provide details)

❏ Please tick this box if you would prefer not to receive occasional mailings from compatible organisations

GRNT 12/97

Please return form (Freepost within UK) to: Literary Review Subs, FREEPOST 39 (WD 2983), London W1E 5HU England
Credit Card Hotline: Tel: 0171 734 3555, Fax: 0171 287 4767

U N B E L I E V A B L E

GRANTA

IAN JACK
THOSE WHO FELT
DIFFERENTLY

PICTURES BY PETER MARLOW

The last day of August, a Sunday, eight in the morning. Like many people in Britain, I was asleep. The bedside radio came on. A solemn voice, a plain sentence or two, the tune of 'God Save the Queen' played at its most mournful pitch. (There are two versions of the British national anthem kept at every radio station: solemn and triumphant.)

'Did you hear that?' said my partner, who was waking beside me.

I had. The BBC had done a fine job on our slumbering reflexes. The news was more than merely important or shocking—a plane crash, an IRA bomb. Its delivery evoked feelings more awkward than sadness and surprise. The national memory was being awoken; the story that the nation tells about itself. And because the national memory has become increasingly blurred and contested, it was interesting to discover the old version still alive in oneself, to realize how much of it one knew and felt bound up with. Reflexively, I thought of the pre-war prime minister Neville Chamberlain and his tight little speech on the radio on another Sunday morning—in September, 1939—which disclosed that Britain was at war with Germany: 'I am speaking to you from the cabinet room at Number Ten Downing Street.' It was ridiculous to think of this. It happened six years before I was born; and Britain, on 31 August 1997, was not at war with Germany, with anyone (though for a day or two the enemy was identified as freelance photographers, helpfully known by a foreign word, the paparazzi). But the happenings that come into the category of supreme national moments have a grammar of their own, literally so. The BBC announcer usually said, 'You're listening to BBC Radio 4,' but that morning he said, 'This is the BBC,' and with that small reversion from modern, market-minded informality to old-fashioned authority so the death of the Princess of Wales became linked to Mr Chamberlain, air raids on the Ruhr (six of our aircraft are missing), the conquest of Everest, the Falklands War.

Or at least it did in my half-awake mind, not that I noticed the reason at the time. My partner said: 'I feel so sorry for those poor boys.'

We went downstairs and watched television. Eventually the prime minister, Tony Blair, came on and spoke for the first time of 'the People's Princess'. Some journalists later wrote that the phrase had been invented for the occasion by Blair's press secretary (which may well be true, his press secretary having previously worked in tabloid newspapers), but at the time it seemed to fall quite naturally in his statement, in which emotion seemed to battle with articulacy. I write 'seemed' but that does not mean I doubted his sincerity; it was just that, having followed his election campaign, I knew how well he could deploy sincerity in his well-considered outbreaks of spontaneity.

We had lunch. My partner explained to our five-year-old daughter that the princess had died. Our daughter asked: 'Is that the woman you said was awful?' We wondered where we should take the children in the afternoon. The television had pictures of people outside Buckingham Palace, some of them crying. We remembered that the pond in St James's Park had ducks, and that this part of London—central, royal, institutional London—can be enjoyed by the people who live in London as well as by the tourists who have claimed it and made it their own. Also, we were curious—who were these people who had gone to the palace?—but I do not think coldly inquisitive. We were perhaps just a little sad.

We drove. The traffic was thick. The Mall had been closed to all but pedestrians. We parked the car near the monument to the Duke of York and walked down the steps and into the Mall. Whenever I drive down this avenue—always in a car or a taxi; nothing so vulgar as a bus route pollutes it—I am always surprised to see Buckingham Palace, the memorial to Queen Victoria, the Horse Guards Parade, the minor palaces and mansions, the statues of explorers, the friezes of army regiments, the sentry boxes, the immobile sentries in scarlet uniforms and black bearskin hats. My surprise is that I live in the same city, so close to this fabled history which in my childhood looked so grand and far away and could only be represented in my home with model soldiers. And yet (another surprise when one investigates it) the setting is not so very historical. There are people still alive who can remember this imperial cityscape under construction. My own father, had he lived in London at that time, could have watched as a boy as masons chiselled the Portland stone of the new façade to Buckingham Palace (finished in 1913),

11

or the bronze statue to Captain Cook (1914) was unveiled, or Admiralty Arch (1910) had its keystones put in place. He could have been there on the day in 1911 when King George V stood beside the new Queen Victoria Memorial and tapped its designer on the shoulder with a sword, transforming him into a knight: Sir Thomas Brock. And then this small boy, my father, could have turned and walked down the new Mall, with its plane trees, flagpoles and galleon-topped lamp-posts, which was widened to make a processional route and pushed through to Trafalgar Square in the same year.

This, then, is a twentieth-century stage, post-Victorian, the whole planned as a tribute to the dead queen; as traditional and historic as the machine-gun or an early Mercedes.

We did not go to the palace directly. We crossed the Mall and went into the park. How would I describe the situation here? I would say it was normal. The afternoon was fine. Tourists strolled around the lake, young people with backpacks scattered bread for the ducks. For a time, our children stood on the bridge and threw pebbles into the water. A pair of handsome swans and some cygnets slid by. Then, as we lay on the grass, I noticed a little black girl in a bed of roses. She had scissors in her right hand and a small bundle of rose blooms in her left. She was snipping more blooms cleanly and quietly.

I went across to her.

'You know you shouldn't be doing that, don't you?'

'Yes,' she said, 'I know.' Her scissors went on snipping.

A quandary for the civic-minded. She might have a father, or several tough brothers, out of sight behind a tree. I summoned some courage.

'Well, don't do it then.'

She skipped off up the slope to the Mall, where she ran alongside the people who were walking towards the palace and looked up into their faces and offered her flowers. As nobody took them, money may have been involved. She was too far away to hear.

We saw her again among the crowd—then still small—which had gathered in front of the palace railings. She was with a woman, probably her mother, who looked like a Somali. The roses had gone; they must have been on the pile, but the crowd was too thick in front of the flowers to see. The Somali woman stood reverently, I thought, near a mounted policeman who was guiding the flower-bringers to a route which ran along the front of the railings to the place where their flowers could be left. People were arriving with bunches every couple of minutes. The people without flowers looked at these people with flowers. They were the spectacle; there was nothing much else to see. The palace yard was empty apart from the sentries, who occasionally stamped and banged their rifles down and picked them up again, and the palace as usual presented its blank, mysterious face to the world. If the Queen and her family had been at home, it would have looked the same—she does not come to the windows and wave, toodle-oo—but in any case the Queen and her family were on their Scottish holidays in Balmoral.

Further off, behind the Victoria Memorial, hotdog and ice-cream sellers and television crews had parked their vans. On the memorial itself, men in T-shirts had begun to set up scaffolding for television cameras, their steel tubes rattling on the marble, of which the memorial contains 2,300 tons. We climbed the steps towards Queen Victoria, who is seated, but measures thirteen feet high, and is surrounded by allegorical figures. Above her, winged VICTORY with COURAGE and CONSTANCY at Victory's feet. Beside her, TRUTH facing south, JUSTICE north, and CHARITY west. The queen herself faces east, away from the palace and down the Mall towards her city, her empire, her people.

I had never been here before. It was fascinating; how unlikely it was that one small woman in one small country could represent so much universal principle, at least in the eyes of Sir Thomas Brock. People leaned in the sun on the memorial's balconies and, though I overheard one or two quiet conversations about the dead princess, their behaviour suggested attitudes like our own. They licked ice cream. They were perhaps a little sad, but mainly they seemed curious. Later on television we would all be described as mourners. Meanwhile, pole by pole, the television platforms rose up towards CHARITY and the two marble children she clutched at her knee.

We walked back down the Mall. I noticed that many people going the other way and carrying flowers were black or brown,

Africans and African Caribbeans, Asians. I remembered how sixteen years before I had been a reporter at the princess's wedding and how, walking the processional route between the palace and St Paul's, I had seen very few black faces in the crowds. I now remembered writing that, and also a remark about the national anthem being a rotten tune, which had been circled on the galley proofs by the paper's editor with a line drawn to his note in the margin: *No, a jolly good tune in my opinion!*

It seemed long ago; the post-war height of the monarchy's popularity, when newspapers thought royalty could do no wrong and there was a frenzy of good wishes in the streets. We drove home through a city which had changed since then, and (I thought, that day) in some ways for the better.

Later that night the telephone rang. It was a friend who edits a weekly magazine. Could I write 2,500 words on Diana by the next evening?

'But I don't know anything about her,' I said. 'What could I write about?'

'You know—Diana the Icon,' he said.

'The Icon? How do you mean?'

'You know—the clothes, the busted marriage, bulimia, landmines, Aids, all those things. What she meant to us all.'

No, I said, I didn't really think I could.

'Look at it another way,' he said, 'it's worth the price of a new kitchen.'

A new kitchen! Even cheap ones, I thought, came in at about £6,000. And perhaps my friend was thinking bigger than that, somewhere up in the Smallbone range.

A kitchen for 2,500 words. In such small ways does an event become a phenomenon.

September was not a good month for those who imagined that human society is, or might one day be, governed by reason. After the People's Princess came the People's Mall, the People's Funeral, the People's Earl (Spencer), the People's Europe, the People's Television Channel (BBC1), all of them promoted and discussed without irony. In London, a man applied to the International Star Registry to have a star in the Andromeda constellation named 'Diana—the People's Princess' (another application wanted a star in the Lyra constellation named 'Dodi and Diana—Eternally Loved'). The leader of the Conservative Party, William Hague, suggested that Heathrow Airport be renamed Diana Airport. The Chancellor of the Exchequer, Gordon Brown, was said to be seriously considering a proposal that the August Bank Holiday be renamed Diana Day. Letters to newspapers made other suggestions for the renaming of hospitals and coins, for statues, for fountains, for special stamps. Three foreign tourists were sentenced to jail for taking old teddy bears from the tributes to the princess which had been heaped on various pavements (none in fact served their sentences, but one was punched by an onlooker on leaving the court). The wholesale price of flowers rose by twenty-five per cent in the London markets, despite special shipments from the polythene growing-tunnels of Holland, Israel, Africa and South America. By 9 September, 10,000 tons of them had been piled outside Buckingham Palace and Kensington Palace. Estimates of the number of individual blooms reached 50 million. Estimates of the total weight of tributes reached 15,000 tons, if cards, bottles of champagne, trinkets, teddy bears and items of crockery bearing Diana's picture were included. Public health officers estimated that the temperature inside these masses of vegetation, cellophane and paper could be 180 degrees Fahrenheit. People waited for up to eight hours to sign the books of condolence and the queue in the Mall sometimes stretched for three-quarters of a mile. As of 15 September, Buckingham Palace had received 500,000 letters and 580,000 e-mail messages of sympathy. By 30 September, three million CDs of Elton John singing the song that he had sung at the funeral had been sold in the United Kingdom (21 million copies had been pressed worldwide; the profits went to charity). Ten new or revised books about the princess had been published (two of them headed the lists of hardback and paperback best-sellers). T-shirts, tea towels, videos, 'antique bronzed' busts, commemorative plates and medals were also doing well. The press-clippings agency, Durrants, said that the coverage in the world's magazines and newspapers by far exceeded that generated by any other event, anywhere in the world, at any time in history.

Could grief for one woman have caused all this? We were told so, and it is true that personal grief can have odd, rippling effects: Queen Victoria, mourning her husband, set a fashion for black dress in Britain that was copied throughout Europe. This, on the other hand, was not the replication of clothes but a multiplication of tears. People on television and in the newspapers said that they grieved more for the Princess of Wales than they had for their wives or husbands. It seemed unbelievable, and yet for a time it was difficult in Britain to question it. There was an oppression of grief. People had not only to grieve, they had to be seen to grieve, and in the most pictorial way, by hugging and kissing. The Queen and her family were not seen to grieve enough. They were told to grieve more, and not only by tabloid newspapers (*Show us you care, Ma'am!*). *The Times* told her that she went against the public mood at her peril. The *Independent* said that it would welcome the sight of the Royal Family in tears and holding on to one another on the steps of Westminster Abbey. The argument became metaphorical, sociological, psychological and political. 'New Labour', a piece of highly-successful political rebranding invented by marketeers, spoke for 'New Britain'. New Britain was the princess, the prime minister, flowers, compassion and the therapeutic benefits of touching and crying—MODERNITY, if the princess gets a memorial like Victoria. Old Britain was the Queen, her son and heir, pensioners with 'stiff upper lips', reticence and the neurosis brought about by repression—HISTORY on the same memorial. As a depiction of 60 million individuals, it was as accurate as Mrs Miniver had been in 1942 or Swinging London in 1966; but it became accepted wisdom that the nation had crossed some kind of emotional fault line.

Two questions arose. Outside the personal sorrow of those who knew the princess, what kind of grief were people feeling? And how many people were feeling it? To judge the quality of other people's grief may be a risky enterprise, but my guess about the first is this: that it was recreational grieving ('look-at-me grief' was how the writer Julian Barnes described it), that it was enjoyable, that it promoted the griever from the audience to an on-stage part in the final act of the opera, which lasted six days. The dead heroine had provided the most marvellous story, and the grief of her spectators may have been genuine in the sense of unfaked. But it was grief with the pain removed, grief-lite. When people telephoned each other that Sunday morning, they spoke eagerly—'Have you heard that . . . ?'—and not with the dread— 'How can I tell him that . . . ?'—familiar to bearers of seriously wounding news, which the hearer may recover from only in months or years or sometimes never at all. It was possible, after all, for the readers of Dickens to weep at the death of Little Nell, whom they too felt they knew.

In September, in the week that separated her death from her funeral, it was sacrilege to talk openly in this way. I don't think I exaggerate this. The public mood, as relayed and reinforced by the media, became vindictive towards dissension. To be sceptical was to be unfeeling. Organizations which thought that life might go on as normal, as the Scottish football authorities did with an international match that was to be played on the same day (though not at the same time) as the funeral, became enemies of this thing, the public mood. Politicians and newspapers pilloried them and their ways were corrected. And yet privately—or so it seemed to me—it was difficult to meet people who fully shared the emotion that we were meant to feel. Letters began to appear in a few newspapers which suggested another kind of community; the angry, puzzled and beleaguered, the people who were not quite sad enough. How many of them were there—were we? No reliable quantification can exist. In Britain, 31 million people watched the funeral on television, about half the population, but watching (as I did) and feeling tearful (as I did) is no indicator of grief. Still, it was the largest audience that British television has ever had. According to the BBC, the next largest—30 million—was for an episode of the soap, *EastEnders*, in which Angie the barmaid served her divorce papers on Dirty Den.

I interviewed nine people who felt differently. It would be a shame if, in history, the variety of individual feeling at this time was buried under a large monolith called GRIEF; as true and as false as the depiction of the British Empire's guiding principles on the monument to Queen Victoria. The interviews begin overleaf.

Maggie Winkworth

A counselling psychologist, she wrote to the Guardian in response to a piece which had attacked 'knee-jerk cynicism' about the mourning from members of the 'Old Left'.

I'm a light sleeper and I often listen to the BBC World Service in the early hours. I heard the earliest reports which said that Dodi was dead and Diana was injured and my first reaction was: God, we're going to have a year of this grieving princess. I didn't dislike her. Good for her, I'd thought when I looked at the pictures. Obviously, she's having a lovely sexy summer. She was beginning to look sexy—the fuller belly, the flat hair. Then when I heard that she was dead I thought: Oh God, this is going to go on and on and I am going to have to keep my head down. Of course, my feelings weren't entirely that. There was the horror of the smash, the children left without a mother. And I grieved for her as the eight-year-old girl whose parents had separated, whose mother left her. It's a story I deal with all the time in my work and I realize it triggered a lot of that in lots of people.

But then fairly soon back came the Marxist stuff I'd known in the 1960s and '70s. I was on the fringes of a Marxist group then. False Consciousness—two words I haven't heard anyone utter in twenty years—and yet that is what it was. I'd call it mass hysteria, a kind of mania. You saw the power of the crowd. To me, those pictures of mounds of flowers were quite repulsive. I felt *scared* when I saw all those flowers. It seemed a kind of floral fascism . . . a country patrolled by the grief police. I was deeply rattled by it.

Yes, I remember where I was when Kennedy died. I remember it because I was eight and a half months pregnant, having been raped as an eighteen-year-old. The baby was adopted. Somewhere I have a thirty-three-year-old daughter. So when Diana died I remembered Kennedy dying, and remembering Kennedy dying I remember the rape, the pregnancy and the baby. So that was the grief that was triggered in me by Diana's death, which had absolutely nothing to do with Kennedy or Diana as people. 'Defining moments' can have more complicated effects than people imagine.

Diana was very good at being a celebrity. But if she'd had a harelip, none of this would ever have happened. I don't mean to be cruel, but can you deny that truth?

in
ire

nd
es,
lso
he
no
n,
ts
we
ve
ot-
ia-

cause for grief?

It was reported this week that the gap between rich and poor in this country continues to widen. You don't have to be a raging Marxist to believe that it is the duty of a compassionate state, and not a parasitic aristocracy, to direct us into effective ways of redistributing wealth.
Maggie Winkworth.
46 Quick Road,
London W4 2BU.

Peter Ghosh

A historian at St Anne's College, Oxford, he wrote to the Independent to protest about the media's lack of critical detachment in their coverage of 'a soap opera which was prematurely interrupted before the ratings began to fall'.

I'm as happy as the next man to look at pictures of Diana in leopard-skin swimsuits, but there was plainly media manipulation here on a massive scale. OK, there was a pre-existing constituency—the coverage didn't come out of a vacuum, there were people who liked to read about her—and it was only fair to please it. But on every TV channel! The total deployment of the media in one direction! You know, BBC2 only reverted to normal schedules in the evening because of audience protest. Ninety-eight out of every hundred calls to the BBC about its coverage complained at the extent of it. I don't want to exaggerate this, but I think what happened in Britain between her death and the funeral provided just an inkling of what East Germany must have been like when it was the German Democratic Republic. Let me give tiny examples. A friend of mine who's keen on music made the trip to London to hear Poulenc's *Gloria* done at the Proms. You don't often get the chance to hear it performed. But when he got there they'd changed the programme at the last minute to Fauré's *Requiem* as, I quote, 'a mark of respect'. Then on the day of the funeral they closed the Bodleian Library—another mark of respect. Who told them to? Why? Who makes these decisions?

There were fantastic overestimates about the number of people who would turn out for her funeral. The media said that five or six million would come, when the figure turned out to be somewhere between one and two million. I think it was to a very large extent a metropolitan phenomenon. A lot of people present were tourists—it was a very superior tourist experience.

We kept being told that the country was united, which it was in the sense that we were all watching the same television programme. But in any other sense—that divisions of class and race were being healed, for example— well it's crap, obviously. Among people I know in Oxford, mine was the common reaction. I felt sorry for her sons.

Sir: *The Independent* appears to
have forgotten its original policy of
relegating royal affairs to the inside
pages. Was it so entirely foolish?
The media generally were bound to
be distraught at the loss of a goose
that had laid so many golden eggs
but surely we could have asked for
a degree more critical detachment
from you?

After all, what is this fuss about?
"Palace and people"? It's not a
credible social description of
anything found outside Grimm's

Elizabeth Stern

A student of piano accompaniment at the Guildhall School of Music, in London, she wrote to the Guardian about the 'delusion' of people who felt they were suffering real grief.

I heard it several times, people saying: 'Oh, it was just like a member of my family dying.' What on earth were these people talking about? My parents died in February. They were also abroad, and they were also killed in a car smash, so the two events were quite similar. What happened to me was that a policeman knocked on my door about six one evening, about twenty-four hours after the accident. We still don't quite know how it happened. My parents were on holiday in Florida and my dad was driving and he seems to have gone too far over to the right and then over-corrected the steering and hit a car coming the other way. Two people died in that car also. The Foreign Office and the insurance company told us different things. It took two and a half weeks—not six hours [as was the case with Diana]—to have their bodies flown home. My father was sixty-one and my mother fifty-seven and they were full of life—my parents loved life. I think I had a delayed reaction for about five months. I thought I'd got over my initial shock and grief and was beginning to feel fine again. Now I can't see the process ending.

What I feel and what those crowds outside the palaces felt seem completely unrelated. Flowers, cards, teddy bears—you don't send condolence letters to the person who's died, for heaven's sake! People wanted to feel grief so that they could feel part of it all. Fine. But they shouldn't imagine they were grieving. When I was on the Tube and I saw all those women with flowers in their arms on their way to Buckingham Palace, I just wanted to go up and shake them. One of my friends spent fifty pounds on flowers and sent them to the palace. And yet she didn't buy flowers for me when my own parents died. I find it hard to speak to her. My brother, who's a doctor, feels the same as I do, and so do all his colleagues. During the minute's silence one of the doctors at his hospital carried on working—somebody had to—and the nurses there actually shouted at him to stop. It was unbelievable.

I only watched a few seconds of the funeral and then I went to the park and read. I felt very alone. I felt everybody else had gone mad. I felt angry.

SIX months ago, my middle-aged parents were both killed in a car accident whilst on holiday in Florida. Their deaths were as sudden and shocking as Diana's. I have heard and read that many members of the public believe themselves to be grieving for Diana as much as for a member of their own families. They are vastly deluded by equating the loss of those who are

John Bradshaw

A public relations man who specializes in 'crisis management', he lives in a loft above a farm near Stratford-upon-Avon, where he keeps cats and a rare breed of hens–Cochins. He is divorced. His letter to The Times drew eighty-four letters in response, almost all in passionate agreement.

I was in bed when I heard this sepulchral voice on the radio and when I realized it wasn't the Queen Mum who'd died, my first thought was that she'd killed herself. Well, I was immensely sad, to the brink of tears I'd say. When I heard Tony Blair later, I have to say that my eyes did moisten. It was almost a classic tragedy, she'd been living her life in such a way that somehow this wasn't a surprise. It was as if her death had been ordained by the gods. So I found it tragic. But I didn't expect the world to stop turning. I got irritated pretty quickly by the repetitive nature of the BBC's coverage. The same people were saying the same things again and again. When by Tuesday morning they'd got the Mayor of Northampton saying the same thing over again, I thought they'd cast the net wide enough.

I signed the book of condolence by e-mail and sent a message to the Prince of Wales. I quite like the bloke. He seems a reasonable egg. Like me, he's interested in rare breeds and he shoots things. Also like me, he's divorced. I kept trying to imagine how I'd feel if my former wife had died like his had done. I'd be beside myself—there would be a strange mixture of feelings. Likewise, my guess is that there isn't a jilted or divorced woman in the country who didn't identify with Diana.

I'm a Catholic and Catholics have a more participative approach to death. But this thing gave me unease. There was this symbiosis between the object of the media [Diana], the media, and the customers of the media—a great snowball effect. I also have a feeling that there was a piece of demography at work here, that it was C1, C2 and D dominated. Then the touchy-feely fascists got to work and it began to seem that not to feel unqualified grief was somehow a heresy. I thought: I don't fit in with this. I noticed that I was having to be careful in the way that I opened conversations, even with people I thought I knew quite well. One needed to be tentative. 'Am I safe here? Can I say what I feel?' So I'd say something neutral like: 'Um, rum business this,' and if they said: 'Going on a bit isn't it?' then I felt safe to carry on. But if they said: 'Yes, what a terrible tragedy!' then I knew I had to shut up. I felt as though we were like an underground movement—the Jacobites, the Maquis. There were times when I felt that this wasn't my country any more. I felt alienated—by the restriction of opinion as well as by the Latin American nature of the event.

From Mr J. E. Bradshaw

Sir, To me the death of Diana, Princess of Wales, was unbearably tragic, her funeral intensely moving. But I have also found the behaviour of the British public and media unbearable. The response and its coverage were totally excessive, the style for the most part mawkish, vulgar, self-indulgent and hysterical. And the conclusion that we are at some kind of national turning-point is presumptuous arrogance.

The deployment of these excesses as an excuse to introduce ill-considered

Janet Tinbergen

A music teacher who plays the cello and piano, she lives alone on the fringes of Oxford. She wrote to the Independent because she was 'appalled by the injustice' of public demands that the Queen should be seen to grieve.

I'm a republican, perhaps because I'm from a Dutch family and the Dutch are less infected by royalty-worship. But I felt for the Queen. I thought: the poor woman, she's done her best for fifty years. It was the equivalent for me of all the pupils I've taught for thirty years turning round and saying I'd given them nothing, that they hated music. It seemed so unkind, so lacking in imagination. I think there are quite a lot of people like me—people who disapprove of the monarchy as an institution but can feel for the monarch as a human being. Yes, I hope this country will become a republic, but I'd hate to see it happen like this—people suddenly turning round and throwing the Queen's life's work in her face. Hysterical is the word I'd use about the public mood if I wanted to be rude. I began to wonder about my own reactions. I thought—oh, everybody else seems to be feeling like this, perhaps I'd better feel this way too.

Has Britain changed? I always tell this story. When I was at school—it was a private girl's day school—I remember we had to go through this narrow door between the corridors. One day, I must have been nine or ten, I was about to go through this door when I saw a woman cleaner about to go through from the other side. So I stepped back to allow her through. But she also stepped back so that I could go through first. I was nine or ten, she was a grown woman. I was middle-class and she wasn't. I don't think you'd get that kind of deference today. I hope not.

Sir: For all my adult life I have been in favour of this country becoming a republic. This has not stopped me also being in favour of fairness, and I have been appalled by the injustice of the public attitude to the Royal Family, particularly the Queen, during the last week.

Whatever the grief felt by the public, it can only have been a fraction of that felt by two young boys losing their mother in such traumatic circumstances. Of course the Queen's first priority was to

Ron Press

A retired chemical engineer, he lives alone in the suburbs of Bristol. He wrote to the Guardian.

I come from South Africa and I've worked for the ANC for most of my adult life. That's why I had to leave. I was involved in the treason trials in the 1950s and then I was confined by the government to the town where I lived. My wife was schizophrenic and we had a small daughter. I decided to leave and we came to Britain in 1962.

People are very complex. I don't know how much they're governed by reason or unreason. And it's very difficult to get into the minds of so-called ordinary people. Remember how we used to talk about the hysteria of China, Mao and his *Little Red Book*? But now it's everywhere—the same fever and unreality. I felt it was horribly demeaning, as if people were saying: 'I have no light in my soul, I can only bathe in the reflected light of others.' And you can't just blame the media. The media bangs the drum, but the drum's got to be there to bang. That week [after Diana died] my daughter went to a friend of hers who'd organized a wake for the princess—you know, drinking and crying and so on. Her husband just shrugged his shoulders—he didn't understand it either. Diana was somebody they didn't know, had never met. But the country was in a funny mood, you had to be a bit careful what you said. I remember in South Africa in 1954 or '55 there were black riots in Port Elizabeth and two white nuns got killed. It was bad, and I went to see an ANC official to see if he could do anything about it. He said: 'Ron, when the people are like that, you put your head down.' They're too polite to beat you up in Britain, but you got the same sort of feeling. In Germany, remember, they couldn't criticize Hitler, not because they were scared of Hitler in person, but because of what the neighbours might say.

The ANC were nice people, and I had great friends among them. It was a rational, reasonable organization. But I know that when Nelson Mandela dies, it'll be the same. Wailing in the streets, tears. OK, Nelson's a good bloke and a clever politician, but frankly I feel the same way about him—he's only one man and I think unreasonable bowing-down is very anti-democratic.

I suppose my attitudes come from my own history. My family were working-class who had migrated from England. They had no heroes. And I'm Jewish. The wandering Jew who has become a non-Jew. I've never had a god with a capital G, nor anyone like a god in science or politics, the things that matter to me—no single person who epitomized everything that was important.

28

Isabel Hilton

*A writer and broadcaster, she wrote a column in the Guardian two days after
Diana died which attacked the media's fevered response.*

We were in Argyll on holiday, it was eight-thirty in the morning and I was
in the bedroom when Neil [her husband] called up from downstairs that
Diana had been killed in a car crash. I shouted back. I don't know if I
should say what I said. It was just a flip thing. OK, I said: 'Did the Queen
fix the brakes?' But of course I was shocked. I thought, as everyone did,
'Oh, those poor children.' And then I was just extremely curious about
what had happened and how. We were driving home to London that day so
we listened to the car radio for about ten hours. By the time they got to the
fashion editor of *Vogue* talking about Diana's clothes sense I was ready to
scream. For all the size of the coverage there was very little journalism in it.
Certain basic facts weren't there—the name of the driver, for instance, or at
least for several hours that a fourth person in the car had survived. It was a
tabloid response. 'How do you feel?' was the favourite question.

I went down to Buckingham Palace a couple of times that week as a
reporter. On the Wednesday, I certainly picked up the mood of 'Where are
they?' about the royal family. I heard somebody say: 'There's that poor girl
lying all by herself' [her body was in St James's Palace]. There was a kind of
vengeful glee. One man said: 'It's her revenge on them.' You felt that if a
powerful demagogue had arisen from the crowd, they would have stormed
the palace gates. I suppose it was largely a tabloid crowd, and I was struck
by the general kitsch of it—the cards, the teddy bears. It reminded you of
religious parades in a place like Mexico, and I think it showed our
tremendous need for religiosity, if not religion. People seemed to be
inventing religious ritual on the hoof. An Argentinian journalist friend of
mine was outside Kensington Palace and she said that in the middle of one
night a whole troupe of Arab women came on the scene, ululating. And yet
it was a touching thing—you couldn't help but feel touched by the sheer
weight of emotion around you.

Here were crowds demonstrating the urgent need for institutions that had
failed them—the church, the monarchy. From which the magic has gone.
The Windsors are a stuffy old family and how many people go to church
these days? We desperately wanted a fairy princess. I suppose I'm an
intellectual and emotional republican. Would I march for a republic? No, I
wouldn't march. But we'd be a healthier and more grown-up country
without the monarchy.

Isabel Hilton

. . . .

I T WAS well into the
tenth hour of unbroken,
unrelieved and repeti-
tive Diana coverage that a

Brendan Martin

A trade union consultant, he lives in London. His letter to the Guardian contrasted the space devoted to Diana with 400 deaths in Haiti.

I was in bed. My partner who'd got up before me came into the room and said: 'A terrible thing's happened.' Then she said immediately: 'Don't worry, it's got nothing to do with the kids.' I was shocked. I thought it was very sad. I also thought it was sensational. That day I had to catch a plane to Glasgow, where I spent an afternoon wandering the city in the rain, oblivious to the fuss—in retrospect, blissfully so. Then on the Monday I walked into George Square [in the centre of Glasgow] and found a long queue bending round the corner to sign a book of condolence. And there were flowers and cards. I remember one: TO DI AND DODI. TRUE LOVE AT LAST. YOU'LL BE TOGETHER IN HEAVEN. I read every word in the newspapers on the flight back. Everybody was talking about it—it was a genuine phenomenon—but I began to sense a feeling of exclusion. I felt, contrary to the popular idea that it was 'unifying' the country, that it was actually dividing it. The last straw for me was an e-mail from a friend in Washington [Her message in part: *I was shocked and saddened to learn of Diana's death. So sorry for all of you Brits.* His reply in part: *Actually this is a heterogeneous country and the reaction to her death has been heterogeneous*].

So here I was. I felt excluded and angry and yet I wanted to read about it. The crowds were really feeling something and they shouldn't be denigrated for that, but it seemed to me bizarre, absurd, preposterous that people should fabricate this fantasy around a thirty-six-year-old woman called a princess. My strong sense was that she was a consumer item, and that this was mass-consumption post-mortem, a feeding frenzy partly fuelled by guilt. This was how people defined themselves, how they felt connected to the world, and I felt it was completely pathetic. It made me despair. There was a mood of intolerance that week, an intimidating atmosphere—you felt that you had to be careful in what you said.

But I'm torn. Yes, I found it mawkish and distasteful, but I also thought that I'd like to be part of something like that. Not this, but something else. Perhaps when Nelson Mandela dies—it would have to be the death of somebody who had made a huge difference. I seem to be the kind of person who finds it difficult to share a common experience. Sometimes I think, here I go again, always finding some bloody way to be bloody different. And you must remember I speak as a former Trot[skyist]. I mean: how wrong can you be?

FOLLOWING acres of news-print praising Diana's compassion and concern for victims of injustice, the Guardian buries news of the drowning of 400 poor black Haitians at the foot of page 12 (September 9). The contrast illustrates why some of us in this, thankfully, heterogeneous country have felt it so important to resist, if not the mood, then certainly the dominant messages of the past week.

Ian Hislop

Editor of Private Eye magazine, which in the issues after Diana's death satirized the media's response. Several retail chains and many individual shops refused to sell it. The magazine lost many thousands of sales.

My children came up to the bedroom and said the Teletubbies weren't on the TV, so I knew that something Very Important had happened. I had until four the next afternoon, our deadline, to produce a humorous magazine. It was about as hard as it's got for me, but when I read Monday's papers I knew what my reaction was and what the magazine had to do. The speed with which grief turned into self-righteousness—an angry self-righteousness, perhaps born of guilt—I really hated that. We were witnessing the biggest U-turn in media history, with the press pretending that their behaviour over the past ten years simply hadn't happened.

Then the tabloids decided they would have a go at the Windsor family. One's read a lot about the power of the mob in history, and now I felt: this is how it happens. I mean, you couldn't make it up. Here were people kicking the paparazzi on the one hand, and on the other lining up in their thousands to take pictures of the coffin with their Instamatics. Here were people tut-tutting about invasions of privacy on the one hand, and on the other demanding that the royal family line up and weep for the TV cameras. There was just so much rubbish, so much brain-out-of-window stuff, written and spoken. We kept being told that the crowds showed how Britain had changed, no more stiff upper lip, we were all huggers and weepers now. But how could that be when the most impressive thing about the funeral was two boys walking behind their mother's coffin and *not* crying. I was the same age as Prince Harry [twelve] when my father died. It's not a wonderful age to lose a parent but I didn't cry at my father's funeral because it was fairly important that I didn't—not crying was what was expected of you. And I think of all those people who saw their friends die in the Second World War, and how they coped. How is it possible for people to fall apart when someone they've only seen on the telly dies?

It sometimes seems to me that because we can't bear death, everybody who dies has to be canonized. I remember how Freddie Mercury was deified after he died. He was an icon, a martyr, etc. And yet the truth was he wasn't any of these things. He was a singer in a pop band.

I'm not a republican. As I always say, on balance I'd rather be a disloyal subject than a loyal citizen. Watching Blair that week, you realized what a presidential system would be like. Basically, Blair became king for a week.

The Late Princess Diana
An Apology

IN recent weeks (not to mention the last ten years) we at the Daily Gnome, in common with all other newspapers, may have inadvertently conveyed the impression that the late Princess of Wales was in some way a neurotic, irresponsible and manipulative troublemaker who had repeatedly meddled in political matters that did not concern her and personally embarrassed Her Majesty The Queen by her Mediterranean love-romps with the son of a discredited Egyptian businessman.

We now realise as of Sunday morning that the Princess of Hearts was in fact the most saintly woman who has ever lived, who, with her charitable activities, brought hope

flamingo

JOAN DIDION

the Last thing He wanted

'The technique of writing is, as usual, unique, an incantation
with repetitions and rhythms to entrance the reader, meant to
restore full weight to a language made weightless by misuse...
I should perhaps also mention that I read it twice for pure
delight before reading it for review'
Veronica Horwell, *Guardian*

http://www.harpercollins.co.uk

GRANTA

LINDA GRANT
ARE WE RELATED?

Linda Grant, aged seven, and her mother on the cross-channel ferry to Ostend, 1958

My mother and I are going shopping, as we have done all our lives. 'Now Mum,' I tell her, 'don't start looking at the prices on everything. I'm paying. If you see something you like, try it on. You are the mother of the bride, after all.' At long last one of her two daughters (not me) is getting married.

In recent years my mother has become a poverty shopper; she haunts jumble sales looking for other people's cast-offs. I don't like to think of her trying on someone else's shoes which she does not because she is very poor but because footwear is fixed in her mind at 1970s prices. Everything she sees in the shops seems to cost a fortune. 'You paid £49.99 for a pair of shoes?' she would cry. 'They saw you coming.'

'But Mu-um, that's how much shoes cost these days.'

'Yes, but where do you go looking?'

In my childhood, my mother had aspired far beyond her station to be a world-class shopper. Her role models were Grace Kelly and Princess Margaret, Ava Gardner and Elizabeth Taylor. She acquired crocodile shoes and mink stoles, an eternity ring encrusted with diamonds, handbags in burnished patent leather. In her shut-up flat in Bournemouth were three wardrobes full of beautiful, expensive garments all on wooden or satin hangers, many in their own protective linen bags—a little imitation Chanel suit from the Sixties that came back into fashion every few years; her black Persian broadtail coat with its white mink collar and her initials, RG, sewn in blue silk thread in an italic script on to the hem of the black satin lining, surrounded by a sprig of embroidered roses; her brown mink hat for high days and holidays.

And so today I want the best for her, as she and my father had always wanted the best for us. 'The best that money can buy,' my father always boasted when he bought anything, 'Only show me the best,' he told shopkeepers.

'So we're looking for a dress?' A nice dress. The sales are still raging through the summer's heat, hot shoppers toiling up and down Oxford Street. We should, I think, find something for £60 or £70. 'John Lewis is full of them,' a friend has said. She has an idea of the kind of dress someone's mother would wear, an old biddy's frock, a shapeless floral sack.

'I don't think that's her kind of thing,' I had told her,

39

doubtfully. But then who knew what was left? Could my mother's fashion sense be so far eroded that she would have lost altogether those modes of judgement that saw that something was classic and something else merely frumpy?

'I'm not having a dress, I want a suit,' my mother says as the doors part automatically to admit the three of us, for tagging along is my nephew, her grandson, who also likes to shop.

'OK. A suit. Whatever you like.'

And now we're in the department store, our idea of a second home. My mother has never been much of a nature lover, an outdoors girl. We used to leave the city once, years ago, when we motored out of town in the Humber Hawk, parked in a lay-by, ate cold roast chicken from silver foil, then drove home early so my father could watch the racing and my mother refold her clothes. By the Sixties we considered a day out to be a drive to the new service station on the M6 where we enjoyed a cup of tea as the cars sped along to London below. My mother has never got her hands dirty in wellingtons, bending down among the flower beds to plant her summer perennials. Or put her hands to the oars of a boat or tramped across a ploughed field in the morning frost or breasted any icy waves. She shrinks in fear from sloppy-mouthed dogs and fawning kittens. But show her new improved tights with Lycra! They never had that in my day, she says admiringly on an excursion to Sainsbury's, looking at dose-ball washing liquid.

And no outing can offer more escape from the nightmare of her present reality than shopping for clothes, the easiest means we know of becoming our fantasies and generally cheering ourselves up all round. Who needs the psychiatrist's couch when you have shopping? Who needs Prozac?

Through the handbags, gloves and scarves and utilitarian umbrellas. Not a glance at fabrics and patterns for neither my mother nor I have ever run up our own frocks at the sewing machine, shop-bought *always* being superior to home-made in our book. Why do an amateur job when you could get in a professional?

Up the escalators to the first floor where the land of dreams lies all around us, suits and dresses and coats and skirts and jackets. And where to begin? How to start? But my mother has started already.

At once a sale rack has caught her eye with three or four short navy wool crêpe jackets with nipped-in waists, the lapels and slanted pockets edged in white, three mock mother-of-pearl buttons to do it up. My mother says she thinks she is a size twelve. She tries the jacket on right then and there and it takes fifty years off her. She stands in front of the mirror as Forties Miss, dashing about London in the Blitz, on her way to her job in Top Ops. She turns to us, radiant. 'What do you think?'

'Perfect.' The sleeves are too long, but this is a small matter. We will summon the seamstress and she will take them up, her mouth full of pins. As my mother folds the sleeves under I steal a covert look at the price tag. The jacket is reduced to £49.99, and this, in anybody's book, is a bargain.

'Now I need a skirt and blouse. I've got to match the navy.'

She disappears between the rails and I am anxious for it is not hard to lose sight of her, she has shrunk so in recent years. Five feet two all my life but I doubt if she is that now; perhaps she is under five feet. Her only grandson, the one whose mother is belatedly marrying at long last, doing the decent thing by her mother, at eleven is taller than her. How long will it be before he can lean his chin on the top of her head?

She's back quickly with her selection. The navy of the skirt and blouse she has chosen match each other and the jacket exactly, which isn't the easiest thing in the world to do so that I know that her perception of colour is quite unaltered and whatever else is wrong with her, there is nothing the matter with her eyes. I take the garments from her as we walk to the changing rooms, for everything apart from the smallest and lightest of handbags is too heavy for her now. A full mug of tea is too heavy for her to pick up. In cafés where they serve coffee in those large green and gold cups from France, she is stymied, remains thirsty.

What she gives me to hold is a Karl Lagerfeld skirt and a Jaeger blouse, both substantially reduced, at £89.99 and £69.99, but not within the £60 budget I had estimated when the old biddy dress came to mind, like those which hang from rails ignored by my mother. She has obeyed my instruction. She has not looked at the prices. Half-submerged in whatever part of the brain contains our capacity to make aesthetic judgements, her old good taste is buried and my injunction to ignore the prices has been the key that released it. A young woman of twenty-five could attend a job interview in the outfit she has put together.

In the changing room, she undresses. I remember the body I had seen in the bath when I was growing up, the convex belly that my sister used to think was like a washing-up bowl from two Caesarean births. The one that I have now, myself. She used to hold hers in under her clothes by that rubberized garment called a roll-on, a set of sturdy elasticized knickers. She had been six and a half stone when she got married which rose to ten stone after bearing her daughters, and she would spend twenty years adhering to the rules of Weight Watchers without ever noticeably losing a pound. She more or less stopped eating when my father died, apart from cakes and sweets and toast with low calorie marge, on which regimen she shed two stone and twice was admitted to hospital suffering from dehydration.

As she removes her skirt, I turn my head away. It is enough to bear witness to the pornography of her left arm, a swollen sausage encased in a beige rubber bandage, the legacy of a pioneering mid-Eighties operation for breast cancer which removed her lymph glands. The armpit is hollow.

The ensemble is in place when I look back. The pencil skirt, a size ten, is an exact fit but the blouse (also a ten) is a little too big, billowing round her hips, which is a shame for it is beautiful, in heavy matte silk with white overstitching along the button closings.

And now my mother turns to me in rage, no longer placid and obedient, not the sweet little old-age pensioner that shop assistants smile at to see her delight in her new jacket.

Fury devours her. 'I will not wear this blouse, you will not make me wear this blouse.' She bangs her fist against the wall and (she is the only person I have ever seen do this) she stamps her foot, just like a character from one of my childhood comics or a bad actress in an amateur production.

'What's the matter with it?'

She points to the collar. 'I'm not having anyone see me in this. It shows up my neck.'

I understand for the first time why, on this warm July day as well as every other, she is wearing a scarf knotted beneath her chin. I had thought her old bones were cold, but it is vanity. My mother was seventy-eight the previous week. 'Go and see if they've got it in a smaller size,' she orders.

My patient nephew is sitting beneath a mannequin outside watching the women come and go. There are very few eleven-year-old boys in the world who would spend a day of the school holidays traipsing around John Lewis with their aunt and their senile gran looking for clothes but let's face it, he has inherited the shopping gene. He's quite happy there, sizing up the grown ladies coming out of the changing rooms to say to their friends, 'What do you think? Is it too dressy?' or 'I wonder what Ray's sister will be wearing. I'll kill her if it's cream.'

'Are you all right?' He gives me the thumbs-up sign.

There is no size eight on the rack and I return empty-handed. My mother is standing in front of the mirror regarding herself: her fine grey hair, her hazel eyes, her obstinate chin, the illusory remains of girlish prettiness, not ruined or faded or decayed but withered. Some people never seem to look like grown-ups but retain their childish faces all their lives and just resemble elderly infants. My mother did become an adult once but then she went back to being young again; young with lines and grey hair. Yet when I look at her I don't see any of it. She's just my mother, unchanging, the person who tells you what to do.

'Where've you been?' she asks, turning to me. 'This blouse is too big round the neck. Go and see if they've got it in a smaller size.'

'That's what I've been doing. They haven't.'

'Oh.'

So we continue to admire the skirt and the jacket and wait for the seamstress to arrive, shut up together in our little cubicle where once, long ago, my mother would say to me: 'You're not having it and that's final. I wouldn't be seen dead with you wearing something like that. I don't care if it's all the rage. I don't care if everyone else has got one. You can't.'

My mother fingers the collar on the blouse. 'I'm not wearing this, you know. You can't make me wear it. I'm not going to the wedding if I've got to wear this blouse.'

'Nobody's going to make you wear it. We'll look for something else.'

'I've got an idea. Why don't you see if they have it in a smaller size.'

'I've looked already. There isn't one. This is the last . . . '

'No, I must interrupt you. I've just thought, do you think they've got it in a smaller size?'

'That's what I'm trying to tell you. They haven't got one.'

Her shoulders sag in disappointment. 'Anyway,' I say, to distract her, 'the seamstress will be along in a minute to take up the sleeves.'

She looks down at her arms. 'Why? They aren't too long.'

'That's because you folded them up.'

She holds the cuffs between her fingers. 'Oh, that's right.' She looks back at herself in the mirror, smiling. 'I love this jacket. But I don't like the blouse. Well, I do like it but it's too big round the neck. Why don't you nip outside and see if they've got a smaller one?'

'I've been. They haven't. I've told you already.'

'Did you? I don't remember. Have I ever told you that I've been diagnosed as having a memory loss?'

'Yes.'

Now the seamstress has come. My mother shows her the blouse. 'It's too big round the neck,' she tells her. 'Can you take it in?'

'No, Mum, she's here to alter the jacket.'

'Why? There's nothing the matter with it.'

'Yes there is. The sleeves are too long.'

'No they aren't.'

'That's because you've turned them up.'

'Well, never mind that. Go and see if they've got this blouse in a smaller size.'

And so it goes, like Alice in the garden, on the path where whatever she does always leads straight back to where she started. We are through the looking-glass now, my mother and I, where we wander in that terrible wilderness without landmarks, nothing to tell you that you passed here only moments before.

We pay for the jacket and the skirt which are wrapped, the jacket remaining, ready to be collected absolutely no later than the day before the wedding, which is cutting it a bit fine but what can you do? We leave John Lewis and walk a few yards to the next store which is D. H. Evans.

Up the escalator to the dress department and on a sale rack is the very Jaeger blouse! And there are plenty of them and right at the front what is there but an eight.

'Look!' I cry. 'Look what they've got and in your size.'

My mother runs towards me, she really does pick up her legs and break into a trot. '*Well*, they didn't have that in John Lewis.'

'They did but it was too big and they didn't have a smaller one.'

'Did they? I don't remember.'

She tries the blouse on in the changing rooms. The fit is much better. She looks at the label. 'Jaguar. I've never heard of them.' Her eyes, which could match navy, sometimes jumbled up letters.

'Not jaguar, Jaeger.'

'Jaeger! I've never had Jaeger in my life before.'

'You must be joking. You've got a wardrobe full of it.'

'Have I? I don't remember. Have I told you I've been diagnosed with a memory loss?'

'Yes,' I say. 'You've told me.'

'And now,' my mother announces, 'I need a jacket and a skirt.'

'We've bought those already.'

'Where are they then?'

'The skirt is in this bag and the jacket is being altered.'

'Are you sure?'

'Positive.'

'What colour are they?'

'Navy.'

'Well, that's lucky,' she says pointing triumphantly to the blouse, 'because this is navy.'

My mother wants to take the tube home (or rather to the Home in which we have incarcerated her) for a taxi is an unnecessary extravagance. 'I'm fresh,' she says. But I am not. A moment always comes, towards the end of these outings, when I want to go into a bar and have a drink, when I wish I carried a hip flask of innocuous vodka to sip, sip, sip at throughout the day. Most of all I want it to stop, our excursion. I can't put up with any more and I fall into cruel, monosyllabic communication. 'Yes, Mum.' 'No, Mum.' 'That's right.' 'Mmm.'

Here is a taxi and do not think for a moment, Madam, that despite the many burdens of your shopping, however swollen your feet or fractious your child, that you are going to take this cab before me.

'Get in,' I order. As we drive off up Portland Place I am calculating how much her old biddy outfit has cost. It has come to £209.97 which is more than I have paid for mine and has beaten out all of us, including the bride herself, on designer labels.

My mother holds on to her two purchases, from which floral prints have been rigorously excluded.

She looks at us both, her daughter and grandson. She's puzzled about something. She has a question she needs to ask. 'Just remind me,' she says. 'How am I related to you?'

What is wrong with her? It isn't Alzheimer's disease but something called Multi-Infarct Dementia or MID. Tiny, silent strokes had been occurring in her brain, mowing down her recollections of what she had said half a minute ago. They were not the kind of strokes that paralysed or blurred her speech, far from it. She isn't confined to a chair but can walk for miles.

'Why do we have to go back now?' she complains. 'I'm still fresh. You know I've always been a walker.'

Apart from the physical wasting, she looks normal—she looks like a sweet little old lady—and people start up conversations with her which proceed as they expected until a question answered a moment before would be asked again—'No, I must interrupt, you haven't told me yet where you live.'

'As I just said, Birmingham.'

And then asked and asked and asked until you lost your patience because you thought you had been entering a dialogue which had its rules of exchange, and it turned out that what you were really talking to was an animate brick wall. Questions asked over and over again not because she couldn't remember the reply but because a very short tape playing in her head had reached its end and wound itself back to the beginning to start afresh. She knows the conventions of conversation—these have not deserted her—but she cannot recall what she has said herself a few moments before.

Sometimes the question is repeated before the person she is asking has finished getting through their response. There are little holes in her brain, real holes in the grey matter, where the memory of her life used to be and what she has done half an hour or even a few minutes ago.

She has no sense at all of the progress of her memory's ebb. I do. She does not know what lies ahead and I'm not going to tell her. Soon, she will no longer recognize me, her own daughter, and if her disease progresses as Alzheimer's does, her muscles will eventually forget to stay closed against the involuntary release of waste products. She will forget to speak and one day even her heart will lose its memory and forget to beat and she will die.

'Does she know you?' people ask, with that concerned, sympathetic tone in their voices. There is this thing which everyone can tell you about senile dementia, that after a while the most extraordinary event occurs—sufferers no longer recognize their closest relatives and believe that a wife of fifty years is an impostor and a beloved son changing his mother's sheets is a burglar who has entered the house to steal her valuables. When people ask me in that particular way, 'Does she know you?' what they imagine is a vacant drooling wreck in a chair from whom the last vestige of personality has fled, or perhaps a desolate wandering soul in house slippers condemned until death to walk the halls of the asylum, mumbling. Not a screaming harridan with eyes sharp for matching navy.

When did it begin, this business with my mother? Where was the start of it? Even now, when we have tests and diagnoses and medical records, I still feel that who my mother was once and who she is now are bound up together. Where did her personality end and where did the dementia begin? There is another aspect of her condition; it is called by doctors emotional incontinence. It causes her to come out with the most surprising things—rages, tears, but also information that she has suppressed for the whole of her life.

Whenever I asked her what her father did for a living she

said, 'He was a cobbler.'

I assumed he had a shop. I always thought that.

'And what did your father do?' someone asked her recently. My mother replied at once: 'He went round the houses where someone had died and bought their shoes then he did them up and my mother sold them on a stall at Bootle market.' She'd kept that quiet for nearly eighty years.

When I sent away for her birth certificate (because she had given her mother's maiden name as a password for a bank account and couldn't remember it any more) I saw that her father signed it with a cross. He lived, it seemed, the most scavenging of lives, a poor illiterate who in another country would have crawled across refuse dumps to find something he could sell. I come, after all, from a family with a dodgy memory, one which mythologized its own past to fill in the gaps it either did not want to tell us about, or didn't know itself.

'I don't remember' was the answer to so many of my insistent questions. And whenever they told me they didn't remember, I always assumed they had something interesting to hide: like the repressed existence of my older half-sister Sonia, whose phone call to the house when I was ten and picked up the phone before anyone else and said in my best telephone voice, 'Who's speaking please?' was the first, rude intimation that I was a middle, not an oldest child.

Or why there was an eight-year gap between my younger sister and me. Or what my father's name was when he came from Poland, or why the family later changed the one they took when they arrived. Did they drop Ginsberg after I was born, landing me with two complicated birth certificates, because my father had been called guinea pig when he was at school? Or was it that letter from Mosley's resurgent post-war fascists promising the extermination of my Daddy and all his line? I still don't know.

When I think about my mother's loss of memory I understand that remembering things implies continuity, but my grandparents on both sides had, nearly a hundred years ago, become immigrants, stepped off the edge of the known world into England and the twentieth century, the century in which my family was to all intents born. She was the last of her line, my

Mum, the youngest of six who married one of six and all the brothers and sisters now dead and their husbands and wives. The world of my forefathers was locked up in her brain which, in certain places, had been turned off at the mains, so to speak.

On the day she revealed my grandfather's true occupation we were looking at old photographs and she began to talk about how her mother and father had come from Russia and how her father had said he would have stayed if only he could have got his hands on a gun to defend himself and 'your father told me that when he was a little boy he overheard *his* father talking—in Yiddish, you understand—and there was a girl and they came one night, and they came back every night and she went mad in the end and when it was born they killed it.'

'What are you talking about? Who came? Who was the girl?'

'What girl?'

'The one you were just talking about.'

'What was I saying? I can't remember.'

It was so ironic that Jews, who insist on forgetting nothing, should wind up, in my mother's case, remembering nothing.

If there was a beginning, I can't place a marker on it now. There is only the chronology of that year in which she went from being an independent widow in her own flat to her first involuntary steps through the doors of the Home, where she was living in the summer of 1996, the day of the shopping trip.

Whenever she had another stroke, she moved further down the stair into the dark cellar of her life. We got the diagnosis in April 1993 when we paid £60 to a man in Harley Street to tell us what was wrong. But the year which began for us at Christmas 1994 was the one in which great tracts of memory started to disappear in quick succession. And it was not just a matter of blouses, for the disease began to turn its malign attention to the very heart of her, her own identity.

We had always regarded Christmas as an entirely commercial festival, editing out the Infant Jesus and the manger and the carols and Midnight Mass. So when I invited my mother and sister and brother-in-law and nephew to my new flat for Christmas what we all anticipated was a good meal and the exchange of gifts.

They arrived on Christmas Eve and we sent her to bed in my room while I slept on an inflatable mattress in my study below. Michele said the next morning, 'I was up with Mum all night.'

'Why?'

'She kept getting up every five minutes and trying to leave because she thought she was in the wrong house. She didn't recognize the bedroom. I wrote out THIS IS LINDA'S NEW HOUSE. YOU ARE IN THE RIGHT ROOM on a piece of paper and propped it on the chest of drawers but she folded it up and put it in the drawer for safe keeping. I found all the keys to the front door in her handbag.'

My mother came down for breakfast: 'I've had a terrible night. I thought I was in the wrong flat and someone would come in and say "What are YOU doing in MY room?"' She said it in the tone of Father Bear asking Goldilocks, 'Who's been sleeping in MY bed?'

She and Michele had gone out to buy me a house-warming present, a radio for the kitchen as I had requested which I had opened with delight and mock surprise. 'Ooh, a radio! *Just* what I wanted. I can listen to music now when I cook.'

Several times as I was preparing lunch she pulled me away from the stove. 'Now this is important. I haven't bought you a house-warming present so I want you to take some money and get it yourself.'

'You've already bought me a house-warming present.'

'Have I? What is it?'

'A radio. Look, there it is.'

She examined it with uncertain eyes. 'I don't remember buying it. Are you sure?'

'Positive.'

After lunch, which was surprisingly good given the circumstances, my mother said, 'I'll wash up.'

'Fine with me.' It would get her out of the way for three-quarters of an hour.

She came back a few minutes later. 'Linda, do you know you've got no sink in your kitchen?'

'What do you mean, no sink?'

'Come and have a look.'

She gestured round the room. 'Where is it?'

'There.'

'Oh, yes. I see it now.'

The following morning, taking a few glasses from the living room to the kitchen, I fell down a flight of stairs. Bruises blossomed across my back and legs. The pain was frightful. When I picked myself up and crawled to a chair Michele appeared. 'I've got the most stinking cold,' she said.

A summit conference was held. 'I vote we abandon Christmas,' I proposed. 'Let's just forget all about it.'

Mark said, 'The presents were lovely, the tree was lovely, the meal was lovely, the only problem was the people.'

We needed one of those smart weapons that would have vaporized the guests but left the trappings of Christmas intact.

'I want to go home,' my mother said. 'I don't like it here.'

Michele made a pretence of ringing the station to enquire about train times, though we had no intention of allowing her to travel home alone. 'There aren't any trains to Bournemouth on Boxing Day,' she said.

'Any to Liverpool?'

'But you don't live in Liverpool.'

'Don't I?'

'No.'

'Do I have a home any more?'

'Of course you do.'

'Where is it, because I can't remember.'

'It's in Bournemouth, where you moved with Dad.'

'Oh, yes, that's right. But sometimes, you know, I look round when I'm in my flat and I don't recognize where I am. Sometimes I start crying and I can't remember what I'm crying about.'

She began another sentence then broke off. 'I don't remember what I was talking about.' She cried again, easy tears that stopped as easily, for like cigarette smoke, the memory of her sorrow had disappeared without trace into the air.

Mark drove Michele and Ben back to Oxford, then my mother to Bournemouth and then back to Oxford. He spent the whole of Boxing Day on motorways, but that was better than spending it *en famille* Grant, he said.

Linda Grant

April 1995. I went to Capri and stayed in a terracotta-coloured hotel built on the spot where the Emperor Tiberius once hurled his victims into the sea. Every morning I went to the deserted dining room for breakfast, came back and worked on my novel, and in the afternoon I ascended by the funicular railway to the town. The island was quiet; it was the week before Easter and the first tourist arrivals from the mainland were due but they weren't there yet. I did circular walks on paved paths in suede shoes and a pale lilac silk jacket and whatever fork I took, my wanderings always ended among the smartest of shops. One early afternoon I had a manicure. I bought my mother a musical box of inlaid wood which played "Twas on the Isle of Capri that I met her'. Some friends who had driven from Rome to Naples took the boat over to spend the day with me. We had lunch overlooking a gorge and the blue Mediterranean spread itself in front of us, like the best kind of dress. This was what living was cracked up to be, privileged, effortless, exquisite. I was cut off from tragedy and tears. I dwelt that week in fairyland.

At home the new flat was full of plaster dust and builder's rubble, squalor on the grand scale. My mother rang me promptly the morning after my return.

'What are we doing for Pesach? You aren't going to leave me on my own in this flat with a box of matzo are you?'

'What would you like to do? Michele and Mark and Ben are in San Francisco but I could come to you.'

'I'm not staying here. I'm the only one who never goes away. I'm always here on my own.'

Later, searching through her things, I found a scrap of paper. On it she had written: <u>People</u> TAKe <u>STRAN</u>geares IN FOR YONTIF I HAVe <u>NOT</u> Bean <u>OUT</u>.

'That's not true,' I said. 'You were here at Christmas.'

'Was I? I don't remember.'

'Should I come and pick you up on the train?'

'Rubbish. I can manage on my own.'

But I didn't think that she could. She did not know any longer that Waterloo was the terminus station. 'Why isn't it called London?' she had asked me. This was the mother who when we took our annual Christmas trips to London confidently navigated

52

buses and tubes and taxis. We went to the Tower of London and Kensington Palace, to little shops on Bond Street she had read about in a magazine at the hairdresser's, to the East End for Jewish food at Blooms. There were photos of me with pigeons on my head in Trafalgar Square, an outstretched hand filled with corn. Now she moved in a restricted universe, frightened of venturing beyond certain well-known routes near her own home.

So I took the train to Bournemouth and walked along the road from the station to her flat, in the bosky south coast air of a spring morning to the avenue lined with pine trees that were deceptively similar to the ones in Capri. I rang her entryphone buzzer and she let me in. I passed through the large empty lobby with chairs that no one sat in, vases with dusty silk flower arrangements which no one admired, came up in the small wood-panelled lift to her silent floor with its four flats. Her door was ajar.

I walked in. I called out, 'Where are you, Mum?'

'Here.'

The worst of her illness for me then and now was seeing her, sitting on the toilet, crying, struggling to put on her tights.

'I don't think I can handle myself any more.' She wept. 'Sometimes I think I'm so brave, what I manage to do. Do you think I'm ready?'

'Ready for what?'

'To go somewhere else.'

'What sort of place are you thinking of?'

'Somewhere they'll look after me.'

'Yes,' I said. 'I think you're ready.'

I saw her loneliness, her isolation from the world, the battle to make it through every day without major mishap, without getting lost or burning herself or falling in the bath or forgetting to take her tablets or turn the gas off or pay her phone bill or eat. I saw the programmes marked with a cross on the television pages of her *Daily Mail*, the programmes which were her only company day after day, her television friends. The casts of all her soap operas were the ones who said goodnight to her and the presenters of the breakfast shows said good morning. They smiled at her and spoke to her as if she had no memory loss at all, never irritated, never complaining. They did her the honour of assuming she had as much sense in her head as they had.

As if she lived in a house that was falling down, she ran hither and thither trying to repair her roof or mend her floor, anything to stop the place from tumbling down around her ears for she fought not just to manage her everyday life but to maintain her existence as a human being, a social animal with rights and responsibilities and likes and dislikes.

I could see now that my family had by necessity reconstructed itself and its past for the life it would live in a new land. Cut off from the previous century, from its own line of continuity with its memory of itself, it made itself up. All the lies and evasions and tall stories are what you must have when you are inventing yourself. Now my mother was bent on a similar task, that of continuously inventing for *herself* (and the rest of the world) a coherent identity and daily history. For a lifetime of practising deceit had only prepared her for her greatest role, dementia, in which she did everything she could to pretend to the world that she was right as rain and could not stop to talk if she saw someone in the street for really, she had to dash, she was meeting a friend for morning coffee. Her neighbours told me that, later. They suspected that there was no date. Instead of cakes and gossip she would return to her empty flat, with neither husband nor children nor grandchildren, to cry her eyes out. Yet she went on presenting a bold façade, a fictitious person for inspection, hoping it would pass muster.

This was a battle which called up everything she had in her. It was her capacity for deception that armed her against the destruction of her self. Only to me, for a moment, who saw her alone and vulnerable, sitting on the toilet trying to dress, did she reveal the bruising exhaustion of that daily combat.

We took the train to London. 'Would you like to live in London or Bournemouth?'

'London. Definitely. You're not making me stay in Bournemouth.'

I knew why. Because of the humiliation; she who had once been a helper would now be the helped. She who had once held the hands of her old dears at the day centre, where she volunteered with other active Jewish ladies, would have her own clutched by her former equals.

There was no trouble that night remembering where she was but the next morning I found all my drawers and cupboards immaculately tidied. In her case, beautifully folded, were some of my clothes.

I raised again the matter of her moving on.

'I will have my own kitchen will I, because I'm not eating other people's food?'

'No, I don't think you would have your own kitchen.'

'I'm not going then.'

'But it's not like you cook much anyway.'

'Yes, but if I didn't have a kitchen I'd feel like I was in a home.'

'What sort of place would you like to move to?'

'Where they have a warden.'

'You mean sheltered housing.'

'That's right, sheltered housing.'

'I'm not sure if that's the right place for you.'

'Well I'm not going into a home and that's the end of it.'

Walking along the street she suddenly exploded like a match thrown into a box of fireworks, remembering an old grudge she bears against my sister.

'You're taking her side, are you? You're no better than her. Where's the bus? I'm going. I'm getting the bus home.'

'Well you can't. You can't get a bus from here to Bournemouth.'

She began to sob. 'I want to go home, I want to go home. I'll get a taxi, then, you can't stop me.'

We reached my house and she went and sat down and cried. I left the room. I came in ten minutes later. 'Do you want a cup of tea?'

'Yes. But tell me. Have I had a row with someone? I think I've had a row but I can't remember who with. Was it Michele? I don't remember.' It was an excellent new tactic this. Whatever was upsetting her, if you left her alone for a few minutes she couldn't remember it.

The next day I mentioned Michele.

'Michele. Who's Michele?'

'Your daughter.'

'I've got a daughter called Michele.'

'Who lives in Oxford.'

'Who lives in Oxford.'

We were at Piccadilly Circus. 'Where are we, Mum?' I asked her. She looked around. 'Bournemouth.'

Like Michele at Christmas I developed a violent, atrocious cold, the kind where you feel nauseous and dizzy if you stand up. How could I take her to Bournemouth and come back in one very long afternoon? We went by taxi to Waterloo and I put her on the train in the care of another passenger. I went home and as soon as I thought she might have returned I rang. She answered the phone without concern.

'Was the journey all right?'

'Yes. Why shouldn't it be?'

The following day she rang me. 'You've left me like a dog all over Pesach. I haven't budged from this flat for a week. I've been all alone with just a box of matzo. What kind of daughter are you to do this to your own mother?'

'Mum, you were here, yesterday. You've been in London.'

'Don't you lie to me, you liar. I've not been out the door.'

'Don't you remember being in London? At my flat. You stayed here.'

'In Brixton?'

'No, the new flat.'

'When did you move?'

'In December.'

'And you've never bleddy invited me for a cup of tea.'

'You were here. You stayed here. You've only just got back.'

'I'm not listening to you another minute. You're telling me I'm mad.' The phone slammed down at the other end.

I rang her back at once. She was crying her eyes out. 'You bitch,' she screamed and the phone went down again. This went on for the next hour.

I rang her the next morning. 'What's new?' she enquired in a calm, bright voice. 'I haven't spoken to you for ages.'

She wanted me to do something. When she asked me if she

was ready, she knew she was but she could not accept responsibility for making the decision for herself. She wanted to rest now, to let go of all the burden of her life, but she needed someone to make her. So she could say, 'I was advised to. I wanted to stay in my own home but they wouldn't let me.' A member of that superior breed, the 'specialist', would be called in and then pride could be satisfied and indignity stared out.

But Michele and I were too taken in by the current fashion in social work and the advice columns: respect the rights of the elderly; consult them; do not force them to do what they do not want. Michele had already rung the Help the Aged helpline. The thinking went like this: old people with dementia were best left to stay in familiar surroundings for as long as possible, where they were habitualized. It was moving that caused crises, where they would have to deal with unaccustomed rooms and would not have, secure in an undamaged portion of their minds, the routes to and from home. When they were taken away, like dogs they tried to find their way back. Then they were locked in, the keys and the bolts got heavier until in the end only a secure mental institution could hold them. Better to keep her where she was. And anyway she had rights. We could not put her away just to suit us, we were told. My mother's rights allowed her to spend twenty-three hours alone, crying, overdosed or under-medicated because fifteen minutes after her taking her tablets she couldn't remember if she had swallowed them or not. Her nightmare went on and on.

I read these sentences from other people's lives: 'Just because I'm old doesn't mean I'm stupid.'

'Just because I'm old doesn't mean I don't see, don't understand.'

So for several more months my mother was treated like an adult, like a fully-paid-up member of the human race.

October 1995. Yom Kippur, the Day of Atonement, the most important day in the Jewish year when even the least observant Jew makes their way to the synagogue.

Yom Kippur is also a day of remembrance. It is the day when we say the prayer of Yiskor that offers up our words to God for the souls of the dead. Children are ushered out and adults whose parents are both still living leave voluntarily. First there are spoken the names of the congregants who have passed away in the last twelve months. Then come the prayers for the dead whose relatives in the congregation have offered money to charity to hear their names uttered aloud. Then there is our public memory of the nameless dead of the Holocaust.

Those who remain offer their own individual prayer for their dead relatives, their mother or father, husband or wife. So we cast our chain of memory down through the generations and link ourselves with all the forgotten ones of the past who have nobody left to mourn them. The synagogue is at its fullest. The old and the sick and frail stumble there any way they can to say Yiskor. To do less is to have done nothing.

This was the most important day of the year, when my mother would pray for the souls of her dead parents, and for her brothers Abe and Harry and her sisters Miriam and Gertie, and Gertie's only child, Martin, who died of leukaemia when he was only twenty-six, and for her own husband. But I thought she was too confused to travel to London and that it would be best if I came to her.

'I will not, I will not stay in Bournemouth,' she shouted at me down the phone. 'This place reminds me too much of your father at this time of year. I want to come to London.'

'I'll come and get you on the train.'

In fact it was all to the good that she had decided that London was the place to be because my long-lost cousin Sefton, who had lived in Israel for the past twenty-five years, was back in town and so I invited him to come and see my mother. 'Sefton!' she cried. 'My favourite nephew.' She remembered everything about him, who his wife was and how they had married and when he had gone abroad.

I rang her just before I left the house to remind her what time my train arrived. I explained that if she was there to meet me with her small suitcase we would only have a brief wait until the return journey.

'Yes,' she said. 'Don't worry. I've got it written down.'

I did not know if she would be there but she was, only a few minutes late, standing without any luggage. 'I've got to buy my ticket,' she said. 'I've been to the bank.' She no longer kept money in a purse or wallet but in a small plastic bag.

'Mum, where's your case?'

She looked around. 'Where's my case. Bugger it, I don't need any clothes.'

'Of course you do. What have you brought with you?'

'Nothing.'

'Have you got your pills?'

'Yes, they're in my bag.'

'Show me.'

'Bugger off. I've got them.'

'I want to see.'

Meekly, she gave me her small handbag, the lightest of all those she owned and held across her shoulder by its strap. She was so little now. Little and old and confused. A mugger's ideal target.

There were no pills.

'We're going to go back now and pack properly.'

'Oh, do we have to?'

'Yes.'

We walked along the road to the flat. She let us in and sat down for a few minutes with her eyes closed, exhausted, in what used to be my father's chair. Then she opened them and said: 'Well, I'm delighted you've come for the weekend. How long are you staying?'

'I'm not staying. I've come to pick you up. You're coming to London.'

She burst into tears. 'Now you tell me. Do we have to?'

'But it was you who insisted. You said you wouldn't stay here.'

Her mood changed like a radio clicking to another station, from sobbing violins to angry drums.

'You're not going to make me stay in Bournemouth. I'll cut my throat if I've got to stay here.'

'Well that's good, because Sefton is coming to see us in London.'

'Who's Sefton?'

'Uncle Louis's son.'

'No, doesn't ring a bell.'

I watched her pack, a few things that didn't belong to each other thrown into a small case.

'Underwear, Mum.'

'I don't need that, do I?'

We went back to the station and caught the train. The orange signal lights inside the tunnel at Waterloo caught her eye as we approached the platform. 'Ooh,' she said. 'Isn't it beautiful, like fairyland.'

As we went towards the tube I saw a newspaper placard announcing that O. J. Simpson had been found guilty. 'I'm just stopping to buy the *Evening Standard*, Mum.'

'Why, anything interesting in it?'

'The verdict on O. J. Simpson,' I told her. Of course she would not know what I was talking about.

'Well, I think he did it, don't you? I've been addicted to the trial.' Thus my mother, who did not know what day of the week it was, what was up and what was down, had for many months been following one of the most complex criminal cases of the century.

I went in to see her as she was getting ready for bed. She was standing with her nightdress on over her clothes.

'Mum! What are you dressed like that for? Are you cold?'

'No. Why?'

'You've got your nightie over your clothes. You don't do that.'

She looked down, uncertainly. 'Don't you?'

The following morning we went in the rain by taxi to the synagogue at Muswell Hill. She gave out little cries and ran to embrace people, complete strangers as it turned out. They saw my embarrassment. I saw the look of pitying understanding in their eyes. She did not follow the service.

On each seat was the congregation's community magazine. It contained an article about a nursing home adjacent to the synagogue. It was called Charles Clore House after the famous Jewish philanthropist who had once owned Selfridges, exactly the kind of man my parents admired and longed to be like themselves.

She read it over and over again. 'Do you think I'm ready?' she asked.

'Shush. Don't talk so loud. Whisper. Remember where you are.'

'Why? Where am I?'

My mother's diabetes ruled out fasting so I took her for lunch in a café where she had a bowl of soup and a sandwich. Someone I knew came in and I saw him start to come over to speak to us but I shook my head. Her voice was so loud though she wasn't deaf, she smiled so brightly at people she did not know and they all, without exception, said, 'Oh, she's so sweet.'

'I must give you some money,' she offered.

'What for?'

'For the pictures.'

'What pictures?'

'Where we've just been. We've been to the pictures. I can't remember what the film was but I know we've been. Have I told you I've been diagnosed with a memory loss?'

And it was then that I thought, 'That's it. This has gone far enough. She's got to go into a home whether she likes it or not. I must *do* something.'

I saw that the mother, who for so long I thought had made my life such a misery, was gone. That I was never going to win the great argument with her about the kind of daughter she expected me to be for my adversary had left the field. In her place was a bewildered infant whom the world insisted on treating as an adult with no one to protect her. My mother, my child.

After half a lifetime of being an inadequate, undutiful daughter, now I was to take on a role I had refused elsewhere, that of a parent. It was up to me to do what I thought was best for her, to tell her how she could and could not behave, to protect her from danger, make sure she was properly housed and fed, to find her the best attention money could buy. Like many women of my generation, I thought I had won freedom and independence. I hadn't of course. Now I was to become my mother's guardian, as tied to her as if she were my baby.

My cousin Sefton came for lunch and as soon as he walked into the room my mother ran to greet him. After an absence of a quarter of a century the visual recognition portion of her brain was intact.

'You're as handsome as you ever were,' she told him. 'My favourite nephew.'

We looked at old photographs.

'Who's that?' she asked, pointing to a picture of his father.

'That's my father.'

'Who is your father?'

'Louis.'

'But you're Louis.'

'No, I'm Sefton.'

'How am I related to you?'

'I'm your nephew.'

'So who is your father?'

'Louis.'

'That's right. How's your wife? She was very beautiful, you know. She used to be a beauty queen.' It was true, she had been.

Why could she remember Anne, met perhaps two or three times and not since the 1960s? Why could she whisper to me when he was out of the room, 'His wife isn't Jewish, you know'?

And why was it, as we waved goodbye to Sefton, that she turned to me and smiled and said, 'He's lovely. Who is he?'

I took her back to Bournemouth on a packed train. I watched her lips moving as she tried to capture the thoughts that drifted through her mind like fast clouds. A woman opposite us was watching her too. She looked at her in pity. She looked at me and I saw in her face what she thought, 'The poor bloody daughter, having to look after her.' Perhaps she thought I was one of those selfless, dedicated women who loved their mothers so much they would never put her in a home. I stared back at her, eyeball to eyeball. I sent out a telepathic message. I'm not what you think. This situation is not as you imagine. I *am* going to put her in a home.

'Mum,' I said. 'Show me your chequebook.' She handed it over. On the day she left Bournemouth she had withdrawn two lots of £30. She only had £30 when she met me at the station. Thumbing back through the stubs, I saw that on various days she had withdrawn multiple amounts of money. I imagined that she had gone to the bank, written a cheque, then forgotten later that she had been.

She rang me the next morning. She was crying.

'I've left my chequebook at your house. Will you send it back to me.'

'No, you definitely haven't left it here because I was looking at it on the train and you put it back in your bag yourself.'

'I *haven't* got it. Why won't you listen to me?'

'Honestly, Mum, I promise you that you have got your chequebook. It is there.'

'It *isn't*. Why are you doing this to me? I've got no money for food. I'm hungry and I've got no money. Please, please send me my chequebook.'

'I can't because I haven't got it.'

The familiar routine began. The phone slammed down then a minute or two later rang again.

'Linda, it's Mum. I can't find my chequebook. Have you got it?'

'No, we just had this conversation.'

'When?'

'Two minutes ago.'

'We didn't.'

'Yes, we did.'

'Well never mind that. I want you to send me my chequebook.'

'I can't. I haven't got it.'

'Please, please, I'm so hungry.'

It went on for two days. The phone calls every hour or so as if they had never occurred before. I went out for a while. My cleaner said, 'Linda, I was cleaning your office and there was the most terrible message on the answering machine. Whoever it was was in the most awful distress. I didn't know what to do. It was something about a chequebook.' The last call came at twenty past midnight on Saturday, the latest my mother had ever phoned me. The first began at ten to eight the next morning.

In the evening people were coming to dinner. It was early October and unusually warm. The last of the first phase of redecorating was over and I was free to entertain, to be gracious, to lay my marble table with my canteen of cutlery and place there the squat, cut-glass tumblers that I had stolen from my father's cocktail cabinet. To be on the safe side I put the answering machine on. The phone rang and everyone went quiet as my mother's demented voice formed a faint but audible backdrop to the Delia Smith beef casserole which we ate in defiance of threats to our own future sanity, just before the BSE scare went ballistic. 'I'm hungry, I've got no money for food. Why won't you help me?'

First thing on Monday morning I rang my mother's bank. I don't think anyone has been so pleased to hear my voice as that young clerk who, it turned out, dealt with my mother's account.

And that phone call, followed by others to social workers and doctors and matrons of homes, marked the end of my mother's adult life. From that day on, she was to be my dependant. When she went into the Home we took her money away from her, her door keys, her chequebook, her credit card, her kitchen, her cupboard with its boxes of dinner services for best, her furniture. We left her in a small room with some photographs and a fraction of her once-fabulous wardrobe. The jewels were gone already, stolen down the years by window cleaners and home helps.

The actual day she went into the Home, I was away. It was Michele and Mark who took her there. To the place of old men and women, drooling wrecks, Alzheimer's cases. Jewish old people's homes had unusual problems. There was a Holocaust survivor there, severely damaged by dementia. When they took him to the shower he thought he was being led to the gas chamber.

I got back and the phone was ringing. 'They've made a new woman of me,' she said. 'I'm ready to go back to Bournemouth now.' They had, in a way. She was fed three times a day, properly medicated, no longer had to struggle to preserve herself intact for daily life.

'No, Mum, you can't go home.'

'Do you mean I've got to stay here for the rest of my life?'

I did not want to tell her, yes. There was silence at my end.

'You bitch,' she said. ☐

ARIEL DORFMAN
SEPTEMBER, 1973

President Allende outside the Moneda Palace during the Chilean coup

I should not be here to tell this story.

It's that simple: there is a day in my past, a day many years ago in Santiago de Chile, when I should have died and did not.

That's where I always thought this story would start, at that moment when history turned me against my will into the man who could someday sit down and write these words, who now writes them. I always thought this story was meant to start on that morning when the armed forces of my country rise against our President, Salvador Allende, on 11 September 1973, to be exact, and the death I have been fearing since I was a child enters my life and, instead of taking it, leaves me to survive. I am left here on this side of reality to remember what ends for ever that day in me and in the world, still wondering why I was spared.

And yet, I cannot bring myself to begin there, that day I should have died.

There is one last night of reprieve; that is when I really need this story to start: the night of 10 September, the night before the coup. By tomorrow at this time Allende will be dead and I will be in hiding, by tomorrow I will have had to accept a future in which I am alive and far too many others will have been killed in my place. But not yet. Tonight I can tell myself, against the overwhelming evidence screaming at me from inside and outside, that there will be no military takeover, that Chile is different from other Latin American countries, all the comforting myths about our democracy and stability and reasonableness.

Perhaps I am right. Perhaps I should not be poisoning my last moments of peace. From the next room, my six-year-old son Rodrigo is calling. Angélica has already tucked him in. Now he clamours for his bedtime story. Perhaps I am right to crush the sudden sick thought that snakes up from my stomach. *This is the last time I will ever see him, the last story I will ever tell him, la última vez*; perhaps I am right to turn a final blind eye to reality.

It is not the first time I have tried to cheat death, pretend it does not exist.

As far back as I can remember, there it was. I see myself then, awake in my bed for hours thinking about death, my eyes wide open in the dark of our apartment in New York, a child lost and found in the first exile of his life, terrified, trying to convince

death to let him go. If I had known that many years later death
would indeed let me go and that what I did or did not do, thought
or did not think, would have no effect on whether or not I
survived . . . But back then in 1947, I didn't even know that it is
dying we should fear and not death. Oh yes, there were monsters
out there, under the bed, inside the soft light breathing from the
hall, dripping in the bathroom, always scrambling away as I
turned my head, just out of sight, behind me, ready to pounce,
and yet, even so, that's not what really threatened me, the
monsters. I was five years old, perhaps less, and I absurdly
assumed that the pain they would inflict on my body when I died
would somehow be swift, somehow be merciful. No, what I could
not bear was the aftermath of death, its loneliness, that I would
have to be alone for ever and ever.

'But will you be there?' I asked my mother, clinging to her,
trying to blackmail her into never leaving. 'Will you be nearby,
when I'm dead?' And she used to answer something that was only
partly a lie: Yes, she would be there. And afterwards, when the
light had been dimmed and she was gone and I thought about my
death and the very thinking dragged me deeper into the pit of its
terror, death was precisely the moment when I would not be there
to think it, when I would be abandoned by myself, by the one
person I could always count on never to turn off the light and
walk away down the hall to another bedroom. That's what I will
do to you, death said, you'll be so alone that not even you will be
able to accompany yourself, and there is nothing you can do to
avoid it. Just as I was spiralling myself into madness, my mother's
words would swim back to me; she had promised to be there in
the midst of that nothingness, and if she was there others might
also find a way, and that's how I could commence the slow ascent
back to the surface of sanity, conjecture death as a vast empty
space filled with horizontal bodies in coffins, none of them able to
touch each other but secure in the knowledge that the other silent
bodies were there, millions of us, each with our own stories, our
own beginnings, our own endings, a brotherhood of the dead
defeating my isolation. It was the first time I conceived humanity
as something wondrous and healing, a hint that if it could not
escape death, a community might at least provide consolation

against its outrage. And because my parents had told me that God did not exist, I prayed to that humanity every childhood night, asking it to allow me to awaken every hundred years to take a quick look around: the afterlife as a screen watched by a silent eye, eternity as one movie every century, the dead as intermittent voyeurs of the living.

That is how I managed to soften myself into sleep in the United States in those days before I found out that another language can keep us company as if it were a twin. Later, as an adult, I discovered a more ingenious way of draining the slime that thoughts of my mortality secrete into my mind. If I couldn't fall asleep at night, I'd banish the sawbuzz of language, say, English, that was keeping me awake, and switch to my other language, Spanish, and lazily watch it erase the residues of dread from me as if I were a blackboard.

But that was later, that is now. My first insomnia struck at a child who had condemned himself to being monolingual in English, who had repudiated the Spanish he had been born into, that boy I used to be who could not conjure up another tongue to save his soul. All I could do to swindle death at that very early age in the city of New York was to make up stories in the night, colonize the emptiness with multiplications of myself, hoping somebody out there would hear me, accompany me, keep me alive after I had died.

What that child could not conceive, of course, is that his adult self would, in fact, survive his own death several times over, that a quarter of a century into the future this day in September of 1973 was awaiting me—and that the language in which I would try to make sense of the series of connected miracles that spared me would be Spanish and not English. By then, by the time I was a young adult of thirty-one, I had renounced and denounced the language of my childhood America as imperial and northern and alien to me. I had fiercely and publicly converted back to my original native Spanish and proclaimed that I would speak it for ever, live for ever in Chile. For ever. I hadn't learned yet that when other, more powerful people control the currents of your life, very few things are for ever.

It is that sort of lesson I will have to learn as of tomorrow, when death catches up with me and makes me face the fact that my imagination can no longer protect me or my country.

I am now going to postpone that moment for one last time, crossing to Rodrigo's room to offer myself and him a final delusion of our immortality. But before I console my son with a story, just as I consoled myself as a child long ago, I will make a call. That call. If I had understood then its true significance, how it was warning me of what was about to befall me, befall all of us.

It is a call to La Moneda, the presidential palace where I have been working for the last two months as a cultural and media adviser to Fernando Flores, Allende's Chief of Staff. Today, so many years later, as I write this, it seems obvious that to accept a minor post of dubious utility in a foundering government was an act of folly. But that is not what I felt then. Then I saw it as my duty.

As a child I had imagined a fictional community as the best answer to death and loneliness—and it was that persistent hunger for a real community that had now led me here, to this revolution, to this place in history. Needing to prove my loyalty to a country I had chosen and a cause I had adopted as my own and that could only materialize if everybody who believed in it, myself included, was ready to give up their life. And I had therefore purposefully, recklessly, joyfully, sought out the most dangerous spot in the whole country to spend the last days of the Chilean revolution— the spot I am neurotically calling right now, even now on my night off duty, to find out if my services are required. They are not. Claudio Gimeno, a friend since my freshman year in college, answers. He's in a good mood; I can conjure up the shy grin of his buck-teeth, his wide black eyes, his sallow, angular face.

In the years to come, he will be there, in a vision. Each time I imagine my death, I will invariably picture myself in a chair, hands tied behind my back. I am blindfolded—and yet, in that picture, I am also impossibly watching myself, and a man in uniform approaches and he has something, a stick, a pair of electrodes, a long needle, something blurred and piercing in his right hand. In that vision which still assaults me unexpectedly, the body about to be hurt beyond repair is the body of Claudio Gimeno. He is naked in that chair. That is his body, but it is my face he wears. My face, because I had been assigned that *turno*, that stint. I was the one who should have been at La Moneda standing guard that night of 10 September. I was the one who should have received the news that the Navy had just disembarked in Valparaíso. It should have been my hand that put the receiver down and then with a heavy heart dialled the President and informed him that the coup had begun. It is Claudio who will receive that information in the next hours merely because last week I had wondered, rather offhandedly, '*oye*, Claudio, hey, would you mind coming to La Moneda next Monday, yes, September tenth, it's the night I've been assigned, and I'll take your shift on Sunday September ninth, what do you say?' And without giving it a second thought, Claudio had agreed.

So now I am here at home and he is at La Moneda and we are talking on the phone. No premonition of how chance is playing with us startles our conversation. On the contrary. Claudio tells me that things are looking up, there may be a way out of the crisis that is fracturing the country and has paralysed it, a democratic and sovereign way of avoiding what seems an imminent civil war. Allende will announce tomorrow that he will submit his differences with the opposition to a plebiscite and will resign if the people reject his proposals. I'm as relieved as Claudio. Neither of us recognizes this peaceful resolution of the political impasse for what it is: a mirage, an outcome that Allende's enemies, moving in for the kill, will never allow.

And yet, we are in a position to understand that, in a sense, the military takeover has already happened.

Just one week ago, Claudio and I, along with another aide, had been ushered into a musty secluded room in the presidential palace by Fernando Flores. The Minister wanted us to listen to an old Mapuche-Indian woman who had come to Santiago from the south of the country to denounce her husband's torture and death. She was one of hundreds of thousands of peasants who had, for the first time in their lives, been made owners of their land by Allende's government. A group of air-force officers had raided the family's communal farm in search of weapons and, when none were found, proceeded to tie the woman's husband to the blades of a helicopter. While the old man went slowly round and round

71

for hours, the men in uniform had smoked cigarettes, taunted him, sardonically suggesting that he ask his President for help now. As the old man died they had forced him to call on his fucking pagan gods for help now, *sus putos dioses paganos.*

She had come to denounce this situation to the President. But the President could do nothing. We could do nothing. It was as if power had already been transferred to the military.

The old woman had looked at me, straight in the eye. '*A lo largo de mi vida,*' she had told me: 'In my life, white people have done many things to us, but never before something like this. They kept on telling my man that now they're going to take away our land.' She paused. Then added: 'They made me watch what they were doing.'

I had looked away. I could not bear what she was seeing, the future she was able to anticipate because the past had already taught her what to expect. I had wanted so ardently to become a *chileno*, to *belong*; and what that meant, ultimately, was that what they had done to her and people like her for centuries they could now do to me. Maybe, for a flash, I had seen myself in her, I had imagined my body reduced to the defencelessness of that old woman, a foreigner in her own land; maybe, but I could not stand her visionary dress rehearsal of the violence that is about to invade the country, so that when Claudio, a week later, tells me everything is going to be all right, I am ready to believe in a miracle.

Not that we've got that much time to talk tonight. Claudio has work to do and I have a vociferous son demanding a story. When we say goodbye, nothing whispers that this is the last time we will ever speak to each other.

I hang up.

And go to comfort Rodrigo in the next room, off to tell my son that death does not exist, that I will be there with him, we can both delude solitude side by side one last time.

I do not inform him, of course, that real monsters are out there and that what they can enact on your body may be worse than death. That it is dying we should fear, the pain before and not the emptiness afterwards. That exile is staring us in the face, that soon he and I and his mother are going to leave this place where we gave birth to him and not return until many, too many, years have passed. I do not inform him that death and the fear of death inevitably lead to exile.

There will be time, tomorrow and the many days that will follow tomorrow, to discover this together.

For now, I say nothing of this to my son. Not a word.

What else can I do?

I turn out the light and tell my son a fairy tale.

2

Where are you from?

It was a question that since the age of two and a half, and until I was eighteen, I had always answered, spontaneously, invariably: I was from America, I was American.

That's what I was about to say, those were the words on the tip of my tongue on my first day of class at the Universidad de Chile in March of 1960. But I did not let them roll off into the politically effervescent air of a Latin America headed for a showdown with the United States.

Where are you from?

Who asked me that, with its implied query: Who are you? I can't remember the face, only my momentary bewilderment, the fact that I did not dare to admit that I was from the United States. Perhaps it was Claudio Gimeno himself. I did after all lay eyes on him that day for the first time, although it would be too bizarre, perhaps too suitably literary and symmetrical, that the man who saved me for this life of exile which has ended up here in the United States should have been the first person in the world to hear me deny my North American origins. I press myself harder to recall that event and it seems that it was just after *Historia de América*, the first class on my schedule, where our radical Panamanian mulatto professor had gone about dissecting the term America itself, how the United States had appropriated that word and denied it to the South, much in the way, he said, that the same United States had stolen a great part of Mexico and occupied Nicaragua and now sat on the narrow strip of the Canal refusing to return it to the people of Panama. Once lost, he said, it was difficult to get territory back, but establishing an alternative history was a start, even if his forced exile from his own country proved that such an intellectual enterprise was not without risks. But it was essential that Americans south of the Rio Bravo think of themselves differently, in freedom and with sovereignty, because from that thinking, from that territory of the imagination, history could be altered. Just look at José Martí who had died in 1895, before his dream of Cuba's independence could materialize, before he had seen his words of warning against the United States prove prophetic: the most powerful nation in the hemisphere had entered the war against Spain and then had kept Puerto Rico as a colony and occupied Cuba for years and invaded it whenever it was felt that 'those people', in General Shafter's memorable phrase, 'who were no more fit for self-government than gun-powder is for hell', deserved to be taught a lesson. But because of Martí and his words, Fidel Castro had staged his first insurrection in 1953 and taken the Moncada and, when captured, had turned his trial into an indictment of the Batista dictatorship and declared that he had rebelled so that one hundred years after his birth the ideas of Martí would not die. And now Cuba was standing up to Eisenhower, was getting rid of the casinos and the whorehouses and taking back the sugar plantations run by US corporations. And that was possible because Martí had thought of Cuba as part of *'Nuestra América,' our* America as opposed to *their* America.

As he spoke, he asked for opinions and we gave them, each of us, and then it was my turn. I don't remember exactly what I said but I do remember the way I said it, the slight smidgen of a gringo accent that still crept into my voice. I can remember becoming aware of how foreign I must look to my new classmates, my hair, my height, my eyes, my skin, my gestures, all revealing that I was from somewhere else. I can remember how all those other students from *la otra América* turned to me with interest, they were already preparing that question, where are you from? A question I would try to circumvent in the years to come, working strenuously at my Chilean accent and my Chilean slang and my Chilean trivia. But for now, I was going to have to face that curiosity as soon as the class was over and my answer would have to take into account that millions of people around the world were rebelling against a colonial and post-colonial order upheld by the United States, that one year before I had stepped into that classroom, Fidel had entered Havana with his band of guerrillas and that right then and there the first US advisers were arriving in Vietnam. I was going to step out of that classroom at the exact intersection in history when the country where I was receiving my university education was being shaken by riots and strikes and protest marches aimed at the conservative government and its American sponsors. I was going to have to answer the question about my identity in a world whose walls were being painted with that famous formula: YANKEE, GO HOME.

De dónde eres? Where are you from?

Somebody whose face and name I can't recollect asked me that question as soon as class was over. I should have answered: I don't know. My parents were from central Europe; I had been born in Argentina; I had grown up in the United States; and now I lived in Chile. I should have answered: all my life I thought I was a Yankee but now I'm not so sure. I wanted to be one so badly that I went to the extreme of changing my name to Edward. So your name's Edward? *Te llamas Edward?* Where *are* you from? I should have answered: You want to know the truth? I'm still attracted to the United States and who knows if I won't end up there because I may hate its politics but I love its jazz and its movies and its people and the language they gave me which is still the language that I use to make sense of the world. You want to know the truth? I've been flirting with Spanish recently, but I don't feel it deep inside me, I don't imagine myself writing anything intimate or relevant in the language you people speak. I should have answered: I don't have a country, I don't have a community, I don't have a cause. Goddamn it, I don't even have a girlfriend who might begin to tie me to a place. I should have answered: I'm alone on this planet and I don't know where I belong.

Instead, quite simply, I said: *'Soy de Argentina,'* I'm Argentinian. I fell back on that accidental birthplace I barely knew and did not particularly care for, because it was a convenient way of not having to examine my own confusion, admit that my fluid life was in transition, suspended between a country to the north that was drifting away from me and this country here in the south I was not yet ready to commit to permanently. It was a way of giving myself time to figure out who I really was.

A decade later, I knew the answer.

Ten and a half years later, to be precise, on the night of 4 September 1970, I was standing on Santiago's main avenue, the Alameda, all around me the delirious dancing throngs of my compatriots celebrating our victory in the presidential elections, and up there was Salvador Allende on the small balcony of the Student Federation building—Allende presiding over the birth of a new nation at two o'clock in the morning.

'Entraré a La Moneda,' Allende told us that night, *'y conmigo entrará el pueblo. Seré el Compañero Presidente.'* That was his promise to the outcast of Chile: he would enter La Moneda and the people would enter with him. He would be no ordinary president. 'I am going to be,' he said, 'your *Compañero Presidente.*' I was there when Allende swore his loyalty to us, his equality to us, his fraternity to us, that he would not betray us. And I called back from the deepest lungs of my *compañero* soul, I called to him as if I were on a desert island and he had come to rescue me, I began to chant, *compañero, compañero*—the echo of thousands of others who were already calling to him, the words came out of my mouth as if they had been waiting for ever to find that night, that place, this moment in history, *compañero, compañero*, calling to him until there was nothing in the world but that tribal sound filling the streets which were ours for ever, which we claimed as our birthright, until all the voices were one voice, we would enter La Moneda with him, the Palace of the Presidents of Chile, *Compañero Presidente.*

I called to him and it was no longer my call: in that sea of words, my word had become theirs.

We had baptized Salvador Allende.

Although, in truth, I was the one who was being baptized. I now fully knew—or at least so I told myself—the answer to that question I had evaded at the start of the Sixties. I knew where I was from and, more crucially, I knew that to formulate the question in this manner was wrong. I knew, standing there in the multitude, that what matters is to know where you are going.

Where was I from? I had just cast the first vote of my life and it had been for Salvador Allende. Where was I from? I was from Chile and this ocean of people stretching for blocks was my community, and by my side, holding my hand, was my Chilean wife. And the language in which I was imagining the future was the same language in which I was writing it. I had banished English from my life in order to become the privileged guardian of this Spanish I was chanting like a mantra and in which I would soon begin to tell, I was sure, the epic story that was unfolding before my eyes. And a few miles away, at home, our three-year-old Chilean son was sleeping, and he would not have to live the dislocations of his father or his grandparents. I had sworn he would be the first of his family in many generations to be born and grow up and have children of his own under the same southern constellation of stars. I had sworn it when he had been born in February of 1967 as if I were the one being born instead of him, and hammered home my point by giving him a name that symbolized my commitment to Spanish and Latin America, Rodrigo, because it was the name of El Cid, the first Iberian hero, and Fidel, because he had freed Cuba from the Americans. And now we were going to free Chile as well.

3

If it had not been for Susana la Semilla, a cartoon character I invented, I would not have survived the coup against Allende.

At least, that is the story I like to tell. Partly because it's bizarrely true but above all, I think, because this less solemn version of my survival gives me the illusion that I somehow created the conditions whereby I thwarted death, that I had a hand in them. When oblivion breathes down your neck, takes you for a ride to the outskirts of emptiness and then yanks you back to the shores of reality trembling and intact, you need to find a reason, you need to find a meaning. Why me? Why was I spared? Questions that burn through the lives of survivors, questions we ask ourselves because the people who might hold the answers are all dead. So we answer as best we can, we try to find one thread in the absurd chain of circumstances which lead to our deliverance and say: Here! This is it! This is of my making!

And for many years my answer, to myself and anyone who made the inquiry, was Susana la Semilla, the smiling character I had concocted as my contribution to forestalling the coup, my secret weapon against the CIA.

An admittedly puny weapon against the gigantic conspiracy financed by Nixon, Kissinger and International Telephone and Telegraph (ITT) to 'destabilize' the government the people of Chile had freely elected in 1970. This aggression was eventually to be exhaustively documented in 1975 by a Senate Investigating Committee headed by Frank Church, but by 1973 it was already being openly discussed in newspapers in Chile and abroad. What had begun as a covert operation was, by then, not a secret at all. In fact, as the end approached, many of those benefiting from American meddling and money were, instead of hiding the intervention, flaunting it.

I myself witnessed such a display when, around ten days before the coup, I had trekked, with a group of Unidad Popular militants, into some hills twenty miles to the north of Santiago. There, under the Andean cordillera, on an isolated knoll that our group leader had explored on another occasion and deemed sufficiently remote, we were supposed to receive our first lesson in firearms, part of a clumsily improvised training programme destined to prepare us for what seemed an impending civil war.

Not only too little (we had one pitiable gun among the seven of us), but too late as well.

Looking back, I realize that those of us who supported Allende were always a step behind our adversaries in our willingness to use violence. While we subscribed to the idea of a peaceful, democratic revolution, without bloodshed, while we danced along the avenues, they were taking lessons in martial arts. I can remember my surprise when, in 1971, a year after Allende had been inaugurated President, right-wing thugs suddenly made their appearance on the streets of Santiago, formed like a militia, swinging chains and lashing out with *linchacos*, as if they had come out of some perverse Bruce Lee film. We responded belatedly by starting to take karate lessons ourselves—I would sweat and strain with a group of friends at six in the morning, ready to take back our city. But by the time we were ready to grunt and kick and chop away, our civilian enemies had graduated to firearms and were shooting at us while the more adventurous among them blew up high-tension pylons, sabotaged government television stations and assassinated Allende's aides. And now here we were, holding a real gun in our hands for the first time: whereas they had already enlisted the armed forces, they would soon have tanks and planes and battalions at their command.

But we didn't know that then and if we had, we still would have had no alternative but to 'train' and pray that some sympathetic god would give us the time to really learn. We pointed the solitary gun by turns at a tin can on a nearby rock and hit the rock more times than we did the can and soon exhausted the fifteen rounds of ammunition (barely two clips) which was all we had been able to negotiate on the black market. The seven of us were left with a smoking gun and no bullets and a battered rock and more courage than confidence on that beautiful sunny afternoon under those mountains. And time on our hands. So we sauntered down to the other side of the hill to scout the area, almost like children on a holiday instead of would-be guerrillas, and discovered during our patrol that the slope where we had been practising was, in fact, not as secluded as our group leader had irresponsibly suggested.

In a nearby clearing, behind some scraggly trees, some fifteen to twenty truck drivers were roasting meat over a colossal fire, drinking away, laughing their heads off, while a smaller gaggle of women seasoned a prodigious salad. A dozen trucks were parked below on the road itself, blocking it: these men, with thousands of other drivers, were staging a transportation strike that had paralysed Chile in the last few weeks by cutting off many of the main highways, interrupting the country's economic lifeblood in the hope that the chaos and confusion would pressure the armed forces into intervening to restore order.

The truck drivers also recognized us for what we were. They had probably heard the shots. But even if they hadn't, it would have been enough to see us materialize out of the hills, like amateur Che Guevaras, to realize immediately that we were their enemies, that we would gladly have torched their trucks and sent them all to hell. They, on the other hand, didn't send us to hell, not at all: they were going to win, they were already winning, they were the owners of a future that they could envisage even if we couldn't and they felt therefore, as people often do when they have the upper hand, charitable and deadly calm. Maybe that's why their leader, without standing up, motioned us, with a Neanderthal joint of meat in his hand, to come near, to join in the banquet. It was remarkable to see that much food, because by then the strike itself, plus economic sabotage, a financial blockade by Washington and quite a bit of government incompetence, had made provisions scarce.

We came closer, though we did not want to share the meal. I guess we were superstitious: never accept food from someone you might have to kill. We stood there, watching them eat and drink and be merry, mesmerized by their presence. And then, their leader put an oversized hand into his pocket and took out a wad of bills—American dollar bills—as if he were a gangster in a movie, and waved them at us knowingly and counted them in our presence and made a signal and the other truck drivers took out their greenbacks as well. I realized that we were the audience for their triumph, that they wanted us to understand how things stood, how incredibly screwed we were. They were exhibiting to us, right now, a day that was not far off, when we would be hunted and they would be back on the road. Above all, they wanted their women to see our humiliation. Chile had become a country where we, who defended the legitimate government elected by the people, had to hide our training, while these men, who were being paid by a foreign power to overthrow that government, had no need to hide their financing. And adding to the personal irony of the situation was something that neither the truck drivers nor their women nor my companions knew, because I had done my best to try and conceal it: that of all those present that day, I was the most 'American', the only one who could have spoken their own language to the CIA operatives who had provided that money and planned the whole damn thing, who could have understood their jokes, their references to Dagwood and Blondie.

But I had renounced my United States identity. I wanted nothing more to do with the country of my childhood. Chile was my land, it belonged to me, I thought, more than to those drivers willing to sell it off to the highest bidder. They could display their dollars all they wanted, because very soon I would be promenading my own weapon against them in every home in the country: Susana la Semilla, my cartoon character.

I had, in fact, conceived her as an answer to their transportation strike, or to be more precise, as a way of dealing with the most devastating of its many side effects: those thousands of trucks blocking the roads had left thousands of tons of fertilizer rotting in the ports, endangering next year's harvest. Because of my post at La Moneda, I had been asked by Jaime Tohá, the Minister of Agriculture, to contrive an angle for an advertising campaign that would put the blame on our anti-patriotic adversaries.

I had come up with more than an angle. I had come up with a love story, an epic, a saga. I conjured up sexy, luscious, loquacious Susana, Susan the Seed, a sort of Chilean version of Chiquita Banana, pining away in the lonely countryside, eager to bear fruit and be a mother. Her aspirations to multiply were, however, being frustrated by the fact that her faraway lover, Federico el Fertilizante, Fred the Fertilizer, is being held captive in a faraway port.

And I had proceeded to write the story of how Federico escapes his captors and goes on the road, foils the saboteurs and finally joins Susana and makes her germinate. I had scripted twenty-five one-minute TV spots to be transmitted week after week, starting in September of 1973 and culminating in an orgasmic finale, my two lovers coupling under the stars of March 1974. Now I comprehend that this socialist soap opera was my Utopian version of a future where the people defeated hunger: the shining anticipation of a victory of love over terror that was about to be resoundingly denied by history.

But in order to give birth to Susana, to move my harvest of visions from my own private page on to the screens of millions of my compatriots, I had to persuade one man to sign on: Augusto Olivares, the congenial Director of National Television—and I was supposed to make the pitch on . . . 'Let's say Tuesday

September eleventh,' he had suggested to me nonchalantly when I had told him in early September that it was urgent that we get together. He had smiled at me through his bushy, overgrown moustache, looking somewhat like a walrus, perhaps thinking that I was a bit loony but then—so was he. Discussing seeds and fertilizers when the ship was about to sink. 'Let's say—ten-thirty. I've got an opening around ten-thirty in the morning. Not at La Moneda. At my office. OK?'

Of all the days he could have chosen he unwittingly chose the day when the coup against Allende was to be launched and of all the times, he chose, again without the slightest prescience on his part, the one and only time of the day that would keep me away from La Moneda that morning, allowed me, exceptionally, to oversleep, allowed me to be awoken late on the morning of 11 September by the sound of military planes flying low over our house, buzzing the neighbourhood.

It was only then that I found out that the coup was in progress. When I switched on the radio and the station was playing a military march and I changed stations and the other one was also playing a march, and on and on, flipping the dial, and I heard the first proclamation of the military junta that had taken over Chile, and at the end of the proclamation the name of General Augusto Pinochet Ugarte who was supposed to be heading the forces loyal to the democratically elected government, and I knew that the revolution had failed, that's when I knew, the exact moment, that death had finally caught up with me, that all my fears from childhood were about to materialize savagely in real life. And a few minutes later, with Angélica's hand in my trembling hand, I listened to Allende's *últimas palabras* from the presidential palace, his farewell speech in which he told his people that he would not resign, that he would die defending democracy, die so others can live. Later I'd find out that next to him as he spoke was his old friend Augusto Olivares, readying himself for death at the President's side. Augusto never heard how Susana la Semilla was supposed to save his life, how in my delirium I had made her symbolically save the nation. He never knew that, implausibly, the only life that my cartoon character ended up saving was mine.

But is that true? I have told the story so many times that I may have ended up believing it, comforting myself with the notion that somehow I had evaded my own death through the efforts of one of my own inventions, that some fiction I had saved from nothingness saved me from that same nothingness, from becoming fictional. It's symmetrical and a bit cute and makes a great story. But is it true?

As far as it goes, yes: it would have been enough for Claudio Gimeno to have said no, he wouldn't swap shifts with me at the palace, for Olivares to have said another day, for Susana not to have said anything, to have stayed silent and not inspired me—one slight variation and I would be dead, I would have made it to La Moneda the night of the coup or the dawn of the coup or the early morning of the coup.

Essential as they were, however, none of these happenstances really guaranteed my survival. Dozens of other activists who were close to Allende or worked at the presidential palace did no guard duty on 10 September, and many of them had, like me, activities planned elsewhere that morning, appointments far from Allende's side—and that did not save them from being killed at La Moneda. They ended up there quite simply because they were called up sometime during the night: there's an emergency, they were told, the coup has started, they were told, they were told to report immediately. Their names were on a list. I had held that list in my hands on the nights when I myself was sleeping at La Moneda. I had read my own name and phone number on that list just two nights before. I was one of those who were supposed to be summoned in case of an emergency.

But nobody had given me a call.

Why not? Had it just been one more crazy coincidence? One more chaotic incident in a chaotic day, a misunderstanding that had, once again, favoured me instead of somebody else? Is that all? Is that it? No more than a series of arbitrary intercessions had spared me? Could the difference between living and dying really just grind down to this: destiny or fate or sheer dumb wonderful idiotic luck?

Or is there an explanation? Is there a meaning in all of this, a message being sent, something I was being taught? Agnostic that I am now, agnostic that I was then, how to make sense of this sudden reprieve: I had deliberately placed myself in harm's way, almost challenging violence to come and ravish me, and that violence, when it had exploded in all its fury, had ignored me. How to avoid wondering, with humility, perhaps with terror, whether there may have been a design, a deeper miraculous meaning to my deliverance from death? How to avoid the temptation of a mystical interpretation, that some sort of power was trying to rescue me, redeem me, forbidding death to come near, saying to that reckless man: No, you don't—you're needed elsewhere. Your time hasn't come yet.

This religious reading of my survival alternately fascinates and disgusts me. What sort of joy can I derive from imagining a God who condemns so many innocents to death and saves me? What sort of comfort is there in assigning responsibility to some equally precarious higher entity for what happened? Isn't randomness preferable, less cruel, than a supposedly superior consciousness playing haphazardly with our lives? And yet, let me confess that for many years I could not rid myself of the suspicion that some benevolent deity had intervened on my behalf. Some benevolent deity had decided to counter the malevolent gods of the Central Intelligence Agency, the demons of the Chilean armed forces, the men in the shadows who were determining my death.

It turned out that there was a benevolent deity, a secret hand, a message: but luckily for my stubborn atheistic convictions, it was not the hand of a God but that of a real human being of flesh and blood, and by the time he gave me the message, many years later, I had more or less figured it out for myself, had confronted the loneliness of survival and had puzzled out on my own why I had been blessed by the random finger of the universe.

The man to whom I owed my life was Fernando Flores, the very minister who had originally given me the job at La Moneda. He was the one who, in the hours before dawn on that 11 September, had decided to cross me off the list of people to be called. When the news of the uprising had been confirmed, his bodyguard had reached for the phone, started to dial—and Flores had interrupted him, asked him for the list and had read it carefully, taking his time. When he had come to me, he had taken out his pen and carefully eliminated my name.

I was only to hear this story a long time later when we both met in exile, when I visited him in the United States. I think it was in early 1978. During the intervening years, he had been in prison. The military had arrested him at mid-morning on the day of the coup, when he left the presidential palace to negotiate a truce with the seditious troops on Allende's behalf. They ignored his white flag and packed him off to the brutal Military Academy for a few days, after which he was dispatched, along with other surviving ministers of the former government, to a prison camp on Dawson Island, off Tierra del Fuego, one of the most barren, forsaken sites on the planet, and later still detained for several more years in a series of other concentration camps, awaiting a trial that never came. So it was only after he had been deported that he was able to tell me how he had intervened to save my life.

Why? I asked him. Why had he done it?

He paused, he turned inwards as if consulting some person he had once been, he thought a bit and then said, in the same offhand way with which he had probably crossed my name off the list: 'Well, somebody had to live to tell the story.'

During the Allende years, from 1970 to 1973, I had constructed my identity as primarily political: fused with Chile and its cause and its people through the revolution that would, we thought, liberate the country. And so, as the end approached, I had accepted the offer of working with Flores at La Moneda, because that is where I felt I belonged if the revolution failed, because I could not imagine myself surviving that failure, because it was a way of confirming who I was and who I wanted to be. Flores, however, in that desolate September dawn when it became clear that we had lost, saw things differently. Maybe he already knew that the tasks of defeat are not the tasks of victory. Maybe he knew that some of us would die, some of us would be jailed, some of us would turn traitors; and if that was going to happen, a witness would be needed who could escape the conflagration and tell the world the story. He thought I was that person and, at the last moment, he had used his power over life and death to correct what he considered had been his error in offering me the job, what he considered my error in accepting it.

It is a comforting idea, that I was spared because I was to be the storyteller. It does not explain why a friend switched places with me, why a TV executive asked me to come and see him at the one time that would save me, why Susana la Semilla came to me as if in a childhood dream to insist there was salvation. It does not explain, in fact, any of the fortuitous chain of coincidences that pulled me back into life just as I was hurtling towards self-destruction. It does not explain why so many of my brothers and sisters, just as talented, just as in love with life, had to die. It does not assuage the mystery that still gropes in the centre of my existence, does not entirely beat back the fear that life is blind and hazardous and that we stumble in the tender darkness and try to fool ourselves into believing there is a pattern to all of this.

But what Flores decided that day, without consulting me, merely because he thought he had to put history right and not let it take its mad course—what he decided for me that day, that does make sense. Principally, because of what happened later: who I became. It makes sense of what I forged with the life that had been given to me, loaned to me, chosen for me by chance or providence or whatever you want to call it the day I should have died.

If it is not true that this was why I was saved, I have tried to make it true.

In every story I tell.

Haunted by the certainty that I have been keeping a promise to the dead.

4

It is late in September.

I have taken refuge in the house of the Israeli Ambassador.

You have said goodbye to me, my love, and now you are going down the stairs. Soon the sound of the door to the Embassy will be heard closing, your small figure will pass to the other side of the gates, and then you will cross the street. That's where the two men come up to speak to you. The conversation hardly lasts as long as it takes for a cigarette to be lit by the smaller man, the one with the checked jacket. The other one looks you in the eyes and your eyes must feel distant and startled at that instant. Then they invite you to get into the car. One of them takes your arm, but he does so with discretion, almost courteously. The motor is running, humming like a well-fed cat, but the car does not move. Now you're getting in, you and the smaller man in the back, and the other one in front. His strong, decisive shoulders form a contrast to his apologetic lips, to the thin impoverished wisp of his moustache. It will not be possible to see you. Only, all of a sudden, your hand which accepts a cigarette and then cups the flickering flame of the lighter. Your other hand can only be seen on one occasion, for a moment fluttering on the top of the back seat, fingers that hesitate, the shine of a wedding ring. Then it withdraws. The man in the front, seated next to the empty driver's seat, is the one asking the questions. Now, with his left hand, he turns off the engine and pockets the keys. That means they do not plan to leave right away. He will remain half-hunched up against the door, one leg raised, the shoe pushing against the upholstery, fingers intertwined at the knee. Once in a while, he scratches under his sock, rubs the skin compressed by his sock. They will not be in a hurry. Children will pass by on bikes calling each other by the names their parents gave them many years ago; the mailman will cross this spring day that seems like summer bringing news and ads and maybe letters from lost loves; mothers will go for a morning stroll and teach their kids how to stand up on two feet, take a step or two instead of crawling. Now a bird perches itself on the warm roof of the car and, without even a trill, flies off like an arrow. Maybe, inside, you've detected that slight presence, that slighter absence, like a leaf that falls from a tree out of season, a bit too late; maybe you've understood that a pair of wings opened up and then was gone. The man extracts a small notebook from a pocket in his jacket, and then a pencil. He passes it to you. During the briefest wave of time, your hand can be seen receiving the pencil, the notebook. Then, as if you were not really there in the back seat of the car, that extension of your body disappears and nothing more can be seen. The man tosses his keys up into the air and catches them neatly. He smiles. He points a key at you and says something, it must be a question. Impossible to know what you answered. A beggar woman stumbles down the street, a flock of ragtag kids in her wake. She approaches the car to ask for something, and then she backs off, half-understanding or not wanting to understand. Now the car window opens and the swarthy face of the smaller man appears, the man who has been sitting next to you. He hasn't slept much, hasn't slept well: there are bags under his eyes and his features are puffy. He blinks under that implacable daylight. Then he looks towards the Embassy for a while, giving the windows the once-over to see if there is somebody watching, if there is somebody behind half-drawn curtains trying to register and remember each movement, each gesture. He stays like that for a good while, motionless, as if he could guess what is happening behind those walls. He takes out a handkerchief and wipes it across his forehead, cleans the sweat from the rest of his face. He needs to shave, he needs to get home for a good shave. Maybe all night while he waited he's been thinking of the bath full of hot water. The air dances with white spores; he blinks his heavy eyelids. The breeze has begun to fall asleep under the spell of the day's heat. He emerges from the car quickly. A stream of sunlight slides down his body. Now he gets back into the car, into the driver's seat. He holds his hand out so the other man can give him the keys. The sound of the back door that opened and closed, the front door that opened and closed, does not disturb the quiet. It's almost like a sound of harmony, sweet metal. The car moves off, passes the house, passes the curtained windows, for an eternal white instant your petite face can be seen, the way your shoulders breathe, that dress which presses to your body like the skin of a lover. You will pass without looking towards the house, your face will pass, your eyes sinking into the abrupt horizon of the street which connects with other streets. But they will not take you away. Now the car brakes a bit further on, sheltered under the generous shade of that tree you have come to know so well, that you have heard moaning and dancing its branches below the weight of the wind last night. All that can be seen is the back of the car, and in a hollow opened by the leaves gently swaying with the rays of this spring that has quickened into summer, a blur of colour that could be your hair or your neck trembling under your hair. If it were not for the leisurely and merciless progress of the minute hand on your wristwatch, where the slow blood inside your arm finds and flows with the mysterious blood inside your hand, if it were not for the imperceptible rotation of this planet, it might be thought that time had stagnated, that all movement is paralysed, that silence is definitive, and that you will stay there for ever, you, the men, the car, the street. No beggar will pass. The mailman will not come back again. The children will have to put away their bicycles and go and eat lunch. When the sun begins to invade the top of the car, when midday has finally concluded and the afternoon has finally begun, when the intolerable heat forces the driver to seek a new refuge, nothing in the world, neither the buzzing of bees nor the yellow cheerful burst of the flowers, will be able to stop that engine from being started up again, that car from inching away from the kerb, and this time it will not pause under the shade or in the sun, this time the car will go on and on and on, nothing can stop it from losing itself there, far away, down the street which connects with other streets, taking you to that place from where you will never return.

This story, seemingly fictitious, really happened. It happened to us, to Angélica and to me, exactly as written here, exactly as I wrote it many years later. Except for the ending. They did not take her away, not for a day, not for a month, not for all time. But the rest is true: by the end of September I had taken temporary refuge in the residence of one of my mother's friends, the wife of the Israeli Ambassador, waiting during the next week for a chance to slip into one of the heavily guarded Latin American Embassies that could guarantee me safe conduct out of the country. And when Angélica had come to visit me and spend the night, the next morning she had been detained by two of Pinochet's secret policemen who had been watching the house under the impression that Senator Carlos Altamirano, the fugitive head of the Socialist party, thin and bespectacled like me, had sought refuge there. An absurd notion, given his pro-Palestinian sympathies. But Angélica managed to outwit those detectives without discussing international affairs and escaped the fate the character in the story was unable to avoid.

When many years later I came to write the experience, I ended it differently, tragically, partly because that is the way most episodes like this one do end, but mainly, I think, because that was the only way of transmitting to myself and others the horror of what went on in my mind during that hour when the woman I loved was in the hands of men who could do anything they wanted to her, anything they wanted and I could do nothing to stop them. That ending did not happen in reality but it did repeat itself over and over in my imagination as I watched from a window, praying I would not have to watch it over and over in the days and years to come in my memory, praying that I would not have to imagine a world without Angélica.

Discovering, after so many days obsessed with my ever-increasing distance from the country, that I would rather lose Chile than lose Angélica, that I could live without Chile but that I could not live without Angélica, beginning to understand that the private home I had built with her was more important and would outlast the public home I had sought to build with Chile and its people.

It was then, I think, that for the first time in my life I clearly separated my wife from the country where she had been born.

Ever since I had met her, Angélica had been confused, in my mind, with Chile. All the readings and all the trips and all the protests and all the snow on all the mountains did less to attach me to that country than this one frail human being.

There I was in early 1961, a stranger in a land that I had inhabited for seven years without finding a real gateway, whose songs and customs and people I hardly knew, no matter how much I had come to admire them, regard them as a potential avenue for liberation. And then, one day, Angélica. To be quite frank, what enchanted me about her to begin with were her dazzling looks and fiery spirit and extreme joy of life, the hot sexual thought of a lithe *moreno* body under her dress, that enchanting smile of hers that the gods of advertising couldn't have coached out of a woman if they had been given a thousand years and a ton of Max Factor make-up. How much of this I identified with the exotic Chile or Latin America that I had been secretly and transgressively hungering for all these years is anybody's guess. I experienced love with the metaphors available to males in Latin America—and elsewhere—at that time, no matter how suspect and gendered I may consider them now, more than thirty years later: the woman as the earth and earth-goddess to be excavated, a territory to be explored by a pioneer, a land in which to root your manhood like a tree, those were the images that surged inside me as we made love. I could never entirely rid myself of the feeling that I was somehow making mine something more than an individual woman, that I was making love to a community that was inside her, that through her body and her life I was binding myself to a permanent place on this planet.

Now that I write this, I have come to understand that it was ultimately not Chile that I desired in her. What attracted me most deeply in the woman who would become my wife were qualities that transcended national origins or boundaries, things I would have treasured in her if she had been Lithuanian or from Mars. Her fierce loyalty, her amazing ability to see through people, her stubborn (and often exasperating) tendency to speak without minding the consequences, her almost animal loyalty, her fearlessness, her unpredictability—none of these were necessarily typical of Chile and some of them, such as her undiplomatic directness or her rejection of compromises, could even be construed as extremely un-Chilean.

And yet, if it was not Chile that finally ended up joining us, without Chile, nevertheless, the Chile I imagined inside her, it is probable that our love would not have lasted. Angélica is wonderful, but she was not then and certainly is not now, in spite of her name, an angel. Not that I was that easy either. We were attracted to each other precisely because we were opposites and if life was never boring and never will be while she is around, it was a constant clash. Given these circumstances and our immaturity, it is quite possible that we wouldn't have made it to marriage and beyond merely sustained by the dim intuition that each of us had found the long-lost half of their soul. An additional something was necessary for our love to survive those rough and desperate break-ups that all young lovers flounder through, and that something, for me, frequently seemed the vast Chile that I felt Angélica contained within herself. I could feel the country bringing me back for more, my need for the identity she gave me fastening me to her, Chile secretly gluing us together. It is the perverse logic of love that the reverse was true for Angélica: what kept her by my side when things didn't seem to work out was, she has told me, the very fact that I came from some other place, her intuition that I would not treat her the way Chilean males treat women, that I could be entirely trusted, that I was transparent, that I was naive: in other words, that I was a gringo. A gringo who happened to be frantically searching for a country that would answer his loneliness and transience.

Angélica possessed that country merely by virtue of having been born here, simply because her forefathers and foremothers had made love under these mountains and mingled their many races and interbred their Iberian and Mediterranean and Indian and African stock at a time when mine had never even dreamed of emigrating; she possessed it in the nursery rhymes in Spanish she had sung when I had been reciting Old Mother Hubbard; she possessed it in the peasant proverbs she had absorbed in the dusty plaza of the small countryside town in the Aconcagua Valley where she had been brought up; she possessed it in every Chilean spice, every Chilean fruit, every Chilean meal that had nurtured her. That was Chile, all of that and more. She had been accumulating every drop of experience inside herself like a reservoir. At some point early in our fumbling and fearful and expectant movement towards one another, I sensed that reservoir, sensed that I could drink from its waters, drink Chile in her waters.

How vast were those waters and how insatiable my thirst was brought home to me the first night we became 'pololos'—a word with which Chileans designate boys and girls who are going steady, a word that comes from a butterfly-like insect that goes from flower to flower making itself dizzy with sweetness. We had slunk into a sort of discotheque and started timidly to explore one another the way you do when you are under twenty and the universe has everything to teach you and an orchestra is remotely playing a bolero, *Bésame, bésame mucho, como si fuera esta noche la última vez,* kiss me, keep on kissing me, as if tonight were the last night, and then Angélica took her mouth from mine and began to sing (a bit off-key, but who cared) the words to that song of Latin American love that I had bypassed so often on the radio as I rushed to hum along with Frankie Avalon. A tango followed, which she also knew by heart, and inside that brain of hers, behind those freckles, was the whole repertoire of popular Latin America that I had despised and that I now wanted to learn by heart to prove my new-found identity. It may have been that very night when I asked her if she danced *cueca*, the Chilean national dance, and she smiled mischievously and grabbed a napkin from the table and waved it a bit in the air and hid her face behind it and suggested that she could teach me some steps, that it was a matter of imagining a rooster out courting. That I had to try and corral her, corner her, that this was the game. She was the treasure and I was the hunter. She would hide and I would seek.

It may have been the next day, when we went down to the centre of Santiago together, that I realized that Angélica had within herself a treasure she barely knew about, a treasure that I was seeking and that she was not even trying to hide. Her presence by my side as we strolled through the centre of the city I had lived in for seven years suddenly transformed me into a tourist arriving at this foreign destination for the first time. I had often passed this café, for instance, and it meant absolutely nothing to me, but for Angélica it was the place where in the Forties her journalist father, after he had put the paper to bed, would meet her mother and a group of Popular Front friends and drink and talk till dawn. As Angélica casually told me the story of the night her father had waited for the news of the Allied landing in Normandy, we were interrupted by a pretty young woman. She came up to us, pecked Angélica's cheek and was introduced to me as the daughter of her 'Mami Lolo', the woman who had brought up Angélica when she was a little girl in the countryside. The two of them chatted for a while about people I did not know and places I had never been. When the young woman said goodbye and we continued on our way, Angélica sketched out the story of her nanny, who had been brought very young into the family house as a helper and later on had cared for the grandchildren, and who, it would turn out, was in fact the illegitimate daughter of Angélica's grandfather. 'You have to come to Santa Maria,' Angélica said, 'where I was raised, and meet my Mami Lolo.' Half a block later, Angélica was greeted by someone else and so it went and so it would go. So many people and so many conversations and so many stories, stories, stories. Perhaps it was then that I began to understand that Angélica was a network of stories, a lineage of stories, a wellspring of stories that had made her, that she was full to the brim with people, with *Chileans*, who had made her. It may have been then or it may have been later, but at some point rather early in our relationship, I realized that Angélica's connection to Chile was the opposite of mine, that it was not and never could be voluntary, that she could not discard it as I was in the process of discarding the United States, that it was as much part of her as her lungs or her skin. In the months and years to come, as she guided me into her life and her body, she also guided me into the mysteries of a continent that should have been mine by birthright but from which I had cut myself off, a country I had seen for years as nothing more than a stop on the road to somewhere else.

And when I had been faced with the loss of that country after the coup, when I had finally agreed that yes, I would seek refuge in an embassy, what had ultimately made that decision tolerable like a secret silhouette inside me was the promise of Angélica, the certainty that I could wander the earth for ever if the woman who had taught Chile to me was by my side.

Now she was in that car with those two men and I had come face to face with the possibility that she would not accompany me in my wanderings, that she would not be there at all. I told myself that maybe this was the cruel and hidden reason behind my miraculous survival: death had spared me, because all along it was going to take Angélica instead. Death was going to punish me for having refused its gift and stayed in this country all this September. I was going to be punished for not having left immediately and sent my family away; this was what I deserved for pretending that I was untouchable and immortal.

But again I was given a reprieve.

When those two men released her and she came back into the residence and we trembled against each other, when I was able to hold my love, my best friend, my companion for life, in these arms that had already despaired of ever touching her again, my hand going through her hair over and over, closing my eyes and then opening them again to make sure that it was still true, that she was still here, I was finally ready to learn the lesson that death had sent me one more time, perhaps one last time. It was then that the coup finally caught up with me, that it descended on me as it had descended on La Moneda and exploded silently inside me like the bombs had exploded all over the city and made me understand, for the first time since Allende's overthrow, the full and irreversible reality of the evil that was visiting us and that would not go away. When I had anticipated my own death, I thought I had discovered what the Inferno is: the place where you suffer for ever without being able to escape. Now I knew I had been wrong: the Inferno is the one place in the world where the person you most love will suffer for all eternity while you are forced to watch, unable to intervene, responsible for having put her there.

And that Inferno was here, the country I had associated with Paradise.

It was time to leave Chile. □

A working people

Portraits of India by Sebastião Salgado
on the anniversary of Indian independence

sponsored by Christian Aid

City Arts Centre
Edinburgh
Nov 1 1997 - Jan 12 1998

Royal National Theatre
London
June/July 1998

Montage Gallery
Derby
Jan 16 - Feb 22 1998

Norwich Arts Centre
Norwich
Oct 5 - Nov 28 1998

London: PO Box 100, SE1 7RT
Telephone: 0171 620-4444

Registered charity no 258003

Christian Aid
We believe in life before death

DON'T MISS OUT ON MAJOR ISSUES

Granta publishes the most lively, original, entertaining and informative writing it can commission, inspire or find, four times a year. There are almost no boundaries. It can be fiction or non-fiction, short story or memoir, reportage or polemic. The only demand that *Granta* makes is the writing illuminates not other literature but life— and that *Granta* publishes it first.

Subscribe now and you'll save up to 30% on the £7.99 bookshop price and get *Granta* delivered to your home!

'Essential reading'
Observer

DON'T MISS OUT ON MAJOR ISSUES

SAVE UP TO 30% (OR £28) WITH A **GRANTA** SUBSCRIPTION

Subscribe to *Granta* and you'll save money and get *Granta* delivered direct to your home, four times a year.

A subscription to *Granta* makes a great gift, too. See the form overleaf for details.

'The quality and variety of its contributors is stunning . . . *Granta* is, quite simply, the most impressive literary magazine of its time.'
Daily Telegraph

GRANTA
FREEPOST
2/3 HANOVER YARD
NOEL ROAD
LONDON
N1 8BR

DEBORAH SCROGGINS
EMMA

When I think of Nasir, I remember the sun. Nothing in that place escaped it. Perched on the great savannah of northeast Africa, Nasir lies a hundred miles east of the White Nile and another eighty miles west of Ethiopia. Early in the century the British established a command post there over the local tribe of extremely tall and fearless cattle-keepers, the Nuer. But when I went there, Sudan's civil war had destroyed most of the old town. The United Nations was delivering food at a crude airstrip made from the rubble of evacuated buildings. The rebel Sudan People's Liberation Army (the SPLA) had located their provincial headquarters a few miles up the Sobat River from the ruins.

I remember how desolate it was, and I think of Emma. I met her there in 1990. I was working for an American newspaper; she worked for a Canadian relief agency. She had not yet scandalized the region's aid workers by marrying the local warlord and going to live with him and his gunmen in a mud compound on the Sobat. But even then there was something unsettling about her.

I had been in Nasir for a week, reporting on the war between the Islamic government in the north and the non-Islamic (pagan and Christian) rebels in the south. I had been interviewing teenage soldiers and starving children: since the war began in 1983 perhaps a million people had died, a quarter of them in the war-made famine of 1988. Still, there was an eerie beauty to this part of southern Sudan. The years of fighting had sealed the area off from modern life, turning the swampy land between Ethiopia and the Nile into a vast wilderness, interrupted only by occasional bombings and machine-gun fire.

At the end of the week I went to the airstrip and waited for a United Nations plane to fly me back to Kenya. The plane had been delayed for several days, for the usual obscure reasons. Perhaps the government had banned flights to rebel-held areas; perhaps the UN was punishing the rebels for threatening to shoot down UN flights to government areas—no one knew. I walked up and down the banks of the Sobat, where a blue heron roosted on an ancient steamer and long-horned cattle roamed through what once had been a market street. By the time I heard the whine of the plane, it seemed like a visitation from a civilization whose existence I had already begun to forget.

The plane came down in the tight corkscrew that the pilots always performed in case someone shot at them from the ground. The engine died, the door opened, and out jumped Emma. She was six feet tall, as slender as a model, and she was wearing a red miniskirt. An SPLA officer was with her, and they were laughing together about something. It was hard to believe that she was flying in on an emergency relief mission. She looked as if she were stepping out of a private plane to go to a party.

In a way I was not surprised. I had heard about Emma: young, glamorous, energetic and idealistic, she had sent a ripple of excitement through the social circles of the aid business. In Nairobi—the headquarters of the humanitarian industry in East Africa—she had a reputation for wildness: adventures in the bush, nightlife in the city. She was an Englishwoman said to feel at home only with Africans. Some admired her nerve; others thought her dangerous. I'd caught sight of her a few weeks earlier in Lokichoggio ('Loki'), the Kenyan staging ground for UN relief operations into southern Sudan. She was in a mess tent surrounded by men. I couldn't hear what she was saying, but I could see that they didn't want her to stop.

Now, in Nasir, I understood the undercurrent of disapproval that followed in her wake. That gorgeous splash of a miniskirt seemed almost indecent in a place filled with sick, hungry people catching their breath between bouts of famine and vicious killing. To look happy seemed tactless—a flaunting of one's good fortune. It occurred to me that the unofficial uniform for most of us Westerners—blue jeans and T-shirts, modest shorts—was one way of desexing ourselves, at least in our own minds. It announced: 'We're not here to have a good time.' It was like a surgeon's scrubsuit, or maybe a modern version of sackcloth and ashes; an unspoken signal that we were wiser than the Sudanese, and in a kind of mourning for them and the things they did. Not that the Sudanese were fooled. The truth was that the average Western aid worker or journalist delighted in the buzz, the intensity of life in a war zone, the heightened sensations brought on by the presence of death and the determination to do good. We wanted to be here; we were paid good money to be here; and the Sudanese knew it.

Emma's miniskirt seemed a refreshing departure from the

usual pieties. It suggested that she was more honest than the rest of us, that she wasn't afraid to admit that she was here because she wanted to be.

Emma and I exchanged pleasantries, nothing more, and I didn't see her again for a long time. But I began to think about her for another reason, which had nothing to do with clothes. In Nasir, I had spent days interviewing the SPLA's 'education coordinator', a man named Lul. He had claimed to be a great friend of hers. He was the sort of man his fellow Nuer used to call a black *Turuk*—a black man who wore clothes and could read and write and had adopted some of the ways of the Ottoman Turks and other foreigners who'd invaded Nuerland a century and a half earlier. Like most Nuer, he was black as a panther, tall and thin with a narrow head and a loping walk. Lul was a former schoolmaster and an elder in the Presbyterian Church. He was also a bore and a bully. In the afternoons, he would lecture me in his straw shack about why southern Sudan was so backward while he drank Ethiopian gin from the bottle. ('The stage which we are at now,' he would say, 'is the stage of the European in the Stone Age. And you, you be careful. You should know you are talking to somebody who knows everything.') He would recite SPLA slogans with noisy fervour, insisting that southerners would never settle for anything less than a new, secular government for the whole of Sudan, though less than a year later he was to be equally enthusiastic when Riek Machar, the Nasir-based leader of the Nuer, split from the SPLA and formed a new movement that wanted the south to secede and become independent.

Emma was working with Lul to try to reopen Nasir's schools, which had been closed for six years because of the war. I wondered how she could stand it, listening to him raving on day after day about fighting for a hundred years to create a 'New Sudan' in that blinding emptiness. But according to Lul, he and Emma got along famously. In fact, he was more interested in discussing Emma than the schools. 'You know, Em-Maa'—he pronounced her name with a satisfied smack of his lips—'is just like one of us. She walks everywhere without getting tired. She is bringing us so many things we need, like papers and chalks and school books. You people should know, our commander likes

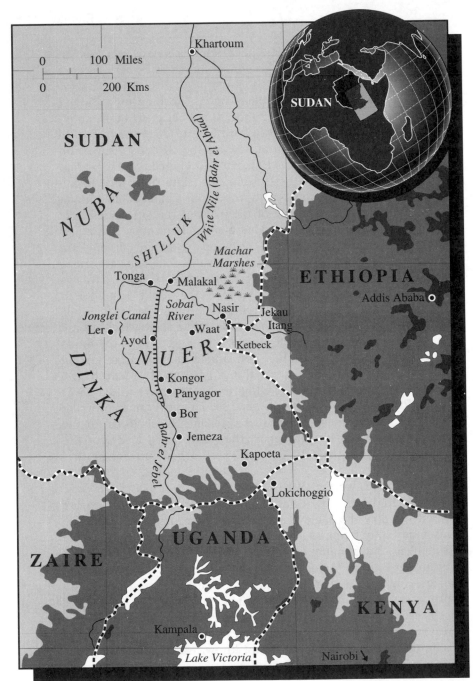

SUE WORTH/LYVENNET

Em-Maa very much. Very much!' Underneath the praise there was something leering in the schoolmaster's voice.

When I learned, six months later, that Emma had actually married Riek Machar, the commander Lul had been talking about, the one who liked her 'very much', I remembered that mingling of lust and envy and contempt in Lul's voice. Naturally I knew of 'Dr Riek'. A black *Turuk*, like Lul, with a Ph.D. from Bradford University in England, he was the best-educated Nuer in the ranks of the SPLA. Westerners found him unusually sophisticated and amiable. But though I knew Emma only slightly, the news of her marriage provoked a jumble of emotions in me. At twenty-seven, she wasn't much younger than me. And the world of the *khawadja*—the Sudanese term for white people, the aid workers, journalists and diplomats working in Africa—is a small one, so we shared many friends and acquaintances. A few months earlier we had both been invited to spend Christmas with mutual friends in Mombasa (an invitation I was not able to take up, as I was reporting on the Gulf War from Khartoum). But I had been writing about Sudan, off and on, for three years: it was the furthest and deepest part of my experience. Now here was Emma going further and deeper than I had even imagined, crossing over from the aid world into a violent guerrilla movement led by men like Lul, men responsible for some of the horrors she had been working to alleviate. What, I wondered, drove her to take such an extreme step? It occurred to me that her story might shed some light on the entire humanitarian experiment in Africa. Or at least on the experiences of people like me, who went there thinking they could help, and came back numb with disillusionment.

And this was before I learned that Lul was later tortured to death, probably on the orders of the man Emma had married.

Aid is an idealistic enterprise, but in Africa, at least, the hard work is done by romantics. A lot of humanitarians are drawn to the world's awful places by urges half-hidden even from themselves. In the heyday of colonialism, when idealists had a lot of firepower at their disposal, the most memorable empire builders tended to be those eccentrics and flamboyants who were open to the irrational—to the emotions, to mysticism, to ecstasy—such as the hero of Khartoum, General Charles Gordon; or those who believed in nothing at all, such as the journalist Henry Stanley. None of Gordon's contemporaries could understand why he did the things he did. He went to Sudan to stamp out slavery, only to appoint the biggest slaver in the country as his deputy. In the days before the Mahdi's troops cut him down, he lay in his shuttered palace reading biblical prophecies that he believed pertained to Sudan. And colonials such as Gordon were engaged in a far more wholehearted attempt than today's humanitarians to remake Africa in the image of the West. Today's aid workers are in one sense an imperial rearguard, foot soldiers covering the retreat of a West defeated by the continent's persistent opacity. They may still be animated by many of the old impulses, idealistic and otherwise, but they have lost some confidence in them. In any case, it takes more than an idea, even an unselfish belief in an idea, to keep today's aid workers in place. Emma had ideals, but in the end it was romance that lured her to Africa.

Where did Emma come from? In London I went to see her mother, Maggie McCune, a trim woman who looks like what she is—the crisp and competent secretary to the registrar at St Paul's Cathedral. She still calls herself an ex-colonial, though the imperial sun was setting by the time she was born in India in 1942. Her parents had been British tea planters in Assam; and she met and married Emma's father, Julian McCune, in India in 1962. Julian, the child of an Irish father and a mother from Yorkshire, was an engineer who had knocked around Britain's colonies for more than a decade before settling down with Maggie at a tea plantation. But by the time Emma and her sister Erica were born, it was plain that there was little room in the post-war world for men such as Julian. The Indian government had started nationalizing the tea companies, replacing British executives with Indians. Julian considered going to South Africa, but Maggie wanted to spare her children the loneliness of her own colonial childhood at boarding schools in Britain. The McCunes moved to Yorkshire when Emma was three.

Emma's father took a job with a security firm, and bought a country house near Bedale, on the edge of the Yorkshire dales, large enough for what would soon be a family of six—Jenny was born in 1967, and Johnny in 1970. There were ponies for the children: Emma's mother saw a moral purpose in outdoor pursuits. 'Ponies are such good discipline,' she said. 'When you come back from riding, you can't just think about yourself, you have to brush down the horse.' But her husband was restless. He never got used to being back in England. He became involved with a woman; there were money troubles. When Emma was eleven, he killed himself.

Maggie McCune, who had never been trained to earn her own living, suddenly had to provide for four children. She was forced to sell the house and move them all into a cramped little flat. Somehow she managed to find the money to keep Emma in private schools, first at a Yorkshire convent and then at Godalming College in Kent. 'I think education is the most important gift you can give your children, don't you?' she said. Emma was never cerebral, but she was smart, and had a gift for getting people to do what she wanted. In 1982 she was offered a place to study art and art history at Oxford Polytechnic.

I asked Mrs McCune how she thought her husband's suicide had affected Emma. She said only that she thought it made Emma 'less materialistic'. Some of Emma's friends think it might have helped create a split in Emma's psyche—between the sensuality and freedom she linked with her father and abroad, and the frugality she associated with her mother and England. In any case, by the time she left home for Oxford, Africa already beckoned.

She was seventeen and in her first year at the polytechnic when she met Sally Dudmesh. Dudmesh holds a British passport, but was raised in Africa and considers herself a white African. She designs jewellery in Kenya, though when I talked to her she was visiting friends in Sussex. There was, she said, an instant attraction between the two. The first time they met, Emma was wearing a long purple velvet kaftan. She was pale and dark-haired, with a seductive whisper of a voice. 'I felt like I was meeting my own sister. She always dressed exotically. She had a wicked sense of humour. At that time, she was really arty. She had a really fun, bad-girl side.' Dudmesh felt sure that Emma was drawn to her because of her connection with Africa.

Dudmesh lived with Willy Knocker, a white Kenyan. Emma joined a circle of would-be Africanists in Oxford who liked to wear African clothes, listen to African music and talk about African politics. These students saw in Africa an escape from the restraint of middle-class English life. 'It was just a sort of wildness, a spirit of adventure,' said Dudmesh. 'There's an incredible freedom and scope to Africa that you don't find in England. In England, everything is so controlled. In Africa, there's an intrigue and a fascination and a sense that you can really expand. In England, you have the feeling that you're always having to play a certain role. You could always see that we would not end up living in England. We were not ordinary English girls.'

At Oxford Emma was not, perhaps, an ordinary student. In 1985 she took the best part of a year off to co-pilot a single-engined plane to Australia. The plane belonged to a friend from Oxford, but the flight was Emma's idea. It seemed a wild notion, but Emma later found it useful: it taught her about maps and radios.

Her Africa-loving friends envisioned Western lives against an exciting big-sky backdrop; but Emma sought a more intimate connection. She was always attracted to African men (later she would joke that white men made her think of earthworms) and especially to African men with power: politicians and generals. On the surface her views on Africa were conventional; mostly liberal platitudes. But underneath she seems to have been instinctively attracted to the high drama of it all, the almost Shakespearean sense that, behind the sham parties and borrowed ideologies, character is all. She spoke of economic development and Western imperialism, but dreamed of heroes, kings and queens.

In her last year at Oxford she took up with a former Sudanese government official, an elegant Muslim intellectual and a well-known critic of Western aid efforts who worked at the Refugee Studies Programme in Queen Elizabeth House. She had volunteered at the centre herself—this was the time of Band Aid and Live Aid, and the programme had a hip aura. When she graduated in 1986 she went, on the centre's behalf, to the refugee camps for Ethiopians in the eastern Sudanese desert.

The trip was not a success—apparently Emma got nowhere with a plan to start a refugee newspaper—but on the plane back to England she met another former Sudanese official. He too was twenty-odd years older than her, but they became lovers. He took her to stay with friends of his near Oxford: a redoubtable British mother and daughter with old ties to Sudan. Dorothy Crowfoot Hodgkin, a scientist who won the Nobel Prize for Chemistry in 1964, had grown up in Sudan, where her parents were teachers. Her daughter, Liz Hodgkin, had spent several years teaching at the University of Khartoum; she now works at Amnesty International in London.

The Hodgkins were disconcerted when their married Sudanese friend turned up with a young British girlfriend. But they quickly agreed that Emma was a 'wonderfully interesting person' and invited her to stay. After a few months, Emma decided to enrol at London's School of Oriental and African Studies for a master's degree in African studies. She and Liz Hodgkin moved to London together. Emma found a part-time job at the Sudanese cultural centre in Knightsbridge. For a while she lived with an Ethiopian man, but after they broke up, she seems to have decided that her future lay in Sudan. Liz Hodgkin said that Emma told her she didn't understand Ethiopians the way she did Sudanese. 'I just don't know what they're thinking,' she said.

Emma's supervisor at the School of Oriental and African Studies remembers her well. 'She was one of the better students we've had,' said Michael Twaddle. 'A very original person.' In 1988, evidence began to come out of Sudan that the government's tactics in the civil war had created a great famine in the south. Emma and Liz Hodgkin joined several London groups trying to promote peace. With Twaddle's help, Emma and some of the other members started a newsletter to collect information about Sudanese human rights abuses. The first issue of *Sudan Update*, as it was called, came out in June 1989, the same month that Islamic fundamentalists overthrew Sudan's weak but elected government in Khartoum. A few months later, Emma took a job in southern Sudan. She was twenty-five.

Twaddle never asked Emma why she wanted to go to Africa. 'We take it as a given that we're all hooked,' he said. Nor was he surprised when she married a guerrilla. 'People who get involved in Africa,' he said, 'often do get involved in terrible things.'

In *The Warlord's Wife*, a 1993 television documentary, Emma told her interviewer: 'Sudan has a magic that takes hold of you for better or worse.' She added: 'It's not a very beautiful country; it's the people who are so charming.' Foreigners entranced by the Sudanese often speak of their charm. But for the British television audience watching shots of Emma (languid in a pink leotard and long flowered skirt) juxtaposed with familiar African scenes— soldiers training, dying babies—the question must have been: If they're so charming, why do they keep killing each other?

In 1989, the standard journalistic answer went something like this. In the north, a Muslim government was determined to turn Sudan into an Islamic state. The non-Muslim south was fighting back. An American-educated former military officer named John Garang had formed the Sudan People's Liberation Army to lead the rebellion. Garang wanted to abolish Islamic law and create a national government that would give power to dispossessed people all over the country, not just in the south. The war started in 1983, though in a sense it was the resumption of a southern insurrection that had broken out soon after Sudan gained its independence from Britain in 1956. That round of the civil war had ended with a rickety peace in 1972, which gave the south regional autonomy. But the north, home to the Arab tribes that had devastated the south with slave-raids in the nineteenth century, proved unable to overcome its contempt for its darker-skinned, culturally African countrymen. The bigger southern tribes like the Dinka and Nuer, Nilotic cattle-herding warriors, rose up again rather than accept second-class status.

Like all such answers, this was true—but not the whole truth. Islam and Christianity were indeed part of the equation, but so were tribal and personal antagonisms less visible to the foreign eye. And money—especially money. As a political community, Sudan was to a large extent an illusion, a vast confidence trick promoted by the country's literate elite as a means of getting foreign aid and investment. Inevitably, when the jobs and money started to dry up, people fell back into more traditional tribal groupings. The north had what was left of urban life and a government. The south had oil, timber, gold and water. The war was messy: sometimes it seemed like an interminable series of bloody cattle-raids, with one side or the other constantly burning enemy villages so that they could herd away women, children and livestock. Most people were so poor and dulled by violence that plenty of them were willing to kill in exchange for some cows, a pair of trousers or a meal of sour sorghum bread.

There were also outsiders, kindling the flames for shadowy reasons of their own. Ethiopia's dictator, Colonel Mengistu Haile Mariam, wanted to retaliate against the Sudanese government for harbouring his enemies: the government of Sudan was sheltering the secessionist rebels who were eventually to overrun Ethiopia's government in those refugee camps Emma visited on her first trip to Africa. So when John Garang mutinied against Khartoum, Mengistu invited him to Ethiopia.

One long-time British investor in the region was Tiny Rowland, president of Lonrho Corporation and owner of the London *Observer*, and a career meddler in African politics. Whenever Garang or one of his associates went to London, they stayed at Rowland's Metropole Hotel. Rowland once commented to a business colleague that 'he had the future of Sudan in the palm of his hand'. When I spoke to him (on the telephone to his country house in Buckinghamshire) he stood by that statement. 'I've been involved with Sudan for over forty years,' he said. 'I was a founding member of the SPLM [the Sudan People's Liberation Movement: the political face of the SPLA]. All their uniforms were supplied by me—boots, everything. I still have a warehouse full . . . I've put about twenty to thirty million pounds of my own money into the SPLM.'

Riek Machar joined Garang's movement in 1984, five years before Emma arrived in Sudan. To most Western aid workers and journalists, he was just an unusually genial SPLA officer. But as the grandchild of a famous Nuer warrior-prophet, and the possessor of a rare advanced education, he was rather more important than we realized. John Garang was a member of the south's largest tribe, the Dinka. Both cattle-herding peoples, the Dinka and the Nuer were old rivals—with some three million people, Nuerland spread across an area the size of England. When Riek joined Garang, it was part of a conscious attempt to unite the two tribes in common cause against the government. Riek told me that back in 1983, when he was finishing his doctorate in England, a private 'contact' arranged for him and a group of southern Sudanese students to visit Libya's Colonel Gaddafi in Tripoli and John Garang in Addis Ababa. It was on this trip that Riek decided to join the SPLA. Riek didn't tell me the name of his 'contact', and Rowland couldn't recall that particular student trip. But Rowland was confident that he must have been the man who paid for it. 'Oh yes,' he said. 'Gaddafi gave me power of attorney for four years. He's a very dear, close friend of mine.'

Emma's job, in this combustible situation, was to organize a schooling programme for southern Sudanese children. Schools had been closed throughout most of the south for up to six years by then. The north had an old, if not especially deep, tradition of literacy, owing to its contact with Islam and, before that, with Christianity. But reading and writing were unknown in the south before the foreign invasions of the nineteenth century. The British left the education of the naked southern tribesmen to the voluntary efforts of Christian missionaries. At the time of Sudan's independence, only a few thousand of the several million people in the south's two largest tribes, the Dinka and the Nuer, knew how to read and write. Their helplessness before the mysterious powers of 'paper' contributed to their feelings of cultural inferiority. One of their main grievances against the north during the years of peace was Khartoum's failure to open more schools for southern children. In truth, the years of war had done more than the most diabolical northern government could have to thwart southern education. A century and a half after the first foreigner invaded and 'the world was spoiled', as southerners say, still only about one in twenty southerners could read.

Emma's programme was the pet project of Peter Dalglish, the founder of the Canadian aid agency Street Kids International (SKI). Dalglish is a bouncy Canadian who gave up his legal career after visiting a famine camp in Ethiopia in 1984. 'It occurred to me that perhaps the world didn't need another corporate lawyer,' he told me. He left his Halifax law firm for Sudan, where he eventually became involved in Operation Lifeline Sudan, a UNICEF programme set up to ease the famine of 1988 by shipping food from Kenya to the rebel-held areas of the south. Dalglish had a British friend at UNICEF called Alastair Scott-Villiers (who happened to know Emma from Oxford). In 1988, Scott-Villiers visited parts of the south that had been closed to foreigners for years. After five years of war, only a few hundred bullet-pocked and mostly roofless brick or concrete buildings were left standing in an area three times the size of Great Britain (there are only four miles of paved road in the south's 322,000 square miles). Wasted refugees wandered through the grassy swamps towards the camps in Ethiopia. So many skeletons lay alongside the path to Ethiopia that the Nuer called it 'The Trail of Bones'.

In some places, Scott-Villiers encountered bands of skinny young boys marching under SPLA guard to Ethiopia. The rebels claimed that the boys were orphans, but the aid workers knew that the SPLA was encouraging Dinka and Nuer families to send their boys to the big refugee camps across the border—telling the boys' parents that their children might get an education at one of the UN-funded camp schools. In fact, most of the boys seemed to end up fighting alongside the rebels long before their education was completed or, in some cases, begun. The SPLA argued that reviving the south's schools was an important first step in the rebuilding of a shattered society. The Westerners saw the schools as a chance to keep southern boys from being forced to join the army. Scott-Villiers's wife, Patta, another aid expert, put together a proposal for Dalglish's outfit to fund a project. Patta knew Emma already, and suggested her for the job.

Emma accepted eagerly. Dalglish met her some months later, on one of his periodic visits to Nairobi. She drove up to the Fairview Hotel in the battered Land-Rover she'd named 'Brutus' (an early sign of her interest in rebel leaders). Dalglish, only a few years older than Emma, was smitten. 'Who wouldn't be?' he said. 'She was extremely dashing. Everything with Emma had a story. You know, a lot of people her age are back in the City of London now, driving smart cars. Emma had no interest in those things. She was very compassionate. She clearly had a real interest in children, in helping kids.' She enthralled Dalglish with tales of her escapades, and invited him to go camping. They looked at flamingos and swam nude in the salt flats outside Nairobi.

Dalglish was impressed by Emma's flair. With help from the SPLA, she had somehow turned a small budget of around $10,000 into a network of bush schools. In just over a year her schools had about 25,000 pupils, most of them boys and girls who had never before attended classes. Emma found that there were more than enough literate southern Sudanese willing to teach in return for soap and salt, which were more valuable than money in the south's barter trade. She convinced UNICEF to lend her two vehicles as well as other supplies. One of the biggest obstacles to her programme was the lack of books printed in the southern languages. Someone had discovered that the missionaries who had worked in Sudan a generation earlier still had the original printing plates for their children's readers in southern languages. The books were reprinted, and Emma gave them to her teachers.

The schools were rough. Classes were held under trees. I once winced through an English lesson at one of her schools in 1990. The teacher pointed to his ears and shouted, 'Repeat after me! These are my eyes!' No one asked whether it made sense to be encouraging southerners to put their faith in Western education in a country whose Western-style society had been withering for thirty-five years. But it was moving to see the joy that the children and their parents took in learning. The woman who took care of the decaying missionary house where I stayed in Nasir counted herself lucky to be able to sit up at night by a kerosene lantern, trying to teach herself to read from one of Emma's books.

It took Emma no time at all to figure out the political implications of her new role. She was giving southern rebels the UN supplies and teachers' salaries they needed to open schools, and, naturally, Khartoum opposed this, out of fear that it would bolster the rebels' authority. But Emma took tremendous pleasure in her power to bestow what the southerners saw as the ticket to a better life. 'It was a wild place with a lot of opportunity for her,' said Sally Dudmesh. 'She had this incredibly powerful job. She was like the Minister of Education! I think she just found out she could have this power. She could go places.'

She discovered something else about herself at this time: she was good at war. Once, she was caught, along with some other Westerners, in a government bombing raid on a collection of mud huts at Bor. Crouched in a shelter dug by the SPLA, the aid workers listened to the whistling of the bombs. When they crawled out, they saw bodies everywhere. People were screaming. Some children were alive, but shrapnel had cut off their legs. The SPLA medical team had run away. One of the aid workers, a Vietnam veteran, climbed into the UN vehicle and drove around in circles, maddened with rage. Emma remained calm: she seemed almost exhilarated. She radioed the UN to divert a plane to pick up the wounded, and organized the Sudanese to dig holes for their dead.

Late in 1990, Emma took Dalglish on a tour of some of the bush schools. They stopped in the town of Kapoeta, an armed SPLA camp that was the drop-off point for trucks carrying relief food from Kenya. There was a young orphaned boy in Kapoeta who was deaf and mute. Emma thought his hearing might be restored with proper medical care, and brought a Walkman with her. She placed the headphones on the boy's ears and gradually turned up the sound. Dalglish told me that he would never forget the moment when the boy heard his first notes of music: he leapt into the air, weeping with happiness. On the same trip, Dalglish recalled, he and Emma were rattling along a mined road one day in the back of a truck when they got into a conversation about *The Iliad*. Didn't this world of warriors in southern Sudan remind her of the heroic age of Greece? Wasn't all this talk about honour and fate and feuds right out of the great epic? And what did Emma think about Achilles' preference for a short but spectacular life instead of a long, dull one?

Oh yes, Emma agreed. She would much prefer the fate of Achilles to that of ordinary mortals.

At the end of May, in 1991, radio operators at the UN's Operation Lifeline Sudan office in Nairobi began receiving urgent messages from Emma in Nasir. As the Street Kids International representative, she was allowed to use the UN radio in emergencies. She warned that hundreds of thousands of hungry Sudanese refugees were fleeing their camps inside Ethiopia and walking back into southern Sudan. She begged the UN to begin airlifting relief supplies to Nasir. She even requested a UN peacekeeping force to provide a safe haven for the refugees.

It was true that Ethiopia was in chaos. Just over a week earlier, on 21 May, Mengistu had fled the country as rebel forces advanced on Addis Ababa. The Operation Lifeline Sudan officials in Nairobi had no doubt that large numbers of people were on the move, but every single delivery of grain inside Sudan was subject to delicate negotiations. They knew that to Khartoum the idea of a peacekeeping force would sound like a declaration of war. They were furious with Emma for using their open radio to broadcast what sounded like flagrant rebel propaganda.

Alastair and Patta Scott-Villiers took a boat from Nasir to Jekau, a village on the border between Sudan and Ethiopia, to find out what was happening. On 29 May, as they later wrote in an article for the journal *Disasters*, they watched 15,000 people cross into Sudan. These people came from Itang Camp, which until three days earlier had been the largest refugee camp in Ethiopia, and one of the largest in the world. Without Mengistu's protection, the SPLA could not maintain its bases there. So on 26 May, the rebels marched all 150,000 inhabitants out of the camp. Over the next few weeks, about 130,000 of them arrived in Nasir.

As the refugees walked the hundred-mile route along the Sobat River from Jekau to Nasir, they were bombed by the Sudanese government and attacked by bandits. Tarquin Hall, a young British journalist, saw them when they reached Nasir. 'On the south bank of the Sobat, as far as the eye could see, huddles of scrawny, dying people lay about on the cracked, sunbaked earth,' he wrote afterwards. 'Skeleton-like figures crawled across the landscape on all fours, too weak to stand. In order to protect themselves from the sun, the returnees covered their bodies from head to toe in a mixture of ash and mud. The substance turned their skin a deathly gray which made them look like corpses awaiting burial in a mass grave.'

There to meet them were the Scott-Villiers, from UNICEF, and Douglas Johnson, an Oxford-based historian of southern Sudan on temporary assignment to the World Food Programme. They were joined by dozens of other aid workers, who set up beds and mosquito nets for themselves in the abandoned houses of the missionaries along the Sobat. But the relief officials had little food or medicine to give the refugees. Khartoum refused to permit the

UN to expand the operation beyond daily flights of a single plane, accusing unnamed Western aid workers of violating the neutrality of Operation Lifeline. To their chagrin, UN officials learned that Khartoum was not wrong. When they arrived in Nasir they found Emma living with Riek in his thatched military compound at a place called Ketbek, a few miles up the Sobat.

Emma and Riek had met briefly in 1989, in Nairobi. They saw each other again when he passed through Kenya four months later. Then, in February 1991, Riek sent her a written invitation to visit him in Nasir. Planes were not flying there at that time, so Emma set off in a car with Willy Knocker. They drove 1,500 miles through the bush, along mined dirt tracks. Riek said later that when they finally arrived it was the first car to have reached Nasir in eight years. Two days later, he asked Emma to marry him.

And now, with thousands of withered refugees converging on the place, she made a decision. On 17 June, Emma and Riek announced that they were getting married that afternoon.

Patta Scott-Villiers, who had been organizing workers to distribute food, was mustered into service as a bridesmaid. She ran around among Nasir's weed-covered ruins picking flowers for Emma's bouquet. The wedding was held in a little Presbyterian church built by American missionaries and badly damaged in the war. The church's Nuer pastor performed the ceremony wearing a pink bathrobe. Riek wore his fatigues. Emma was dressed in an Ethiopian white shawl, and was given a silver ring that Alastair Scott-Villiers had bought for Patta in India. Riek's fellow SPLA commander, Lam Akol, was the best man. Patta Scott-Villiers remembers that a huge red sun was setting over the grasslands as Emma and Riek walked through the mud to the church. The pastor recalls that Riek didn't seem to be paying any cows for Emma, as was the Nuer custom. Otherwise 'it was just a regular marriage ceremony,' he said. 'Everybody was very happy.'

The wedding struck Emma's colleagues as the kind of surreal sideshow that often accompanies awful disasters. When you see starving Rwandans or Somalis or Cambodians staring with such solemn dignity out of your television screen, you get the idea that such camps must be like mass hospitals in the dust. You think it must be all emaciated children lining up for food handed out by

sternly heroic aid workers. That's how it appears on television, but in reality it is more like a Hieronymus Bosch painting—a hallucinatory sea of huts and figures and odd little nightmare scenes punctuated by the rare saintly cameo. I remember how shocked I was in a famine camp in 1988 when I heard that Sudanese soldiers were screwing the refugees. But it's a funny thing about those camps—the less food there is, and the more dead bodies you find in the morning, the more fucking there is.

Power is naked in such places. It comes down to who has food and who doesn't. The aid workers try to cover it up, try to make the men with guns deny themselves in favour of the children and the women. The camp's rulers play along for a while, but then the mask falls away. The strong always eat first. Then the question for the aid workers is: Are we doing more harm by feeding the men with guns than we would by letting everybody starve? In Nasir, the question arose more quickly than usual because there was less food to go around. And very soon some of the aid workers began to wonder where Emma stood in this dilemma—on the side of the refugees or on the side of Riek.

Riek's best man had his own fears about the marriage. With his small, pointed beard, Lam Akol looks like an ebony Mephistopheles. I had lunch with him in 1997 at a café in Nairobi. Spread out in front of us were papers detailing the subtle positions of the splinter group that Lam formed after he and Riek broke up a few years ago. Lam called it SPLA-United, but at that time it had united nobody much outside Lam's own Shilluk tribe. Clever, foxy Lam carries a briefcase full of such documents wherever he goes. Although Emma and the aid workers weren't aware of it, at the time of the wedding Lam and Riek—two of Garang's senior commanders—were in the process of launching a coup against their leader. For the previous year and more, Riek and Lam on one side and Garang on the other had been manoeuvring for position. It had started in 1990, when Riek visited Addis Ababa. Lam—who like Riek holds a Ph.D. from a British university—was then acting as the SPLA's 'foreign minister'. He, Riek and two other SPLA commanders decided to talk to Garang about sharing more power with lower-ranking officers such as themselves.

Garang was not pleased. In fact, Lam and Riek agree that he might have had them both shot if it weren't for the fact that his patron and protector, Ethiopia's Colonel Mengistu, was growing weaker by the day. Garang could no longer rely on the Ethiopian security forces to do his bidding, so to build up support within the SPLA for Riek and Lam's arrest he started a whispering campaign against them. Meanwhile, Lam and Riek were canvassing other commanders to see if they would support a full-blown coup. By June, the situation was very tense. According to Lam, he and another of the plotters, Gordon Kong Chuol, were scheming in their mud hut when Riek walked in and surprised them with his news. Lam was amazed that Riek could be so irresponsible, at such a perilous moment. 'I knew Garang would say she was an agent or whatever,' Lam said. 'It showed me that Riek was a carefree fellow. At that moment I knew we had difficulty.'

It was too late to turn back. In Nasir, the plotters heard that Garang planned to arrest Lam. They asked one of the aid workers flying to Nairobi to take an envelope to the BBC correspondent. It contained their 'Nasir Declaration', a thirteen-point appeal for a new SPLA based on human rights and democracy. It called for an end to the stealing of relief food and to the conscription of child soldiers. It referred to 'self-determination for southern Sudan'.

Lam said he deliberately left that last term vague. But when the BBC correspondent flew up to Nasir a few days later for an interview, Riek started blabbing into the man's tape recorder about how the SPLA shouldn't bother trying to free the whole country, just the south. 'There was no way of stopping it,' said Lam, disgusted. Poor Lam: so clever, so devious, yet forever hobbled by being a member of a smallish tribe. He was obliged to let Riek take the lead for the same reason Garang was obliged to promote Riek. If Riek wasn't in charge, the Nuer wouldn't follow, and without the Nuer the rebellion would go nowhere. The mutiny, however, was in trouble from the start. Through bad luck or bad timing or bad judgement, Riek and Lam failed to secure the overt support of any senior Dinka commanders. By the time Emma returned to Nasir a few weeks later, the coup had already galloped off in directions they say they never anticipated.

Riek had agreed when Scott-Villiers insisted that the UNICEF food was strictly for refugees, not for soldiers. But once a few *khawadjas* had stayed long enough to start recognizing faces, they spotted Riek's cook and driver lining up for rations. The aid workers frequently caught Riek's soldiers stealing, but when they complained, Riek threatened to expel them. An Englishman who yelled at Riek for commandeering two UN motorboats to catch some fish was 'PNG'ed'—named *persona non grata* and flown to Nairobi. Emma was a silent presence at these confrontations. To her former co-workers, it seemed that she had gone over to the other side. 'She was no longer a colleague,' said Wendy James, Douglas Johnson's wife. 'She represented the power.'

James, herself an Oxford social anthropologist, had come to Nasir to produce a UN report on perhaps the most desperate group of refugees, the Uduk. The Uduk are a small but distinctive tribe who used to live north of the Nuer, not far from Ethiopia. James had written two books about them in the 1980s, before they were chased out of their homeland by the war. Caught between the SPLA and the army, they had been chased all over Sudan and Ethiopia by various armed groups. In Nasir, James learned that they had been trying to return to their homeland when the SPLA forced them to turn around and walk to Nasir. They were extremely malnourished, and the UN gave them priority for feeding. But after a few weeks they were still dying. On one occasion James found them eating pythons and water snails. They had not received UN rations for eleven days. The SPLA often presented the Uduk to Western journalists and visiting officials as proof of the great hunger in Nasir. James began to suspect that Riek might be using the Uduk as bait to keep the UN food coming. She pressed Riek to move the Uduk camp to a place where they could grow their own food, but he prevaricated. She expected Emma to back her up, but Emma said nothing. When I visited James in Oxford, she became almost tearful when she recalled the frustration she had felt. 'Emma didn't want to know,' she said. 'I began to feel that she was a part of this.'

For his part, Johnson believed that the SPLA was playing an even more sinister game with about 2,000 malnourished boys. These boys were among those who had gone to Itang camp in

Ethiopia in search of an education back in 1988. Now Riek had settled them in a camp of their own, across the river from his headquarters at Ketbek. No journalist could visit Riek without seeing them—they were a pitiful sight. Photographers turned them into poster children for the relief effort. In UN language, the boys were 'unaccompanied minors'. In fact, they were accompanied at all times by about 300 well-fed soldiers, who claimed to be their teachers and insisted on handling the distribution of food to them. Like the Uduk, though, the boys kept dying.

The aid workers also noticed that the boys' rations of Unimix high-protein meal were disappearing. Some of them went to see Riek and Emma about it. While they sat chatting, Riek's servant served them some fried bread balls called *mendazis* on a bright orange plastic plate—just like the plates in the UN feeding kits supplied to the boys. The *mendazis* were uncommonly tasty, said one of the aid workers. 'Oh, it's Unimix,' Riek explained.

Johnson was appalled, by Emma as well as Riek. 'She made a great crusade for children, but when things began to go wrong, she took no position,' he said. Some of the other aid workers in Nasir did not judge Emma that harshly. It was so hard to pin down facts in Sudan, they said. Maybe the other refugees were getting more food than the Uduk and the boys because they had relations in the area and the Uduk and the boys didn't. Maybe Khartoum was to blame for not letting the UN bring enough food for everybody. So they ate Riek's *mendazis* and hoped for the best. It was pointless to argue with Riek about the Unimix unless they were prepared to stand on principles and pull out, and they weren't. (About a year after the *mendazi* episode, the London *Times* reported that Emma and Riek were eating Unimix intended for the boys. Emma and Riek called the article 'absurd'.)

The longer the aid workers stayed in Nasir, the harder they found it to distinguish right from wrong. Combatants weren't supposed to receive UN rations, but some aid workers suspected that the 'unaccompanied minors' were under-age soldiers. By insisting that children be considered innocents more deserving of food than adults, the UN was inadvertently encouraging the SPLA to starve them in hopes of receiving more aid. Then again, if most of the aid workers and journalists in Nasir never tasted any Unimix, they also never went without a meal. This made some people a little uncomfortable. But—let's face it. Food tastes awfully good after a day that begins at five a.m. and carries on until nightfall with all manner of frustrations in between. Who could blame the Westerners if they enjoyed an extra helping of corn meal and boiled fish? Think what they could be eating if they were at home in London or Paris! True, kids were dying, but if the aid workers didn't keep up their strength, more would die. This was dangerous work—there were cobras under the bedding and puff adders in the latrine pits. And then there were the moral issues raised by the blow-dried politicians and TV camera crews, who came flying in on chartered planes hired at a cost that could have fed Nasir for a week. So the discussions went at the nightly drinking sessions, until some of the old hands who had heard it all before in other famine camps were ready to scream with boredom. To many people, Emma's transgressions, such as they were, seemed only a tiny piece in a much larger and more outrageous puzzle. When she left Nasir to visit Nairobi, they wished her well.

Emma's mother was working in a London bank when Emma telephoned from Nairobi. Emma usually came to England for a few weeks each summer and her mother was expecting her. 'I have good news and bad news,' Emma said, sounding very far away on the international line. 'The bad news is I won't be coming home for a bit longer. The good news is, I'm married!'

It was the first that Maggie McCune had heard about it. She offered her congratulations.

Sally Dudmesh knew all about the romance with Riek: Emma always stayed with her when she came to Nairobi. When she came home that night and went up to Emma's room, she guessed what had happened. 'Oh my God,' she said. 'You've married him, haven't you? Why couldn't you wait?'

'I just couldn't,' Emma said—and told Dudmesh all about the wedding.

When Emma returned to England in August, everyone could see that she was in love. She made a dramatic entrance to a friend's wedding in a designer dress, by Ghost, that must have cost several hundred pounds. 'Who is that stunning woman in black?' the guests were asking. She liked to answer that she was the wife of an African guerrilla chief. She told one person it was so much fun telling people about her marriage that she wished she could videotape their reactions.

Emma knew that she was not Riek's only wife. Ten years earlier, in 1981, he had married Angelina, the daughter of a Nuer politician and schoolteacher. After their wedding, she went with Riek to Bradford University, where she had two children in three years. In 1984, when she was twenty-one, Riek left her and the children in England, returning to Sudan to join John Garang.

Emma actually tried to call on Angelina that summer, having been told that this was the proper thing for a junior Nuer wife to do. But Angelina refused to see her. Later, Emma was often asked how an avowed feminist could marry a man who already had a wife. She would speak about the importance of respecting African traditions. Sometimes she praised polygamy as more honest than the serial monogamy of the West. 'You never have to worry that your husband is having an extramarital affair,' she said in *The Warlord's Wife*. These remarks embittered Angelina, who really had to live by the traditions Emma claimed to admire. 'Who would want to share a husband?' she asked me when I visited her in the north London suburb of Kingsbury. 'The job of the first wife is to make the second wife's life hell, and vice versa.'

I had imagined Riek's first wife as a victim, but there was nothing victim-like about her. The atmosphere in her flat was striving and disciplined. She was raising four children—Riek's children—and was studying at the University of North London to become a nutritionist. She served wine, though like Riek she doesn't drink alcohol herself. The furniture gleamed with polish; textbooks and encyclopedias filled the bookcase. Big studio portraits of Riek, Angelina and the children hung on the wall. After she put the children to bed, washed the dishes and took clothes off the garden line, she told me that the portraits had been taken on the three visits Riek had made to England since he left.

Angelina and Riek had been sweethearts since she was thirteen. When they married, Angelina's father insisted on a Catholic ceremony, fearing that if they married in the traditional

Nuer way, Riek would see it as a licence to take additional wives. 'Men will always take advantage of culture,' Angelina's father warned her. So they were married in the most stridently monogamous Christian church her father could find. 'Not that it made any difference,' Angelina said bitterly. 'A man asked me why I am so devastated. I said "Wait and see how you feel if your wife were to bring home a co-husband."' Of Riek's marriage to Emma, she said: 'It made me feel as if I had wasted all of my years.' She had wanted to divorce him—she had grounds under Nuer law because he had not asked her permission to take a second wife. She said she presented Riek with her ultimatum two years later when he visited London for the first time after his second marriage. But Riek didn't pay much attention. On the contrary: when he left, in 1993, Angelina was pregnant again.

Did Emma feel betrayed when Riek slept with Angelina? Later, Riek told me that the only betrayal she ever complained to him about was something else that occurred on that trip to England in 1991. On 28 August Emma was in London when she learned through the BBC that her new husband and Lam had proclaimed their independence from John Garang. The BBC reported that Riek and Lam were calling for a new SPLA that would concentrate on creating an independent southern Sudan rather than overthrowing the Khartoum government. On one level, Emma was thrilled. She loved the rhetoric that condemned the SPLA's human rights abuses and demanded greater democracy within the movement. But she was furious that Riek had kept such an important secret from her. She flew straight back to Africa to confront Riek. 'You can't take me for granted like that,' she told him.

That, he said, was the last thing he ever tried to hide from her.

At first Emma seemed to think she could carry on as an aid worker in Nasir as if nothing had changed. She sent her boss, Dalglish, a long field report. 'It said "I did this and distributed this much and PS three weeks ago I married Riek Machar in a short ceremony in his community,"' Dalglish recalled. Such breezy confidence was typical of Emma, and Dalglish was so infatuated that his first instinct was to go along with her. But it was impossible. 'My board said no. They said southern Sudan is already highly politicized. We cannot have the representative of our agency married to the commander of the area.' The board wrote to Emma to say that because Street Kids International had to preserve its neutrality, it couldn't renew her contract.

Emma's friends in the aid business had warned her that this would happen. But Emma was strangely blind to the obvious conflict between her humanitarian work and her husband's war. 'She wrote and said "You're firing me because I fell in love with someone and I resent that,"' Dalglish said. 'I had sent her that poem about how the moving hand of time writes ["and having writ, moves on"]. I was trying to say that what's done is done. I was really upset by her letter, really hurt. I cried. She accused me of having betrayed her and betrayed the children.' Later, Riek too remembered Emma's fury. 'It definitely affected her because it was a good source of income,' he said. 'And she was angry with the behaviour of Peter because he wrote her a silly poem.' Did Emma not see that she had put Dalglish in an embarrassing position? Or did she just not care? She certainly regretted the loss of her $12,000 a year salary. She incurred almost no expenses in Sudan, and had saved enough to keep going for a while. But she liked to live well when she was in Nairobi and London, and would come to be irked by her lack of money.

But she was madly in love. Each dangerous move Riek took against Garang heightened her excitement. Even the aid workers were caught up in it. Everyone agreed that Garang's SPLA-Mainstream, as people now started calling it, was a secretive, dictatorial organization. Some said the SPLA's leadership was a mafia bent on plundering the south for gold and timber and stealing aid money. Until now, southerners had had no alternative but to side with Garang against the Islamic fundamentalists. Emma's husband was offering them liberation from both. Emma had persuaded the UN to donate a typewriter and mimeograph machine to her education programme; now she used them to produce proclamations and manifestos in the hut she shared with Riek. She said once that it was 'an incredible high' to get up from lovemaking to draft constitutions for an independent southern Sudan. She was twenty-seven.

Unfortunately, her new husband was no Thomas Jefferson. In September 1991, Riek's breakaway force began attacking the SPLA-Mainstream in Dinka villages near Garang's home town, Bor. Lam and Riek seem to have hoped to persuade wavering commanders to join their side by demonstrating their strength in Garang's backyard. Bor was bigger than Nasir, with a good airstrip which allowed the UN to deliver a lot of food, and the nearby villages were rich in long-horned cattle. Riek had started calling himself 'Riek Machar Teny-Dhurgon'—after his grandfather, the celebrated Nuer warrior-prophet. As it happened, a new prophet had arisen in Nuerland, named Wut Nyang. Wut Nyang had been talking about how Riek was left-handed and how, around the turn of the century, the most famous of all the Nuer prophets, Ngundeng, had foretold that a left-handed man would be the salvation of the Nuer. Others claimed that Ngundeng said there would be peace once civil war came to Bor. Some remembered that Ngundeng prophesied that after the white people left, black *Turuk* would rule for a while. Then all the foreigners would be expelled and the Nuer could go back to raiding the Dinka, as they had done before the first outsiders arrived 150 years earlier.

Amid such portents, unmarked planes started airdropping mysterious bundles to the Nasir forces. Then, in late September 1991, Khartoum for the first time in eight years allowed a barge filled with grain to sail up the river to Nasir from the government-held town of Malakal. Garang was quick to accuse Riek of collaborating with the government against him. At the time, Riek and Lam denied it. But Lam later told me that they had indeed held their first meeting with the government negotiators that October. He added that the meeting was facilitated by the SPLA's old friend Tiny Rowland. 'Yes,' said Rowland, when I asked him about this. 'I thought it was time they came to an agreement with the government. But Garang is an extraordinarily difficult chap. It wasn't just Riek Machar who broke away. There were a lot of us.'

One of Riek's own men was scared by the growing anti-Dinka feeling in Nasir. Captain Michael Manyon Anyang was a Dinka himself, a former circuit judge in his early thirties and the SPLA's 'relief coordinator' in Nasir. Michael spent his spare time

studying Dinka and Nuer traditional law. Whenever the aid
workers went to Nairobi, he asked them to pick up law books for
him. He had been an outspoken critic of the split. He started
visiting the UN camp in the evenings, telling the aid workers he
was afraid. Then one day in November, he disappeared. Riek's
security chief told the aid workers that he had been caught trying
to set a landmine in the UN camp.

The charge was ludicrous. Scott-Villiers and another
UNICEF official took the UN motorboat up to Riek's compound
at Ketbek to protest. Emma was there. She liked Michael, and
seemed horrified to hear that he had been arrested. But Riek was
impassive. 'Look, you don't really know these people,' he kept
telling the Westerners. Finally Riek agreed that they could see
Michael at eight a.m. the next morning. But the next morning,
eight a.m. came and went with no sign of him. At ten, Riek sent a
message to the UN camp apologizing for the delay and telling
them not to worry. Some four hours later, a soldier took Scott-
Villiers and his colleague to one of the ruined houses by the river.
They could tell it was not where Michael was ordinarily kept.
There was no bedding and he appeared to have walked a long
way. He was dirty, sweating, and his eyes bulged with terror. The
Westerners tried to question him. Was he being fed? Was he
allowed to see a newspaper? Would he like his law books? But
Michael seemed frightened to answer. After securing a promise
that they could visit again the next day, the UN officials left. The
next day Michael was gone. They never saw him again. When they
protested to Riek, he flew into a rage and accused them of trying
to abduct a criminal caught planting landmines. Amnesty
International later reported that Michael had been executed.

Emma had wanted to go with Scott-Villiers to see Michael.
She seemed as puzzled and worried as any of the aid workers
about his arrest. When I asked Riek what was hardest for Emma
to accept about their life together, he mentioned two 'murder
cases'. 'A judge, Michael Manyon—that person was murdered,' he
said. 'We heard the shots. And there was another person, a
medical assistant . . . Up to today, we did not trace who killed
them. I think the man who murdered them was making a sabotage
to project us as people who did not care about human rights.'

Emma had nagged him about the cases. 'When you know a
woman is right, what can you do?' he said, reasonably. He said he
called a meeting of his officers and told them: 'This is disgusting.
If that's what you're going to do, count me out.'

Later, when I spoke to Lam, he found Riek's account
hilarious. 'He *will* lie to you,' he said. Michael was executed at
night, he insisted, on Riek's orders. Perhaps Emma did hear the
shots. Lam said that he was in Nairobi the whole time and had
nothing to do with it. Wendy James later heard that two medical
assistants and twenty-eight soldiers from another tribe, the Nuba,
had been executed along with Michael.

So far as Emma's friends were concerned, the main thing was
that she took Riek's side regardless of what he did. 'You saw a
whole new face of her coming out, which was to dig her feet in
and deny,' said one. 'The more you pushed her, the more she saw
that this thing was going wrong, the more she denied.'

Scott-Villiers was in Nairobi in November 1991 when the first
word came that Dinka were being massacred at Bor. The UN had
evacuated its people weeks earlier. Riek's group started issuing
press releases along the lines of 'Bor Captured, Great Victory'.
Before long, Operation Lifeline couldn't hold a relief meeting
without rebel factions screaming recriminations at each other over
Bor. It was decided that Scott-Villiers, some private relief officials
and representatives from both rebel groups should visit the scene
and make an assessment. They flew up to Loki and started driving
north, through the badlands of southernmost Sudan.

Once they crossed into Equatoria, they found themselves
driving through a sea of Dinka refugees, all shrieking and wailing
about what the Nuer had done at Bor. As their Landcruiser
approached Jemeza, a village south of Bor, a silence fell. Then
they saw the bodies. Some were hanging from trees. Others lay
beside the dirt road. They saw three children, tied together and
shot through the heads. They saw disembowelled women. Scott-
Villiers took pictures. They kept driving. In Bor, the huts were still
smouldering. The UN house stank—a soldier's body was rotting
inside. They noticed Nuer government ID cards spilled on the
floor. Garang's forces had just retaken the town. The relief
officials could hear gunfire. An SPLA-Mainstream soldier

soldier approached them menacingly. 'This is what you lot have caused,' he said. They turned around and drove back to Loki.

Scott-Villiers was shaken. In Nairobi, another Operation Lifeline official took him aside and suggested that he take a break from Sudan. 'You must not become part of it,' he warned. Patta Scott-Villiers took one look at her husband's pictures and was afraid. She felt that they had been in the presence of evil in Nasir. 'I felt that anyone associated with it was going to be in moral danger,' she said later. After a few days, Scott-Villiers took his pictures to Emma, who was at Sally Dudmesh's house in Nairobi, waiting for news from Bor. 'Just have a look at these,' he said, tossing the black-and-white photos on to a table. Taut as a cat, Emma snatched them up. They showed a dead child, buzzards eating the naked body of a man, Dinka streaming down the road.

'What are these?' she said impatiently. 'Was it a victory?'

It was not a victory. It came to be known as the Bor Massacre. Amnesty International later estimated that 2,000 people died in nearly two weeks of killing. Looking back, most observers agree that the massacre was the point at which Riek and Lam's rebellion turned irrevocably tribal. Why did they let it happen? 'It got out of control,' was the explanation Riek offered. But there was more to it than that. There were still some Nuer soldiers in the government army, and one Nuer militia was invited to join Riek's forces in the attack on Bor. Swarming among these uniformed troops was the prophet Wut Nyang himself, with hundreds of his followers covered only in ashes or in white sheets tied at the shoulder. He urged the Nuer to stop fighting among themselves. Some say he swore that any Nuer who joined his 'White Army' would be protected from bullets, while those who stayed behind would die of sickness or be eaten by crocodiles. Others say he excited the Nuer with promises of Dinka cattle and women. What nobody doubts is that he stoked Nuer envy of the UN food and mosquito nets that the Bor Dinka had been receiving.

Riek encouraged this 'White Army' to go to Bor. Maybe he was spellbound by Wut Nyang's prophecies; maybe he simply wanted a victory. For Lam, it was the end: 'Everything we had called for was shattered,' he said. 'After people saw the White

Army had the same status as our regular army, discipline broke down. You cannot motivate people with witchcraft. This is where Riek got stuck. He started as a man who wanted to make a revolution, but he became just another Nuer leader.'

I have some pictures of Emma in Nasir. A British friend of hers took them on a visit in 1992. In a black-and-white shot, Emma stands outside a mud *tukul*, squinting at the sun. She's wearing a sleeveless black lace shirt, a long skirt with a belt, and flip-flops. Her dark hair is shoulder-length and stylishly cut; her long hands are clasped behind her back. The next picture is in colour. It shows Emma sitting inside the hut on an iron bedstead with a thin foam mattress. A mosquito net hangs over the bed, and, behind it, you can see Emma's clothes hanging on a line strung across the hut. The walls are painted black, white and brown, with African animals, human figures and geometric shapes. The third picture is my only one to include Riek. He and Emma are sitting in front of a big table covered with ledgers, papers and airmail envelopes, two glasses of tea and a shortwave radio. Riek is looking straight at the camera, dressed like a cartoon African dictator in military fatigues with giant epaulettes and a bright red beret. Emma leans on the table, looking down, half-smiling at something you can't see.

She looks a little self-conscious, as if she were posing on the set of a movie. But people who visited her in Nasir say she took her queenly position quite seriously. Sally Dudmesh managed to fly up with the UN not long after Emma and Riek were married. 'She was very busy with what he was doing and it was just horrible there,' she said. 'There were mosquitoes everywhere. The only thing to look at was that great river, and you couldn't even swim in it because of the crocodiles. Of course, she couldn't drive most places and it was really uncomfortable to walk in the heat. And all they talked about was politics.

'But she didn't mind at all. She would never ask for a single thing. She would never send for shampoo. She would live on rice and boiled fish for months on end without complaining. Then it was like she had two lives because she would come out of these swamps of hell, walk into my wardrobe in Nairobi and come out looking like something out of *Vogue*.'

Emma seemed to revel in her role as the warlord's consort. There was talk of Lady Macbeth. When Garang's fighters began raiding Nuerland in retaliation for Bor, Riek tried to persuade Emma to go to Nairobi because, in a radio broadcast, Garang had blamed the split on Emma. Now, she was a target. She refused to leave Riek, but did begin travelling everywhere with a seven-foot-tall bodyguard named 'Forty-Six'—after a certain machine-gun he liked to use. In June 1992, the *Mail on Sunday* sent Tarquin Hall to Sudan to write about Emma. Hall found his subject carrying a parasol and feeding an ostrich in a village near the Ethiopian border. 'She didn't seem the least bit amazed that I had travelled all the way from Nairobi to see her,' Hall wrote. '"Do you like ostriches?" she asked. "I call this one Burty, because he reminds me of one of my old teachers. Burty used to have a mate, but she was killed on a cross-border raid."'

Hall spent two weeks with Emma at Riek's compound in Ketbek. She had a brown-and-white dog that Riek's soldiers named 'Come-on' because Emma was always calling to the dog to follow her. He saw the cats Emma had imported to catch rats, but which instead caught the soldiers' chickens. 'The soldiers keep threatening to kill them because they are so expensive,' she said of her animals. 'But Riek has forbidden them.' Under Emma's supervision, the soldiers used seeds extracted from UN vegetables to grow tomatoes and melons. She helped women to organize so they might have a voice in local politics. She advised Riek's faction on how to deal with the UN and the private aid groups. 'It has been important for me to help these people,' she told Hall. 'I feel like I'm in a unique position now because I share their lives every day and I'm not just another aid worker pretending to understand their position and telling them how to live.'

Hall had been present when Emma and Riek presided—'like royalty at Ascot'—over celebrations to mark the liberation of Nasir three years earlier. 'Everywhere we went the Sudanese seemed happy to see Emma even though she had learnt little of their language,' he wrote. 'In villages, people would run up to her car as she drove past, bringing presents and seeking her advice.'

In another article, never published, a Nairobi friend of Emma's called Emma Marion wrote that when she arrived in a village, the Nuer women would set upon her, waxing every inch of her body-hair with a caramelized mixture of lemon and sugar. 'They called Emma *Yian,* after the colour of their palest, creamiest cows,' Marion wrote. She added that Emma had developed the habit in Nasir of sleeping from ten in the morning to four in the afternoon. In June 1992, Emma wrote to Marion thanking her for a package that included chocolates, vodka and a copy of the *Observer.* Both Emmas planned to visit England later in the summer. Emma wrote from Nasir: 'I understand that there are two big exhibitions on Piero della Francesca and Rembrandt now on in London—not to be missed by us either!'

Sometimes Emma passed on radio frequencies and news of military manoeuvres to Riek's supporters abroad. Her call sign was Nefertiti. She would often call up journalists like me to talk (off-the-record) about the war. She told her friends, though, that she didn't always know the details of Riek's political intrigues. 'Everyone is in a bit of a spin with peace talks, war and politics,' she wrote to Marion. 'None of which I understand, but I faithfully type out draft constitutions, programmes and plans and policies for my beloved husband.' When Tarquin Hall asked her how she felt about Riek's role as a military man who made decisions to have people killed, she replied, 'I don't think Riek is in the war because he loves it or because he loves fighting . . . Riek has chosen it because of a principle, as a means to an end.'

Emma's former colleagues had more difficulty discerning exactly what principle Riek was fighting for. They began to say that Riek was no better than Garang—and maybe worse, because of the damage he had done to the cause of southern unity. The tension grew between them and Emma. The UN banned her from its flights after Garang's faction complained. There was no way the UN could justify letting the white wife of one rebel leader on its flights while banning the families of others. But once again Emma wouldn't see it. 'The UN refuses to allow me to fly on their planes for some unknown reason,' she wrote to Marion. 'Anyway, come hell or high water I will be [in Nairobi] by the end of the month.' She convinced a UN pilot she had known as a relief worker to smuggle her aboard listed as a spare tractor part.

In England that summer, she went to see Amnesty

International's head Sudan researcher, Andrew Mawson, who had written his dissertation at Cambridge on the Dinka religion. Mawson was an acquaintance of Emma's from the Sudan peace groups. He remembered her as an energetic advocate of human rights. When she began to tell him that human rights reports had overblown the Bor Massacre, he was embarrassed. 'She spent a lot of her time trying to persuade me that it didn't really happen,' he said. 'I always felt she wasn't actually being very frank. She didn't seem to understand that she was acting as Riek's ambassador. She wanted to play it as a friend. I found her manipulative, and became very uncomfortable.' People who challenged Emma about the atrocities learned to drop the subject or risk losing her friendship. If her alienation from the humanitarians bothered her, she didn't show it. 'I am so happy,' she told Tarquin Hall. 'Whatever happens, I'm glad that I followed my instinct, married Riek and came to live in Nasir. I have no regrets.'

Towards the end of 1992, Riek and Emma made a pilgrimage through the swamps on foot to the town of Ayod, to a ceremony in which Riek would be given a leopard skin, a Nuer symbol of divinity. This would give him the spiritual authority to absolve men of murder and to settle blood feuds. From the town of Waat, where they started, it was eighty miles to Ayod. The trip took five days. Sometimes they walked through chest-deep water. Riek's men offered to carry Emma, but she insisted on walking. Emma later dubbed the area between Waat, Ayod and Kongor 'the Hunger Triangle', and the media picked up on it. The war, at this time, had become a hopeless three-sided affair—the conflict between the government and Garang (and, despite Riek's secret deals, between the Nuer and the government) ran alongside the feud between Garang and Riek. There was so much fighting that Operation Lifeline shut down. People were dying of hunger and sickness. Nearby, at Nuerland's most sacred shrine, the giant earth Mound of Ngundeng, tribesmen offered prayers for victory.

For a moment, it seemed as if they had been heard. In October, the prophet Wut Nyang and his White Army attacked the government garrison town of Malakal, a hundred miles to the west of Nasir, on the Nile. (According to Lam, Wut Nyang had dreamed that the *mor-mor* termite would come to his aid against the government's mechanized troops. And Douglas Johnson heard that before the battle Wut Nyang proved his power over life and death by killing and resurrecting a goat.) When Riek learned that the White Army had overrun a few suburbs, he was overjoyed. In a delirious press release, he announced that his forces had captured Malakal, a town of more than 10,000 people with its own electricity and schools. But government forces swiftly drove Wut Nyang and his army away, reportedly slaughtering hundreds of Nuer civilians in revenge. 'By then I think even Emma realized how weak Riek was,' said Lam.

Riek and Emma were still in Waat when, in January, an incident took place that Emma could not ignore. Lam says that Riek had begun to fear that his underlings were plotting against him. It's certain, at least, that the Nuer had begun feuding among themselves, and that Riek's lieutenants were beginning to divide along lines of kinship. One officer, Hakim Gabriel Aluong, fell foul of the others in some murky dispute and was dragged away in Emma's presence to be shot. Riek's men paid no attention when she pleaded for Hakim's life. 'Emma came [to Nairobi] and she was very angry,' recalled Lam. 'She talked to everyone about it. Now it was really in front of her eyes. But she didn't blame Riek. She said it was the officers.'

She was admitted to Nairobi Hospital, feverish with hepatitis and malaria. But after a few weeks, she left the hospital and threw herself into the preparations for a big political meeting that Riek planned to hold in the Dinka settlement of Panyagor. The plan, she told journalists, was to hold a rally with all the Nasir leaders, to show the Dinka and the other tribes that the struggle within the SPLA was not tribal, but about principles. Before the war, Panyagor had been the site of a Western development project: the Dinka were there because it had an airstrip, and the UN offered food. A few weeks earlier, the US Center for Disease Control had reported that rates of malnutrition in Panyagor were 'among the highest ever recorded'. A Frenchman named Jean François Darcq was responsible for feeding the people in Panyagor. On 26 March, Darcq and several thousand others in Panyagor listened to Riek and his comrades appealing to the Dinka to rise against Garang.

At six the next morning, Darcq was in the UN's storehouse, talking on the radio. When he heard shooting, he thought that Riek's forces were holding a parade. Then the UN watchman told him they were under attack by Garang's SPLA. The watchman ran, but Darcq stayed in the brick storehouse. When the mortars and rocket-propelled grenades died down, he peeked outside. People were running and falling and lying on the ground bleeding. A couple of Garang's young fighters appeared with rifles. They ordered Darcq to take off his shirt, trousers, shoes and socks. They left him with his underpants. Darcq knew what this meant. 'They were shooting the guys whose underwear they had taken off. Because they don't like to dirty them with blood. So then I thought that they would not kill me.'

A long, terrifying day passed in which Darcq was shot at and forced to run through the bush before Riek's forces recaptured the town and released him. Emma came limping in along with Riek's soldiers. She later said she had hidden under an overturned cupboard until Forty-Six, her huge bodyguard, rescued her. She ran from the gun battle barefoot through the thorn scrub, lacerating her feet. One of the Nasir group's most venerable supporters, an elderly politician who had once served as Sudan's minister of sport, couldn't keep up. When he fell, Garang's fighters shot him in the back. Garang's men caught Emma's dog and beat it, calling it 'Emma'. For half a day Emma believed that Riek too had been killed. When she and Darcq met up afterwards, they sat in front of a concrete *tukul*—a remnant of Panyagor's development project—and smoked an entire packet of Dunhill cigarettes.

Emma's narrow escape seemed to sober her. She had spent all her savings; she and Riek owed money to everyone. The electricity and the telephones were always off at the office that Riek's faction kept in Nairobi, even though the UN gave it money to pay the bills. In London she had met a literary agent who was interested in her story. She started writing her autobiography: *Wedded to the Cause*. Bit by bit, crumpled sheets began to arrive in London, after a circuitous journey involving friends and friends of friends. The first chapter described her departure from Panyagor.

'I climbed in and bent to kiss Riek goodbye at the door. The door closed, the engine started and we sped down the airstrip and turned sharply away from the fighting. I looked down and saw Riek and his men watch us go until they became mere dots on the earth's surface. Part of my heart remained behind with Riek. As we soared up, as if magically lifted from hell, the vastness of this great flat land overwhelmed me ... Unstoppable tears poured down my cheeks, washing away all the shock, the fear and the grief. I grieved for those who had died and those who would die in this endless struggle.'

She had always wanted to have a child. She started taking fertility pills. In the summer of 1993 she became pregnant.

In August of that year, twelve little boys straggled into Riek's military compound in Waat. Emma was visiting Riek there and heard the boys say they had been walking for three months to escape Garang's forces. The SPLA had drafted them for its 1992 assault on Juba and for months of hard fighting afterwards. Emma had always felt that Westerners gave Riek too little credit for taking a stand against the use of child soldiers. Since 1992 Riek had been allowing UNICEF to reunite many of the 1,500-odd boys still in Nasir with their families. By contrast, Garang had refused to let any of the more than 10,000 boys under his control go home. One eleven-year-old boy in Waat described firing mortars and carrying ammunition for Garang's men. When Emma returned to Kenya, she smuggled him into the country with her. Over the next few months, he was often at her side. She badgered her friends to contribute to a fund for his education.

Riek and Lam continued their secret talks with Khartoum. In September 1993, Emma chartered a plane so that she and Riek could pick up Lam from one meeting with government officials in the Shilluk town of Tonga. When they returned to Nairobi, they were put up at the InterContinental Hotel by Tiny Rowland ('Food, cars, hotels—it was all paid for by me,' he said). In late October, the US government invited the two rebel leaders to see if they couldn't patch up their differences in Washington. Jimmy Carter, the former US President, had been trying for years to engineer a peace. Now, the Carter Center in Atlanta, Georgia, paid for Riek to travel to the US. Emma stayed behind at the InterContinental: because of her pregnancy, she had been advised not to fly. After the talks in Washington collapsed, she phoned me in Atlanta, where I worked, urging me to see Riek and get his side of the story. She sounded worried, but when I saw Riek he was suave and relaxed, patiently recounting the obscure affronts that made it impossible for him to sign an agreement with Garang.

Riek stopped in London on his way home to see Angelina and the children. When he returned to Nairobi, Emma had found a house, again courtesy of Tiny Rowland. It was a white stucco bungalow off Riverside Drive, a smart area where the Kenyan bigwigs and Western diplomats live. To Emma's brother Johnny, and her sister Jenny, who arrived in November for their first visit to Africa, she had never seemed happier.

Lam Akol believes that it was during this period that Riek gave orders for the arrest of Lul, the lecherous education coordinator I had met back in Nasir. Gordon Kong Chuol was in charge in Nasir: he accused Lul and thirteen others of plotting to bring a well-known Nuer politician back from exile in Sweden to overthrow Riek. A few weeks later, Lam and a Nuer lawyer, one of Riek's lieutenants, heard that Lul was dead. They asked Riek about it. Riek said that Lul had died of typhoid. The lawyer was suspicious. He went to Nasir to investigate. There he heard another story. Every evening at seven p.m., he was told, the prisoners were taken out of their huts and beaten, one by one. One night, Lul was not brought back until after midnight. He was nearly unconscious and vomiting blood. That night, he died.

When the lawyer returned with his report, Riek swore that he hadn't known that Lul was tortured to death. He said he would court-martial Gordon. But nothing much happened. Gordon continued to reign in Nasir, undisturbed. Then, in January 1994, Riek expelled Lam from the Nasir forces. He said he did it because Lam was in the pocket of the government. But I heard about a more sordid tussle involving Tiny Rowland's money. Apparently, Riek had gone to see Rowland in Nairobi to ask for a ticket to London. Rowland obliged. But Riek said something about not being ready to sign an agreement with the government unless Garang did too. After that, Rowland cut off funds to Riek. Since Lam was the one who usually dealt with Rowland, Riek accused him of sabotage. That was the story. But Rowland denied cutting off anyone. 'I never fell out with any of them,' he assured me. 'No. It's quite wrong to say so. I was everybody's friend.'

But two years later, Riek had Gordon arrested, in the town of Akobo near the Ethiopian border—not for killing Lul, but for plotting against Riek himself.

On 24 November 1993, Emma was busy writing a proposal for the UN to finance a new aid group run by southern Sudanese women. 'Womenaid,' Emma typed, 'wishes to help people displaced by war and famine to help themselves and their families.' She was alone in the house off Riverside Drive. Her brother and sister had decided to spend an extra day on the coast. Riek was away at a meeting. She planned to meet her friends Sally Dudmesh and Willy Knocker for dinner in the Nairobi suburb called Karen. Midway through a list of Womenaid's proposed 'small income-generating projects'—restaurant, $5,000; tea shop, $3,000; vegetable gardens, $3,000—she stored the document and turned off her computer. For some reason, Forty-Six wasn't around, so she borrowed a neighbour's Suzuki Landcruiser and drove off. She was five months pregnant. She didn't bother with a seat belt. Hardly anyone in Africa ever does.

She stopped briefly at Knocker's sister's house, then continued west on Argwings-Kodhek Road. When she reached the intersection with James Gichuru Road, she slowed, then started to cross. Naturally, there were no traffic lights, and Emma didn't see one of Nairobi's notorious little private buses, a *matatu,* barrelling down the road towards her. When the *matatu* hit the Landcruiser, she was thrown through the window. The car rolled on top of her.

'My baby! My baby!' she was crying when the first Kenyan passers-by reached her. She died on the way to Nairobi Hospital.

When I heard that Emma was dead, I had just returned to Atlanta from Somalia. It was Thanksgiving Day in 1993. Visions of Emma being crushed by a *matatu* bus in Nairobi mingled with other images: of the queer, insect-like look that starving children get when their bodies shrink out of proportion to their heads; of the twitchy eyes of stoned Somali gunmen. I found a copy of the London *Times* and read Emma's obituary. It referred to her, inevitably, as a 'British aid worker'.

At the time of her death it was wrong to call Emma an aid worker. She hadn't been employed by an aid agency for two years. But the clichés of mercy are powerful, and it was beyond the obituarist's imagination to see her as anything but a humanitarian. She was British, she was in a poor and angry part of Africa, therefore she must be helping. Here are some of the things Emma was called in Sudan: First Lady; Concubine; Traitor; Spy; Heroine. She was not easy to label. She passed over the barriers between different worlds without appearing to notice them. And she had taunted death in so many exotic ways that her friends could hardly believe it would sneak up on her in an everyday accident. There had to be more to the crash than careless driving. But the Kenyan police declared her death an accident. In the end, most Westerners accepted that.

The Nuer took a more complicated view. In the old days, they didn't believe in accidents of that sort. They assumed that someone was to blame for every violent death, if only through the agency of *wiu*, a bleak thing like an evil eye that punishes people for their sins or the sins of others close to them. Nowadays, some Nuer believe in *wiu*, some don't. Some say Emma was a victim of sorcery, others say it was an accident.

For a few years after Emma died, Riek Machar seemed to avoid talking about her. Emma's mother mailed him a new Church of England diary every year at Christmas, but he didn't write back. He spoke on the phone to an old friend of Emma's, but failed to turn up for an appointment. Maybe he was busy—he had a war to fight, after all—or maybe, as he told me, the subject was too painful. At first he didn't answer my faxes and letters either. But in April 1997 he signed a peace agreement with the hated Islamic regime in the north. Many southerners branded him a traitor. Desperate for any favourable publicity, his supporters pushed him to see me. I flew to Khartoum in June.

The government had lent Riek one of those big, half-empty stucco villas that drowse along the avenues of old Khartoum. Human rights groups say the Sudanese security forces torture their opponents in some of these decaying mansions, or 'ghost houses'. In the empty hotels and crumbling government offices along the Nile there are haunting echoes of British colonial Sudan. But the British, along with the other *khawadjas* who built old Khartoum, have been dribbling away since independence. After the Gulf War, when Sudan supported Iraq, only a few hundred diplomats and aid workers remained. The Greek merchants began to leave when the Sudanese government confiscated much of their wealth back in the 1960s. There are more teachers than students at the Greek Orthodox school. Westernized Khartoum is fading away.

The Arab-African city, however, keeps growing. Across the Nile Omdurman, the heart of Muslim Sudan, swirls with men in spotless white gowns and turbans, drinking sweet tea and greeting each other in melodious Arabic. In Khartoum North, concrete mansions rise, nourished by the wages of Sudanese working in the Gulf. And peeping out of abandoned lots and on the edge of the desert are the *tukuls* that the refugees build out of discarded boxes and plastic sheeting—round huts so stubbornly African that to the north's Islamic rulers they must seem like unruly weeds.

When we drove up to Riek's big brown villa on University Avenue the morning after I arrived, my Arab taxi driver clucked disapprovingly at the teenage Nuer boys hanging off the fence and swaggering around the grounds in their startlingly green fatigues. At eight a.m. it was so hot outside that sand blowing in my face felt like a dirty flame. The boys grinned sweetly, hurrying me into the house and up an unlit staircase carpeted in a stained pattern of roses. 'Dr Riek is expecting you,' they sang. They flung open a door, and I walked into a room dominated by a giant bed.

I could picture Emma in this place. I remembered hearing about the time Emma and Riek were staying in an expensive Nairobi hotel. Riek's fighters kept trooping in and out of Emma's bedroom, flushing the toilet, examining her Tampax. Some of them had never seen running water and, of course, there is no such thing as a private bedroom in the traditional African home.

Riek came forward with a dazzling white grin and offered me a chair in a little seating area at the foot of the bed. One aspect of Sudan that might have attracted Emma was the sheer height of its people: it was the one place where she wouldn't have felt gangly. Riek is nearly seven feet tall, in his mid-forties, not gaunt like most Nuer, but rather fleshy, with small black eyes. He was wearing smartly pressed blue jeans, a matching denim shirt, new shoes and socks. He fetched a Coke for me out of a sweaty little refrigerator by the wall. His voice was thick and sweet. I remembered something a Washington negotiator once told me—how he got the feeling that Riek was either a very nice guy or a very effective murderer. All I could see was a huge, handsome man, a little on the masterful side, but with a friendly grin.

He sat down opposite me and we talked for a long while before I got up the nerve to ask him about Emma. We talked about his upbringing: born in 1952, he was the twenty-sixth child of a headman in the town of Ler. I've seen photos of Ler. It's a village of mud houses and cattle byres with conical thatched roofs. When Riek was growing up there was no plumbing, no electricity, no doctor, and no secondary school—only the civil war. It's the same today. Most people still live on millet porridge and cow's milk, sometimes flavoured with cow urine. Riek told one journalist that his family was the first in Ler to own a tin-opener.

Not many people from Ler go to universities overseas. Riek said he owes his unusual education to his mother. Illiterate herself, she was the third of his father's five wives. But she had a cousin who was one of the first southerners to attend university, and developed a fierce ambition for her sons to do the same. Riek became one of the first hundred southerners admitted to the University of Khartoum after the war, and his brother ultimately became a professor of veterinary medicine. Out of their father's thirty-one children, only Riek and his brother went to school.

Because Riek was educated he never had to prove his manhood by lying perfectly still while an older Nuer man carved marks into his forehead. His father thought the marks wouldn't be necessary for one so well-educated. Riek later came to regret his alienation from his own cattle-centred culture. When he returned to Sudan in 1984 to fight against the government, he discovered that Western political slogans meant little in village Africa. Eventually he realized that 'the basic values of our own society are our roots. Whatever we want to create in town, that has no roots. Maybe after generations, it will have roots. But for us, the village children, from village schools, what we have acquired in towns, it's just a beginning.'

I asked him why he was so willing to fight—why peace wasn't more precious to him. 'One individual success, to us, was nothing,' he said. 'We southerners are just downtrodden.'

Finally we reached the year 1989, when he met Emma. He started to tell me about their first encounter, then stopped. I was astonished to see his face pucker up in an expression almost like a pout. He cocked his head at me. His voice turned sentimental. 'Do I have to?' he said coyly.

What could I say? I said nothing.

He began speaking in a more normal voice. A schoolfriend had introduced them, he said. He was in Nairobi on a break after five years in the bush, most recently as the commander of Upper Nile province. He didn't say that it was 'love at first sight'; merely that he was attracted by her interest in education. He told me about her bold car journey to see him in Nasir in 1991.

'Were you flattered by that?' I asked.

'Beyond flattered,' he said huskily.

I sat up in my chair.

'She—there were no inhibitions on her side,' he added.

'I see,' I said. I was afraid that I might blush or burst out laughing. I thought about the answers others had given when I asked them what had attracted Emma to Riek. 'She just adored being with him,' said Sally Dudmesh. 'He was a big sexual powerhouse,' said an American journalist who knew them both. Liz Hodgkin said Emma told her that she sometimes asked herself whether she would have fallen in love with Riek if he hadn't been 'an important person'. An SPLA comrade of Riek's explained it by saying that they were both chain-smokers who liked computers. To Riek, the question was too obvious to bother answering. 'What are the reasons that a man marries a woman?' he said.

A gaggle of Riek's advisers came into the room and sat down on a sofa next to me, at the foot of the enormous bed. I noticed that the men were all decked out in new blue jeans, plaid shirts and tennis shoes. The advisers were in Khartoum to draft the provisions that would, supposedly, make Riek's peace agreement part of Sudan's constitution. (Three months later, Riek and the government were still arguing, and the constitution remained basically unchanged.) They needed Riek's approval for their latest work. While Riek tapped away on his laptop computer, I looked out the window. Outside on the grass, two soldiers armed with automatic rifles lolled under red carpets strung up like an Arab tent. I asked the advisers about the villa's age.

'I think it was built in the 1970s,' said one man.

A sad-eyed Nuer, one I had met before, corrected him.

'No, it was built earlier than that, because this is where Numeiri held the officers who tried to overthrow him in 1971,' he said. 'This is where he had them executed—right in this house.'

We looked at each other. The air-conditioner in the window droned feebly. Later, this same man would turn to me and quote from Richard II: 'In the base court! Base court where kings grow base; To come at traitors' calls and do them grace.'

A book of Indira Gandhi's collected speeches lay on Riek's bedside table. It was covered, like everything else, with dust.

R iek has a lazy eye. As our interview wore on, and he wearied of my questions, it rolled back and clouded over. Suddenly, he didn't seem so genial. I thought I had better change the subject. I mentioned the profile I had written back in 1990 of the schoolmaster, Lul (I had no idea at this point what had become of him). 'I thought I might go see him while I'm here,' I said. 'Do you have any idea where he is?'

'Lul Kuar Duek,' said Riek, rubbing his chin as he repeated the name. 'Yes, he was arrested and killed by Gordon Kong Chuol. It was a pity. It was something personal between them.'

'Gordon Kong—you mean, in Nasir?' I said, dimly remembering the cat-faced old warlord who had acted as Riek's deputy, and who had been arrested.

'Yes, it was a pity,' Riek said again.

I had one more question. What did Riek think about Emma's death? An accident? *Wiu*? It was late in the afternoon. Outside the bedroom, a dozen or so people were waiting to see him. I could tell that Riek was anxious to go. But he leaned back for a moment, still courteous, a long man in stiff blue jeans. Yes, he admitted, he'd had his suspicions. He'd concluded, though, that his and Emma's enemies weren't sophisticated enough to use a *matatu* bus half-full of people as a murder weapon. As for the question of *wiu,* he didn't want to talk about it. 'Some would say it was bad luck because of a curse or something. They will give it many interpretations. I am truthfully not going to go into it.'

I apologized for bringing up painful subjects.

'No, it's OK,' said Riek. 'It's been a day of remembrance.'

And it was over. Riek stood up. I could see that his mind was already with the chattering men waiting for him on the faded couches in the hall. I went back to my hotel room and lay in the gloom, watching the ceiling fan go round.

In London I met Emma's brother Johnny for a drink. He helps produce television comedies at studios in Covent Garden. It was a warm summer evening. The pubs and restaurants overflowed with young people, their laughter rising up to the pale lavender sky. We found a table in a crowded brasserie. Johnny is slight, with sandy hair and wire-rimmed glasses. He has his sister's fine features, and her silvery charm.

'I still hear her voice sometimes,' he said. I heard it, too.

'It wasn't until I was at the funeral that I realized she had made such an impact,' he said. 'You know, after she died, her friends came to me in Nairobi, and they said, "You'd better get Nairobi Cathedral for the funeral." I told them, "You must be mad." Because, you know, if I died, I really don't know if I could fill a village church. But we did get the cathedral and when we went there it was packed to the rafters. Then we took her body up to Ler, where Riek is from. She's buried there. It's quite a pretty place, but, my God, the sun! And people had walked for days to get there. When our plane landed Riek had to get a megaphone to get them to step back so we could get off. There were thousands of people—thousands. We were the only white people there. They were all rushing forward. We thought we were going to end up in the grave ourselves.'

He laughed. Then he said: 'Emma wasn't out to better herself. When I think about her, I feel a bit guilty about my life. I'm doing something really selfish. I'm not bettering anyone.'

There it was again: the noble cause, the great saving illusion. I didn't say anything. I thought of Somalia and Sudan, of all that vainglorious rhetoric about saving a nation by throwing bags of food at it. I remember how Emma laughed at the aid workers in Sudan who fondly imagined that they were in charge of events. At least Emma took Africa seriously enough to see how little aid could accomplish. She loved Sudan so much that she was willing to sacrifice her ideals to become part of it.

At home in Atlanta, I called Tiny Rowland in England to ask him if he had known Emma. It took him a few moments to remember. Then it clicked. 'Yes, of course I met her,' he said. 'Yes. And when she died Riek was in a dreadful mess.'

How important a figure was she? I asked him. He paused. 'My dear,' he said. 'She was a white woman, a married white woman. I'm sure she helped him enormously. But in terms of Africa, she didn't play a role.'

It struck me that the saddest thing about Emma was the waste of it all. She had beauty, passion, talent, a radiant spirit. Yes, she had been up to her neck in horrors. But the horrors would have happened even if she hadn't been there. Certainly they continued without her. I don't know if she helped many Sudanese. Once she surrendered so wholeheartedly to her intoxication with the place, she might have harmed more people than she helped. She never appears to have seen the damage she did to her best self when she followed Riek into the wilderness of that war. But the lure was too powerful for her to resist. She had grandeur. She was not ordinary. She loved her fate. □

GRANTA

THE NUBA
JACK PICONE

The photographs in the following pages show people without recorded names, often without clothes, identified as Nuba villagers from Sudan. Archaic in appearance—a girl's cicatrized torso, a trance-bound healer—they reveal very little of the circumstances in which they were taken. Are these people naked because they are poor? Or because that is the way they want to be? Why has the photographer singled them out? Are they typical of the Nuba? Who are the Nuba anyway?

The Nuba are not Nubians, ancient inhabitants of the land on the border between present-day Egypt and Sudan. Nor are they Nubi, Ugandan descendants of soldiers recruited in Sudan by nineteenth-century European adventurers. The Nuba are a distinct group of hill-dwelling peoples on the border between the Arab-Islamic north of Sudan and the non-Muslim south. An enclave of black Africans almost encircled by plains-dwelling Arabs, they speak many different languages, but have in common the experience of being treated as second-class citizens in Sudan's Arab-dominated political culture.

For over a decade the Nuba have been trapped in the middle of Sudan's long-running civil war. Control of their territory is divided between the government in Khartoum and the Sudan People's Liberation Army (SPLA), which controls much of the rural area of southern Sudan. These pictures were taken in the SPLA-controlled area of the Nuba Mountains, which has been cut off from government services since the mid-1980s. They show people denied access to markets that they enjoyed before the war, people impoverished by the fight to preserve their culture and to assert control of their territory.

The Nuba are no strangers to photography. In the 1970s they were the subject of two books of photographs by Leni Riefenstahl, the German film-maker. Before that, during the colonial era, the British photographer George Rodger documented the wrestling matches and body-decoration for which they are renowned. Today the culture of display that lured these and other photographers to the Nuba hills is threatened, not by the incursion of modernity, but by the immiseration of war. Today in the Nuba Mountains there are Nuba guerrilla fighters in fatigues and tyre-sandals, as well as women, children and wrestlers like these.   JOHN RYLE

148

Two boys await medical treatment in Chingaro, a village in the Nuba Mountains

Two boys bathing in Chingaro. Today, the vast majority of Nuba people live in Khartoum. Only an estimated 300,000 remain in the mountains

A hilltop view over the village of Chingaro

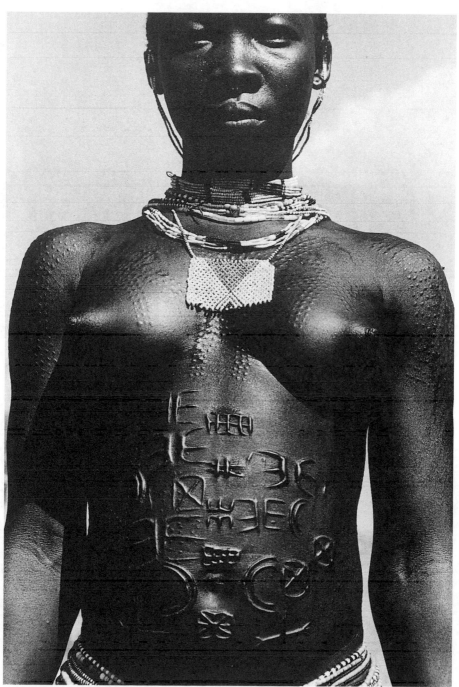

Nuba scarification: the scars represent different stages of a woman's development

Villagers in Touche dance at the end of the rainy season, one of many traditional Nuba customs strangled by Sudan's civil war

Young women in Touche: some parts of the Nuba Mountains have been cut off from government support and services since 1980

A 'kujul'—a traditional healer—from the Tira tribe, one of fifty Nuba tribes

Two wrestlers near Touche

Wrestlers prepare for a bout in the hills near Touche

Wrestlers run to deliver a challenge to the men of Touche

The horn blower signals to nearby villages that a wrestling match is about to take place

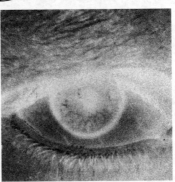

GRANTA

AIMEE BENDER
LOSER

Once there was an orphan who had a knack for finding lost things. Both his parents had been killed when he was eight years old—they were swimming in the ocean when it turned wild with waves, and each had tried to save the other from drowning. The boy woke up from a nap, on the sand, alone. After the tragedy, the community adopted and raised him, and a few years after the death of his parents, he began to have a sense of objects even when they weren't visible. This ability continued growing in power through his teens, and by his twenties he was able to actually sniff out lost sunglasses, keys, contact lenses and sweaters.

The neighbours discovered his talent accidentally—he was over at Jenny Sugar's house one evening, picking her up for a date, when Jenny's mother misplaced her hairbrush and was walking around complaining about this. The young man's nose twitched and he turned slightly towards the kitchen and pointed to the drawer where the spoons and knives were kept. His date burst into laughter. Now that would be quite a silly place to put the brush, she said, among all that silverware! and she opened the drawer to make her point, to wave with a knife or brush her hair with a spoon, but when she did—boom, there was the hairbrush, matted with grey curls, sitting on top of the fork pile.

Jenny's mother kissed the young man on the cheek but Jenny herself looked at him suspiciously all night long.

You planned all that, didn't you, she said, over dinner. You were trying to impress my mother. Well you didn't impress me, she said.

He tried to explain himself but she would hear none of it and when he drove his car up to her house, she fled before he could even finish saying he'd had a nice time, which was a lie anyway. He went home to his tiny room and thought about the word lonely and how it sounded and looked so lonely, with those two *l*s in it, each standing tall by itself.

As news spread around the neighbourhood about the young man's skills, people reacted in two ways: there were the deeply appreciative and the sceptics. The appreciative ones called up the young man regularly. He'd stop by on his way to school, find their keys, and they'd give him a home-made muffin. The sceptics called him over too, and watched him like a hawk; he'd still find their lost items but they'd insist it was an elaborate scam and he was doing it all to get attention. Maybe, declared one woman, waving her index finger in the air, maybe, she said, he steals the thing so we think it's lost, moves the item, and then comes over to save it! How do we know it was really lost in the first place? What is going on?

The young man didn't know himself. All he knew was the feeling of a tug, light but insistent, like a child at his sleeve, and that tug would turn him in the right direction and show him where to look. Each object had its own way of inhabiting space, and therefore messaging its location. The young man could sense, could smell, an object's presence—he did not need to see it to feel where it put its gravity down. As would be expected, items that turned out to be miles away took much harder concentration than the ones that were two feet to the left.

When Mrs Allen's little boy didn't come home one afternoon, that was the most difficult of all. Leonard Allen was eight years old and usually arrived home from school at 3.05. He had allergies and needed a pill before he went back out to play. That day, by 3.45, a lone Mrs Allen was a wreck. Her boy rarely got lost—only once had that happened, in the supermarket, but he'd been found quite easily under the produce tables, crying; the walk home from school was a straight line and Leonard was not the wandering kind.

Mrs Allen was just a regular neighbour except for one extraordinary fact—through an inheritance, she was the owner of a gargantuan emerald she called the Green Star. It sat, glass-cased, in her kitchen, where everyone could see it because she insisted that it be seen. Sometimes, as a party trick, she'd even cut steak with its bevelled edge.

On this day, she took the Green Star out of its case and stuck her palms on it. Where is my boy? she cried. The Green Star was cold and flat. She ran, weeping, to her neighbour, who calmly walked her back home; together, they gave the house a thorough search, and then the neighbour, a believer, recommended calling the young man. Although Mrs Allen was a sceptic, she thought anything was a worthwhile idea, and when the phone was answered, she said, in a trembling voice:

168

You must find my boy.

The young man had been just about to go play basketball with his friends. He'd located the basketball in the bathtub.

You lost him? said the young man.

Mrs Allen began to explain and then her phone clicked.

One moment please, she said, and the young man held on.

When her voice returned, it was shaking with rage.

He's been kidnapped! she said. And they want the Green Star!

The young man realized then it was Mrs Allen he was talking to, and nodded. Oh, he said, I see. Everyone in town was familiar with Mrs Allen's Green Star. I'll be right over, he said.

The woman's voice was too run with tears to respond.

In his basketball shorts and shirt, the young man jogged over to Mrs Allen's house. He was amazed at how the Green Star was all exactly the same shade of green. He had a desire to lick it.

By then, Mrs Allen was in hysterics.

They didn't tell me what to do, she sobbed. Where do I bring my emerald? How do I get my boy back?

The young man tried to feel the scent of the boy. He asked for a photograph and stared at it—a brown-haired kid at his kindergarten graduation—but the young man had only found objects before, and lost objects at that. He'd never found anything, or anybody, stolen. He wasn't a policeman.

Mrs Allen called the police and one officer showed up at the door.

Oh it's the finding guy, the officer said. The young man dipped his head modestly. He turned to his right; to his left; north; south. He got a glimmer of a feeling towards the north and walked out the back door, through the backyard. Night approached and the sky seemed to grow and deepen in the darkness.

What's his name again? he called back to Mrs Allen.

Leonard, she said. He heard the policeman pull out a pad and begin to ask basic questions.

He couldn't quite feel him. He felt the air and he felt the tug inside of the Green Star, an object displaced from its original home in Asia. He felt the tug of the tree in the front yard which had been uprooted from Virginia to be replanted here, and he felt

169

the tug of his own watch which was from his uncle; in an attempt to be fatherly, his uncle had insisted he take it but they both knew the gesture was false.

Maybe the boy was too far away by now.

He heard the policeman ask: What is he wearing?

Mrs Allen described a blue shirt, and the young man focused in on the blue shirt; he turned off his distractions and the blue shirt came calling from the north-west, like a distant radio station. The young man went walking and walking and about fourteen houses down he felt the blue shirt shrieking at him and he walked right into the backyard, through the back door, and sure enough, there were four people watching TV including the tear-stained boy with a runny nose eating a candy bar. The young man scooped up the boy while the others watched, so surprised they did nothing, and one even muttered: Sorry, man.

For fourteen houses back, the young man held Leonard in his arms like a bride. Leonard stopped sneezing and looked up at the stars and the young man smelled Leonard's hair, rich with the memory of peanut butter. He hoped Leonard would ask him a question, any question, but Leonard was quiet. The young man answered in his head: Son, he said to himself, and the word rolled around, a marble on a marble floor. Son, he wanted to say.

When he reached Mrs Allen's door, which was wide open, he walked in with quiet Leonard and Mrs Allen promptly burst into tears and the policeman slunk out the door.

She thanked the young man a thousand times, even offered him the Green Star, but he refused it. Leonard turned on the TV and curled up on the sofa. The young man walked over and asked him about the programme he was watching but Leonard stuck a thumb in his mouth and didn't respond.

Feel better, he said softly. Tucking the basketball beneath his arm, the young man walked home, shoulders low.

In his tiny room, he undressed and lay in bed. Had it been a naked child with nothing on, no shoes, no necklace, no hairbow, no watch, he could not have found it. He lay in bed that night with the trees from other places rustling and he could feel their confusion. No snow here. Not a lot of rain. Where am I? What is wrong with this dirt?

Crossing his hands in front of himself, he held on to his shoulders. Concentrate hard, he thought. Where are you? Everything felt blank and quiet. He couldn't feel a tug. He squeezed his eyes shut and let the question bubble up: Where did you go? Come find me. I'm over here. Come find me.

If he listened hard enough, he thought he could hear the waves hitting. ☐

Subscribe to "the leading intellectual forum in the US"

—New York magazine

Since we began publishing in 1963, *The New York Review of Books* has provided remarkable variety and intellectual excitement. Twenty times a year, the world's best writers and scholars address themselves to 130,000 discerning readers worldwide...people who know that the widest range of subjects—literature, art, politics, science, history, music, education—will be discussed with wit, clarity, and brilliance.

In each issue subscribers of *The New York Review* enjoy articles by such celebrated writers as Elizabeth Hardwick, V.S. Naipaul, Timothy Garton Ash, Milan Kundera, Susan Sontag, and many more. Plus, every issue contains the witty and wicked caricatures of David Levine.

Subscribe to *The New York Review* now, and you'll not only save over 60% off the newsstand price, but you'll also get a free copy of *Selections* (not available in bookstores). With this limited offer, you'll receive:

➤ **20 Issues** A full year's subscription of 20 issues for just $27.50/£37—a saving of 50% off the regular subscription rate of $55/£53 and a saving of $42.50/£18 (60%) off the newsstand price.

➤ **A Free Book** *Selections* is a collection of 19 reviews and essays published verbatim from our first two issues. In it you'll discover how works such as *Naked Lunch* or *The Fire Next Time*, now regarded as modern classics, were perceived by critics when they were first published and reviewed.

➤ **A No-Risk Guarantee** If you are unhappy with your subscription at any time, you may cancel. We will refund the unused portion of your subscription cost. What's more, *Selections* is yours to keep as our gift to you for trying *The New York Review*.

The New York Review of Books

Return to: Subscriber Service Dept., PO Box 420382, Palm Coast, FL 32142-0382

Yes! Please enter my one-year subscription (20 issues) to *The New York Review* at the special introductory rate of only $27.50/£37 (a saving of 60% off the newsstand price). With my paid subscription, I will also receive *Selections* at no extra charge, as well as a no-risk guarantee.

FREE with this offer!

Name

Address

City

Country/Postal Code

A7L43G

❑ $27.50/£37 enclosed*   Charge my: ❑ Am Ex ❑ MasterCard ❑ Visa

Credit Card Number

Expiration Date/Signature

☏ **For faster service on credit card orders, fax to: (212) 586-8003.**
Please include your own phone and fax number in case of questions. *If you fax your response, do not also mail it.*

*Make checks or US money orders payable to *The New York Review of Books*. We accept US Dollars drawn on a US bank, Canadian Dollars drawn on a Canadian bank, or Pounds Sterling drawn on a UK bank. If paying by check in CDN$ or Pounds Sterling: return to Mike Johnson, *The New York Review of Books*, 1755 Broadway, 5th Floor, New York, NY 10019-3780. We cannot accept international money orders. Rates outside the US: Canada: $53/CDN$72.50, Rest of World–Regular Post: $57/£37, Rest of World–Print Flow Air Post: (2-3 week delivery time; strongly recommended for the Far East, Australia, Africa, New Zealand, and South America) $84/£55. Credit card orders will be charged at US Dollars rates shown. Please allow 6 to 8 weeks for delivery of your first issue.

DAN JACOBSON
ARGUING WITH THE DEAD

Heshel Melamed

M y childhood was spent in Kimberley, the diamond-mining town in South Africa.

In those years most of the mines were no longer being worked. They did not even have fences around them. You could, if you dared, go right to the edge of the two biggest open mines, the Kimberley Mine and the De Beers Mine, and look directly into the depths below. Their central pits were hundreds of feet across, thousands of feet in depth.

It was terrifying to stand above them. Yet from time to time I would feel compelled to do so. The contrast between the banality of the earth underfoot and the emptiness that yawned fatally from it, a single pace ahead, was irresistible. There was no compromise between the two. Only an edge. On this side, life. On that, its unimaginable opposite.

All of it man-made too. That was part of the fascination of these places. Everywhere else, flatness, flatness, flatness.

Later the pits were fenced in. After forty years of inactivity the search for diamonds in the De Beers Mine was resumed; the Kimberley Mine was turned into a tourist attraction. An open-air museum was established nearby. Only on the outskirts of town did a few smaller mines remain unfenced and unguarded. One of these was called Otto's Kopje. It had its own diminished version of an open pit and several vertical shafts at varying distances around it. The shafts did not have any broken ground near them to warn you of what was ahead. You just came upon them: perfectly square, black holes in the ground, each as big as a room, and apparently bottomless. At night, in bed, I would occasionally be racked out of sleep by a sudden involuntary step into that black space.

In early adulthood I left South Africa and went to live in England. There too, quite by chance, I was able to make solitary visits to various disused mine shafts. Near the house owned by my wife's father, in south Devon, were many acres of woodland riddled with disused copper-workings. These were much older than the mines in Kimberley; they had been abandoned decades before the opening of the diamond fields in 1870. Their shafts did not go down nearly as far as those I had looked into, or looked away from, in earlier years. But they too were cut square and were unfenced, half-hidden by overhanging fronds of bracken and branches of trees. Inside the shafts it was possible to make out a rough layer of clay and pebbles, like a thick skin; then, as one's eyes became accustomed to the darkness, a further level of hewn rock, the rough flanges of which seemed to reach out to one another, across the vacancies of the pit itself. Further down rock and emptiness merged into a gathering of shadows, visible as misty colours only—mauve, green, brown, blue. Below that, darkness. An absence of texture and colour. An absence of everything.

I could never visit one of these pits without looking for something to throw into it. Once I tossed in a book I had been carrying in my jacket pocket. Call it an act of literary criticism. Most of the objects—stones, lumps of earth, bits of branch— simply went straight down; others I would throw up in the air, for the pleasure of seeing how they appeared to hang momentarily over the middle of the shaft before falling.

Then I waited for the sound each made when it hit the bottom. The reverberations from below were sometimes no louder than a discreet cough; sometimes almost as loud as a train shunting. Occasionally I also heard sounds like chimes or cries.

Now try to imagine a man dropping a stone into a pit and waiting for a reverberation which never comes back to him, no matter how long he stands there. The thing that had been in his hand, that had hung briefly above the vacancy below, is dropping silently into a deeper silence. Let him leave the shaft, go elsewhere, sleep, work, eat, travel, watch television. The stone is falling still, dropping further and further from the square of darkness which had yawned under it, before being transformed instantly into a square of light receding above it. Dwindling rapidly in size from something like a room to a box, a book, a postcard, a stamp, a pinpoint, the light has long since vanished. Still the stone drops, never meeting any resistance, never producing the sound of having at last come to a halting place.

That is what the past is like: echoless and bottomless. Only its shallowest levels, those closest to us, have recognizable colours and forms. So we fix our gaze there. Below them is a darkness that gives back nothing.

2

Since I never met my grandfather, Rabbi Heshel Melamed, I never lost him. For me he has always been one of the dead. He has always belonged to that region where shadows give way to unchanging darkness. How could we have met? I was born more than a decade after his death, in a country he never visited.

In fact, if he had not died prematurely, I would never have been born.

No doubt many grandchildren could say the same about their grandfathers. Deaths occur, families move, as a result new connections are made, children are conceived who would not otherwise have come into existence.

In his case and mine, however, there lies between us a gulf of unspeakable history.

And I know something that would have seemed utterly grotesque to him, had anyone been able to say it to him during his last illness. I know that the kindest thing he did for his wife and children was to die quite suddenly, at the age of fifty-three, leaving them penniless and helpless.

Yet encoded in the loops of DNA in every cell of my body are discrete physical, mental and emotional potentialities which are my grandfather's as much as mine; mine because they were once his. The genes I have inherited from him cannot be changed or done away with; they were and are capable only of combining in unpredictable fashion with countless others from other sources. Some of those which he passed on to me have doubtless been 'expressed', as the geneticists say, this time around, my time around; I would see them in the mirror, if I knew where to look; I would recognize them, if only I knew how, in the states of mind they give rise to, in the sensations I experience, in the feelings which move me. In my habits of perception too. Other encoded potentialities, dormant in him, still dormant in me, wait to be summoned forth in other combinations and occasions, in persons still to be born.

The pit of the future is quite as deep as the pit of the past. Through it, too, all things fall endlessly. Genes included.

Dan Jacobson

He is the only one of my grandparents I never met. Of the four of them he alone does not lie in the pale brown, quartzy soil of one or another of Johannesburg's Jewish cemeteries. When I think of the other three I face the stubbornly indisposable memory of their presence. But him? Heshel Melamed? He is a fateful absence, a bodiless name, hardly more. He has always been the one who owned death or was owned by it. The deaths of each of my grandparents was different: each was an event, if only a remote one, in my life: known through a sequence of letters, telephone calls, parents' emotions and journeys, which I remember not so much as a loss of my own but as one belonging to an adult world I had yet fully to enter.

Heshel Melamed was different, however. He still is. Death, closure, 'existlessness' (Thomas Hardy's word) was always his lot. When I was a child this rendered him particularly distant and mysterious. Now that I am so much older, he has become far closer to me than he was then. The corridors of thought which lead to him are shorter than they used to be. He, who stood behind my coming-into-being, now waits for my ceasing-to-be. He is the expert on both conditions. His is the absence into which my absence will eventually be absorbed.

As a little boy I believed that he died because his 'blood turned to water'. I understood this phrase in the most literal fashion. No doubt I had misheard something said by the adults. The idea of it, the magical chemistry involved in such a death, was a source of worry to me. Could it happen to anyone? Could it happen to me? Was it the consequence perhaps of drinking too much water? Or of not drinking enough? Did the red fluid inside him actually become as thin and transparent as water? I did not dare to ask any of these questions aloud, for fear of being laughed at, but I turned them around in my mind.

Now I know better. The truth must have been the exact opposite of my fantasy. So far from his blood turning to water, it must have thickened into clots which attached themselves to the walls of his arteries. One seizure was followed by another until all was over with him.

That, more or less, was what had happened to his oldest daughter, my mother. It had already happened at a much earlier

178

age to one of her younger sisters, Rae. I was not with my mother when she died, but I was on a visit home when she suffered her penultimate heart attack, a few months before the end. How she laboured for breath! How bright and wide open her brown eyes were, staring from below! The ambulance men carried her out of the house on a stretcher covered with blue blankets. She was supine. She saw me leaning over the stretcher, but could not speak. It was as if my presence told her only how much closer she was now to her father than she was to me. How little chance she and I had of reaching each other.

It was just before sunrise, on a morning no different from any other. Except for what was happening to her.

She was sixty-seven years old then, exactly as old as I am now. No angioplasty for her. No triple bypass operation. Such procedures were not known in those days. All they could do, once she had been taken into hospital, was to cover her nose and mouth with an oxygen mask. Would clot-busting drugs have been available at that time in a small-town hospital like the one in Kimberley? I doubt it.

So what chance did he have, in Varniai (Vorna to him), Lithuania, forty years before? With the same ailment? In 1919, less than a year after the end of the First World War?

There is just one photograph of Heshel Melamed in my possession. It is not large—about six inches by four inches—and is printed in the sepia tints of the time. It remains strikingly clear and unfaded, however, given that it is about ninety years old. Taken from the front, though not directly so, it shows his head and shoulders only, with a top hat affixed above. Because it reaches to such a height, and because of the elaborate curl of its brim, the hat is as prominent as anything else in the picture. Its salience is emphasized also by a highlight that runs vertically from the band above the brim to a vanishing point just right of centre.

Nothing else in the photo is as bright as that bar of light; not even the two smaller highlights shining within his wide-open eyes. Shaped like a French circumflex gone slightly awry, each shows up as a tiny white gleam just above his black pupils. Looking at them I can still see today, reflected in his eyes, the light that once shone in some photographic studio in Kaunas (Kovno to him) or Siauliai (Shavel to him). The reflections bear some indubitable witness to the consciousness that was then his. Obedient to the photographer's command, he had self-consciously stiffened his gaze and directed it into the black lens of his camera. Focusing at that point, he was aware, too, though much more fuzzily, of the brass rim and wooden casing around the lens.

I speak so confidently of what he saw then because I know about that kind of camera. They are only to be found in museums now; but when I was a boy in Kimberley there was a photographer in town who still used one of them. From time to time my father and mother dressed up themselves and their four children to have photographs of the family, individually and collectively, taken by him. Because he was of 'restricted growth', I remember, he did not crouch as the other photographers did in order to get under his black cloak and look through the aperture. He had to stand on a special box to get there.

That is not all I see, or find myself remembering, as I look into this representation of my grandfather's gleaming eyes, which is as faithful as the technology of the time could make it. In and through the eyes, and beyond them, I see my mother's eyes too. His have the same shape as hers; the same curvature of the eyeball too; the same structure of surrounding bone into which it fits. Like his, her eyes were brown and exceptionally bright: brightest of all, as I have just said, when she was carried on a stretcher out of the house in Kimberley.

What else does the photograph show? Cheekbones also deeply familiar to me: not from my mother in this case, but from her siblings. A straight, shapely nose. A clear skin. A black, full beard with a grey tinge and an upward curl at the edges. A moustache, still wholly black, conceals most of his upper lip. Where his beard mingles with the hair of his head (no dangling ringlets of a fanatical, Hasidic kind for him), one ear emerges clearly. The other is all but hidden. It is thus apparent that the photographer has chosen to stand slightly to one side of him.

A fragment of black bow-tie can be seen just beneath his beard; below that is a small, triangular section of white shirting.

The rest of him, or what is shown of him, is clad in a black frock-coat. Only one of its lapels is on view; also one arm, two large buttons, several creases.

His expression is severe, I would say, but not unkind.

Looking more closely at this picture than I have ever done before, I realize something else about 'our relationship' I had not previously understood. Because he died more than ten years before I was conceived, I have always, in a quasi-instinctive fashion, thought of him as someone older than myself. Permanently older, I mean. Born older, living older, dying older.

In fact, when this picture was taken he was much younger than I am now. So far from being my reverend senior, he was my junior. Now. Then, too.

The occasion for the taking of this photograph was Heshel Melamed's forthcoming departure for the United States. He made the journey in 1912, seven years before his death, eight years before his widow and her children sailed for South Africa.

It is a true portrait, however; no passport-job. A fine one, too, in its sharpness of outline and expressiveness of gaze. Look at the crisp curl of the beard, the clarity of the line of his nostrils. And those alert eyes, to which I cannot stop myself returning. The picture was taken, I have no doubt, in a *nunc dimittis* spirit: as a pre-journey act, a gesture towards the future, a way of leaving something of himself behind. How could the hazards of travel which lay ahead, and the uncertainty of events at home, not have been at work in his brain? And not only in his brain but elsewhere too: producing hollow pangs in his stomach, a tightness in his chest, a faintness in his head.

He was to go all the way (and his address book, which I also have, provides the evidence of it) from Varniai to Cleveland, Ohio—and back. Or not, as fate and God and he himself would eventually decide. First he would travel by train (with several changes) to Hamburg; then by steamer to New York, to stay with relations of his wife's in Brownsville; then once more by train to Cleveland, where, it had been suggested, he might become the rabbi of a community of Lithuanian Jews (Litvaks) who had established themselves there. En route he would also be making calls in Newark, New Jersey, and in Akron, Ohio, where other *landsleit* and members of the family had established themselves.

A big deal, a step into a strange world. I am not tempted to patronize him for what he felt about it; all else aside, I remember too clearly my own alarm and excitement when, at the age of twenty, I stepped into an aeroplane for the first time in my life. Like him, I was leaving the country of my birth, also for the first time. (An old tin tub of a Dakota the plane was, discharged from service once the Second World War had come to its end, several years before.)

He knew Hebrew, he knew Yiddish, he was able, as a speaker of Yiddish, to make himself understood in German; he had more than a few phrases of Lithuanian and Russian as well. Now he was about to enter another world, one filled with speakers of Polish, French, Dutch, English and God alone knew what other Babel-born tongues. To be a bearded, top-hatted, frock-coated rabbi 'at home' in Lithuania was to be conscious of estrangement and exile, local hostility (sometimes), and legally enforced restriction (always). Nevertheless he regarded himself, and took it for granted that he should be regarded by others, as the most important figure in the Jewish community of Varniai; even the gentiles agreed in assigning that position to him. His people deferred to him and respected the rulings he issued to them on innumerable personal and religious problems. He was the head of his own large household and, the obscurity of his own background notwithstanding, he was connected by marriage with one of the most distinguished rabbinical families in the province. (Or so its members liked to believe.) The fields of Lithuania may have been those of exile, but he had never walked on any other. The country's soft but distant horizons had surrounded him from his infancy. The pattern of its woodlands, marshes and fallow spaces was imprinted on his eye and mind. The shape of its low, wooden houses was as familiar to him as the ever-fading, ever-cracking hues of blue, green and yellow in which they were painted. In Varniai he instinctively took his bearings, whether or not he was conscious of doing so, by the town's high-towered, modestly domed churches; he measured the passing of the day by the sound of their bells. When he travelled to other towns he knew as if by instinct who and what were to be avoided—and when; who was to be placated—and how; where, among his fellow-Jews, shelter and succour would be found. All over the country, not to speak of cities like Vilnius (Vilna to him) and Kaunas, the Jews made up such a large proportion of the population—in some areas almost as much as a half of it—he was confident he would never want for a welcome among them.

But out there? In Poland and Germany which he would have to cross by rail? In a ship sailing the mighty ocean? In the New World?

He didn't stay. It wasn't the children shouting 'Sheeny-Viskers' after him in the streets that decided him never to return to the United States. Nor was it because so few words of the language spoken there were comprehensible to him. Nor because he found the country overwhelmingly huge and populous to a degree for which nothing in his previous experience had prepared him. None of that. What made the United States uninhabitable, as far as he was concerned, had nothing to do with what the gentiles got up to. It was the degradations the Jews inflicted on themselves there that were intolerable to him.

He came back to Varniai and reported that once they had landed there all but a tiny number of Jewish immigrants forsook the ways of their forefathers and the laws of Moses. They shaved their beards; they worked on the sabbath as if it were a day like any other; they attended *shul* rarely; they ate forbidden foods; their women wore indecent clothes; they gave up saying the prayers that should have accompanied their daily actions—rising, washing the hands, eating, leaving the home, retiring to sleep. Worse still, perhaps, was the contempt with which such people, some of whom had been in the country for a few years only, had taken to speaking of those like himself who clung to the old ways, to the ways God had laid down for them. If that was how the new arrivals behaved, what would become of their children in a place like that? And their children's children? What abominations would they commit?

Yes, an appointment had been offered to him in some dingy, noisy quarter of Cleveland; but no, he had not been tempted to take it up. Life in Varniai was poor and uncomfortable: that he knew. For reasons he could never understand he was apparently

183

condemned to remain the rabbi of a *shtetl* inhabited largely by ignoramuses and paupers. (His words for them, in his darker moods.) But if that was the price he had to pay for preserving everything he most valued, so be it. At least he knew that he was keeping himself, his wife and his children safe from the corruptions and contaminations that threatened them elsewhere.

Here in Lithuania he would never be alone, not even in his poverty. He would continue to take his modest place among the generations of scholars and pious rabbis who had made the country's name a byword all over Jewish Europe for austere devotion and intellectual rigour. Some of his predecessors had established famous *yeshivot* (talmudic seminaries) and houses of study in cities like Kaunas and Vilnius and Telsiai; others had lived and died in towns only a little bigger, or even smaller, than the one in which he served. They had not been fanatics; nor did he ever think of himself as one. He despised the outlandish garb and messianic antics of the Hasidim: a sect which had come into existence precisely as an act of rebellion against the traditions of book-bound learning to which he attached so great an importance. He regarded it as an honour to bear the title given to those who were unremittingly hostile to the Hasidic movement: he was a *mitnagid*, an opponent. He was contemptuous too of the political activism of the Zionists, who imagined that they could re-establish the people of Israel in the promised land without God's help. He knew that Israel would earn its redemption, however long it might be deferred, in one way only: not by crossing the seas and adopting the ways of the gentiles in distant continents, but by prayer, study, teaching, preaching, the observation of every biblical commandment and every rabbinical injunction to its last insignificant and mighty letter.

Not that he found everything to his liking when he got back to his brick-walled, wooden-verandaed house in Varniai. (It was then the only brick-built house in Varniai, my mother told me; the only double-storeyed one too. Half of it, however, was owned by, or perhaps let to, the cantor of his synagogue.)

Soon after his return he discovered, by chance, that his wife, Menuchah, had managed to get hold of a German translation of

Ernest Renan's *Vie de Jésus*, which she had been reading in her spare time.

My mother did not know how the book had come into her mother's possession. She guessed that either it had been borrowed from someone in the town, or Menuchah had brought it back from one of her visits to Siauliai or Kelme (Kelm to him). Or Raseinai perhaps.

There it was, anyway, this triply heretical item; first, it was a book about Jesus of all people; second, it was in one of the gentile languages (Russian, German) for whose literatures his wife had a deplorable fondness; third, it was notorious for being 'atheistical' in tendency.

So after a row which spoiled the homecoming for him and everyone else, he seized the offending book, and carried it at arm's length out of the house and across the little front yard. Watched in silence by his wife, the children, and the Lithuanian maid, Annele by name, he threw it into the road. The book flew through the air, its pages open and fluttering, and fell face down in the mud.

It was raining at the time. It had rained the previous night too. The road was 'all mud' according to my mother. Yet he would not let Menuchah go out and pick the book up. 'He grabbed her, he held her by both arms,' my mother said. 'She tried to get away but he was much stronger than she was.'

She had never seen her parents behave in this manner before. None of the children dared to go out and rescue the book. It lay where it had fallen.

'The next morning—well, you can imagine the state it was in. There was nothing left of it; nothing you could read.'

What followed was that which follows all serious marital rows: a sense of mutual betrayal and injury; solitary starings out of windows; retreats to darkened rooms; children with lowered voices and miserable, alert eyes; the mechanical performance of whatever domestic or public duties had to be done; the spiritless contemplation by husband or wife of a future which appeared to promise nothing but more of the same, indefinitely.

There had always been a kind of warfare between him and his wife. Menuchah's habit of reading books—novels and other

185

items—in Russian and German, and her eagerness to see her children follow her example, had been just one of the fronts they fought on. He demanded of himself and of everyone else in the family and his congregation the utmost strictness in the practice of their religion; whereas she—the *rebbitzen*, the rabbi's wife, herself the daughter of a rabbi, granddaughter of a rabbi, great-granddaughter of a rabbi—was as sceptical about the religion, and as recalcitrant in carrying out the duties around the home that it demanded of her, as she dared to be. She was ready, also, to let her children know how she felt. The two of them were always 'wrangling' about it, according to my mother.

It amazed me to hear this from her. The grandmother I knew, and whom I saw about twice a year on family visits to Johannesburg, could hardly have been more devout. She was so devout, in fact, that our home in Kimberley was effectively barred to her. In all the years of my childhood and adolescence, she visited us just once, for two or three days only; and that was it. During her visit she lived, so far as I could see, on boiled eggs cooked in a little pan which she had brought with her. (All the other utensils in the house were *treif*—unusable, not kosher.) Not even the birth of my baby sister, or the bar mitzvahs of myself and my brothers, had been enough of an attraction to lure her back.

But when I said something like this to my mother she answered impatiently, 'Oh, she was always perverse!'

Perverse? My quiet, undemanding, sombrely clad grandmother? To me she looked as if she had gone to a kind of finishing school—*finishing* indeed—where they taught old women the arts and necessities of grandmotherhood. How to shrink in height, lose weight, develop deep wrinkles, grow larger joints. How to bow the shoulders, lower the head, subdue the gestures, soften the voice. How to wear black skirts and jackets with white blouses, live alone in a single room, eat tiny meals, and deploy a range of small, self-deprecatory gestures and facial expressions. How to keep in their place—mantelpiece, table, window sill, bathroom ledge—many valueless, small objects.

No doubt my view of her was affected more than I realized by the stories I read and the movies I watched. In effect I was doing my best to make her over into some kind of traditional, story-book grandmother, with Jewish orthodox, immigrant trimmings attached. The fussiness of her religion, its innumerable injunctions about diet and domestic ceremonial, not to mention synagogue-attendance, struck me as wholly appropriate to an aged widow who had never adjusted and never would adjust to the loss of her 'old country' and to the acquisition of a new one.

Much of this, I was to learn from my mother, was no more than my own fanciful yet wholly conventional reading of her character. I learned that as a married woman she had tried to test to the limit what might be permissible for someone in her position to do and to say, to read and to think. Only after she had been widowed—that is, only after her husband's attempts to dominate her had been brought to an end for ever, and she herself was settled in naked half-pagan South Africa—only then did she choose to become everything he had always wished her to be.

Perverse indeed.

For Lithuania I never hankered. If anything, it was like a wound within me. So far from being a country to which my childhood longings and ambitions could attach themselves, it was the place my mother had escaped from: nothing else; nothing more. The same applied to Latvia, my father's country of origin, which he had left many years before her departure from Europe. I can remember the shock I felt, at about the age of seven, two or three years before the outbreak of the Second World War, when I learned that my father's much older and wealthier brother had gone 'home' with his family for a brief visit there—i.e., on a *holiday*. It seemed to me uncanny that he should have done so: as if, say, a meteorite should suddenly start up from the spot on earth on which it had fallen and make its way back to the moon or Mars or somewhere even further afield. The peasants, woods and snows my parents sometimes spoke of may have sounded exotic, but they made no appeal to me. Their exoticism was indistinguishable from too many of its dire accompaniments: pogroms when Jews were attacked; *yeshivas* where they studied nothing but the Talmud and swayed for ever over dusty bibles and prayer books; *shtetls* where they huddled together for comfort in the midst of a great darkness. Stark hunger, through much of my father's childhood, had been another accompaniment. That my mother's father should actually have chosen to remain in those bleak territories, though he had been given the opportunity to move to the United States—a country where they made movies, where they made Buicks, where they built skyscrapers and spoke English—struck me, when I heard about it, as bizarre and incomprehensible; even mad. Or if that was too strong, then revelatory of the unfathomable strangeness of the place he had lived in, the people he had shared it with, and his own stern nature.

To put it bluntly: like most Jews of my generation I believed that our parents and grandparents had come from Nowhere. They might occasionally refer to *der heim* in affectionately sentimental terms; they might even try to remind us that Vilnius had been so great a centre of Jewish learning it had gone by the name of the 'Jerusalem of the north'. Yet none of them wanted to go back there. So we knew we were right to think of it as we did. In migrating from Lithuania to South Africa they had moved from Nowhere to Somewhere.

It never occurred to us that in certain respects the opposite may have been true: that they had actually exchanged Somewhere for Nowhere. (I know many people who find it impossible to believe still.) We could not imagine that Jewish Vilnius and Kaunas—I specifically exclude here, as I must, the riches of their then-predominant Polish and Russian cultures—might have been centres of a high civilization, compared with anything the immigrants would find in Johannesburg and Cape Town. Let alone in comparison with what awaited them in the tiny, lost-in-space dorps in the backveld, where so many of them first made their homes.

Perhaps I would have felt differently if I had grown up in a city like Johannesburg, in which Jews made up a substantial part of the city's white population. But I grew up where I did: in a town with a small Jewish population (about 120 families, at most, none of them related to us). Moreover, this was at a time when Jews everywhere were being subjected to a worldwide, systematic campaign of vilification, originating in Nazi Germany and unprecedented in scale and degree of malevolence. Its effects were manifest in Kimberley too—at school, in the streets, in the newspapers. Every anti-Semitic jeer or threat I encountered was like a burn on my consciousness, for which no remedy or redress could be found, since it had nothing to do with what I actually did and everything to do with what I undeniably was. Still, when I look back on that period, when one of the world's great powers was tirelessly devoting the resources of its propaganda machine (itself a brand-new invention) to the spreading of crazy lies about the Jews, I am now faintly surprised at how peacefully we lived, at how much respect was shown to my father in the town, at how many of my closest friends were gentiles.

(Had Germany won the war, we would of course have learned soon enough what transformations respect, friendship or neutrality could hastily undergo. We would also have been shown to what extremes hostility could be carried, once it was licensed, even demanded, by officialdom.)

So I am not interested in telling a hard-luck story here. Rather, the point I want to make reaches as deeply as anything can into my relations with my parents, my grandparents in Johannesburg, and my solitary grandfather left behind in Lithuania. It is this. Everything I have so far said describes my childhood feelings about Lithuania before the outbreak of the Second World War; or at any rate before we knew the full extent of what was being done to the Jews of Europe during the war. Even in those pre-war days—I will not call them innocent— Lithuania had essentially been for me a country to abjure. In so far as it was inhabited by gentiles, it was an arena of deprivation and threat. In so far as it was inhabited by Jews, it belonged to what the Russian Jewish poet, Osip Mandelstam, called 'the Talmudic wilds'—a region darker in my imagination than anything I was likely to see around me in the sandy, suburban Africa I knew best.

3

When did reluctance turn to curiosity, curiosity into something stronger—a sense of obligation, even a kind of compulsion? I cannot say exactly. What I do know is that it was not until 1996 that I went to Lithuania for the first time, accompanied by my elder son.

My first impression of the country was of its emptiness. The further east the plane flew, the less demarcated the landscape became, the fewer were the roads crossing it, the more rarely were vehicles to be seen. Ploughed fields turned into pasturelands, pastures into woods, woods into water, water into tussocky heaths and marshes. Each change was marked by a simple, limited change of colour. No one appeared to be moving in the villages randomly dotted about. There were no mountains; hardly any hills. Dirt roads stretched between one cluster of steep-roofed habitations and the next. The plane hissed, hummed, tilted, straightened itself out with a purposeful groan, lurched lower once more. The sun was setting directly behind it. We were dropping into shadow.

The place looked almost as empty after we landed as it had from above. Quiet too, inside and outside the airport. There was no bustle of arrival. The plane had been barely a quarter full, so little time was lost in debarking or waiting for luggage in the dimly lit hall. To judge from the newspapers they had read on the flight, the other passengers were almost all Lithuanians coming home. By the time my son and I emerged from the terminal—all angled walls of glass and a plethora of tubular green banisters—they had already cleared off. No more than three or four cars and a battered, lifeless bus were still in the parking lot. Also waiting near the exit was a man holding a sign bearing the name of the hotel I had booked into. I was relieved to see him. It soon became apparent that he had no English at all; no German or French either. The only other definitely non-Lithuanian person who had been on the plane with us, a frail-looking Indian in a double-breasted suit, with the inevitable flat, hard, black, business-man's briefcase in his hand, had also evidently been expecting to be met, and was now going through the painful process of learning that his hosts had let him down. He looked about him anxiously and followed our departure with envious eyes.

Close to the airport, but apparently not part of it, was a group of houses two or three storeys high, roofed with tiles, fronted in dusty reddish or lemon-coloured stucco; handsome and elaborate in appearance, though shabby too, with bits of mock-rustication, like frayed elbows, at their corners. Nobody was to be seen in them or near them. Next came some humbler, single-storeyed wooden cottages, each with a gabled protrusion in front—a place in which to shed coats and boots before entering the dwelling proper—and a window poking out of the half-attic above. Village-like in appearance, but without a shop or bar to serve them, they too seemed to be deserted. It was only about nine in the evening, in midsummer, not raining: so where were all the people?

I could not ask this question of the driver. Silenced, diffident, middle-aged, he kept his eyes on the road. Not even the sight of a fox dashing across it provoked him to utter a sound. At ground level it was easy to understand the curiously bland appearance of the country from the air. It was virtually without fences. The edges of ploughed fields, copses and meadows met and parted on equal terms, with never a sign of greeting or mutual exclusion between them. Only the gardens of the occasional houses were fenced off; and a group of smallish, multi-windowed factories standing on a cleared slope. Modest boards outside them told us nothing we could understand. No advertisement hoarding gave a clue as to what might be manufactured within. Bottle-tops? Shoelaces? Matchsticks?

A car. Another one. At last, a couple walking. Another couple waiting at a bus stop. The huge red ball of the sun stands proud of the serrated treetops on the horizon. Some blocks of flats appear. Even they look unpeopled. Only when the road passes through the middle of a heavily wooded cemetery within an elaborate, miniature topography of hills, hollows and rocky knolls, do we come on anything resembling a throng. It is made up entirely of stone and bronze figures: angels, life-size images of Jesus carrying his cross or already mounted on it, many Marys with heads bowed or arms held out. There are also a few effigies of the human departed, in frock coats. The tallest of them are lit up momentarily in random rays from the sun. Then a few more roads come together and sidle off from one another—and here we are, on the edge of the Old Town of Vilnius.

It looked as if the city was inhabited by about fourteen people. We went up some narrow, cobbled alleyways and through irregularly sloping squares. Street lamps with lights inside them were almost as rare as people. Admittedly it was by now approaching eleven o'clock on a Tuesday night; this first impression of vacancy was to be somewhat modified in the days that followed. Amid the darkness and general depopulation there were a few large plate-glass windows behind which one could make out displays of chairs or glassware aspiring to elegance and high modernity: to a positively Finnish finish. But most of the shops were meagrely and dirtily windowed, still under the Communist blight, as if nothing had changed since the death of the old order, or ever would.

After some wandering about we found a couple of open cafés. Our attempts to communicate with the waitress in the one of our choice were met with helpless shrugs and giggles. But the menu eventually brought to us had English alongside the Lithuanian version, and we indicated with our fingers what we wanted. I chose a glass of beer and what the menu called 'Beer Accompaniments'. These turned out to be pieces of a hard, brittle, sour cheese so unfamiliar in taste and texture it could have been made out of pig's milk or squirrel's sweat. The beer, on the other hand, was excellent. 'Ustena Ale' it was called. The other English words on the label read: 'Is brewed with malt, rice, hops, yeast, and pure water only.' The choice of my son, Simon, was 'roasted fish'. The smell of garlic that came from it was so strong I was relieved to think we would not be sharing a room for that night, at least.

He ate with pleasure; but his air remained disconsolate. Fatigue, the bathos of our attempts to communicate with the three people we had so far encountered, the spooky emptiness of the streets around us, had evidently affected him. He suddenly said, 'I've never before been in a country I know so little about.'

To my own surprise, and with a feeling of relief at making the confession, I answered, 'Neither have I.'

That was exactly how I felt: family history notwithstanding. Now that I had at last arrived in Lithuania, and was sitting in a café in its capital city, eating peculiar cheese and drinking beer, my presence there felt as arbitrary to me as his obviously did to him. (He had volunteered to come with me, and I had been glad to take up the offer, knowing him to be independent in his habits and well used to coping in foreign parts with conditions much harsher physically than anything I expected to encounter.) What was the point of it? The curiosity which had led me here now seemed frail and wilful; nothing more. I could not connect anything around me with my memories of my mother or grandmother; their lives before I had known them had never seemed to me so remote and inaccessible. And as for Heshel Melamed . . .

So, as much for my sake as for Simon's, I told him in greater detail than I ever had before all I knew about my grandfather and his wife Menuchah—whom Simon had never seen. Then about the nine children produced by the two of them. Some of these great-aunts and great-uncles he had never met; two of them, it turned out, he had never heard of before. This led him to ask when the Jews had arrived in Lithuania (some time in the fourteenth century, not long after the Lithuanian tribes had been united by their first king, Gediminas); and from where they had come (either from Germany or south Russia, or both, depending on which historian one chose to believe); and why they had come (at the invitation of successive kings and grand dukes, who had wanted to use their skills as merchants and scribes in order to build a state out of a semi-wilderness). And what had Lithuania become afterwards? A part of Russia? A 'dual monarchy' with Poland? A part of Prussia? Yes, all of these; while remaining stubbornly itself throughout, in language and in the minds of its native people. And the Jews too had stuck it out, intermittent pogroms and the mass migrations of the late nineteenth and early twentieth century notwithstanding. When the Second World War began with Hitler's invasion of Poland in 1939, almost a quarter of the population of Vilnius was Jewish. Within weeks that proportion was greatly increased by the thousands of refugees who had fled eastwards from Poland after the German blitzkrieg on that country. The 'lucky' ones among them were deported to Siberia during the subsequent, brief Russian occupation of the city; a few managed to flee with the hastily retreating Russian army; the rest were trapped when the Germans arrived. Of every twenty Jews who were alive in Lithuania in 1941, nineteen were dead by 1945.

A strange thought suddenly occurred to me. No wonder the city appeared to be so empty! A quarter—no, a third eventually—of the people who had once lived here had been wiped out. All around us were the spaces they had occupied. We were in the midst of a vacancy their absence had created; the city's silence was that of the words they and their unborn children would never speak.

When I said something of this sort to my son, he was properly sceptical about it: not about the facts I had given him, but about my notion that their effects could be visible still and audible too, even if only by way of absence and dumbness. So long a time had passed since then; the population of the whole of Europe, and of its capital cities especially, had grown greatly during the past decades; many more people were bound to be living in Vilnius today than when the war had ended, fifty years before. They were just a very quiet lot, that was all. They didn't stay out late. Not on a Tuesday night. Not in this part of town, anyway.

It was impossible to argue the point. Yet what I had said was one of those thoughts which, once uttered, is not to be un-thought. It was with me still as we walked back to the hotel, via a different set of romantically ill-lit, decrepit alleyways. (One of them, I noticed, went by the name of Literaturi, as if to show me what a civilized country we were visiting.) All were as silent as before.

Everything passes and is forgotten. That is the one bleak face shown to us by history.

What happens, happens for ever. That is history's other face.

We look first at the one, then at the other, over and over again. Neither offers any solace for suffering undergone.

The strongest emotions I remember from my visit to Lithuania are sadness, a stunned sadness of a kind I had never felt before, and an almost constant sense of humiliation. How feeble my imagination was! How carefully I had protected it, or allowed it to protect me, from the pain that might otherwise have threatened it! How shaming it was that I had to visit the country where these things had been done, and go to some of the places where the murdering took place, to feel the horror of it so intensely! Did I of all people—someone who had mentally reproached his rabbinical grandfather for the gullibility with which he had held to his faith, for the near-fatal rectitude of his innocence—did I really need such 'aids' to reflection and recollection?

Apparently so.

I repeat: only one in twenty of the Jews who were living in Lithuania when the Germans invaded in 1941 was alive four years later. The Lithuanian and Latvian communities share the melancholy distinction of having had more of their people killed in the Holocaust, proportionately, than any other in Europe.

We approached Varniai, the town where my grandfather lived, from the south, at speed, the car radio playing hits from the Seventies. A large lake abuts on the south-east side of the town, and the countryside around it is flat even by Lithuanian standards. Thinly wooded too. Even the individual trees were skimpier and more weedy-looking than those we had seen elsewhere. There are relatively few cultivated fields nearby; instead stretches of barren-looking marshland, covered in an unpalatably reed-like growth, obtrude on the plain.

Earlier, seeing the first road-signs pointing to Varniai, I had felt a strange nervousness, as if the closer I came to it in reality, the more it removed itself in my mind, and not the other way around. For years its old name, Vorna, had been a sound only; then, dressed up in its new garb as Varniai, I had seen it on a large-scale map supplied to me by the Lithuanian consulate in London; now it was a destination, with our distance from it marked in kilometres. Still the car went on. We were travelling directly north. More signs, more empty crossroads, plenty of cottages and ploughed fields. No other vehicles. Here was a turning from the road and just a few minutes later another sign on which Varniai figured at last not as a destination, not as a direction, but simply as a declaration. This was it.

My nervousness left me; or rather, it was replaced by a misgiving different in nature. What threatened me now was anti-climax merely. Discovering that I had come here for nothing.

Our driver, Albertis, stopped the car at my request. To one

side was a dusty, stony space, a kind of parking lot, with some boarded-up kiosks scattered about on it. The largest of these structures—roofed in iron, built of sand-coloured brick—looked like a garage, though it had no sign announcing it as such. It too was closed. Several hoseless, rusting petrol pumps stood nearby; another, more modern in design and in better condition, had its hose padlocked securely to itself, like a prisoner in manacles. Three or four cars waited in front of it. Their drivers and passengers were standing about in the warm sunlight, talking to one another. Presumably they were expecting the garage attendant to arrive; or, I thought later, this was the place where the inter-town buses halted, and they were waiting to pick up friends or to see them off.

No one took any notice of our arrival. Everything was flat and nondescript, as if specially arranged so, for my benefit. There were some telephone poles and wires; a single no-parking sign; across the road a field of newly cut grass; further off an anonymous brick-built public building, too large for a house, too small for a school. Welcome to Varniai. The scent of grass from the field mingled with the smell of oil and dust.

All right then. Having procrastinated long enough, I got back into the car and we drove on. The trees that were gathered together ahead of us separated themselves to form an avenue of young limes. Bare or grassy verges gave way to neat kerbstones. Houses and small apartment blocks appeared: unplastered, unornamented places, built of the familiar, sandy-looking brick; then a cluster of shops, the same; then a few older, lower, more 'picturesque' wooden houses. I remembered my mother's proud recollection that the family home had been the only two-storeyed, brick-built house in the place (even though it had been shared with the cantor). There were hundreds of such houses now. The town hall, more imposing than some we had seen on our travels, overlooked a neat plaza; it was adorned with wide steps below and a pediment above. On the far side of town a tall red-brick factory chimney rose above yet another blur of trees.

Empty of traffic, empty of people too, the main road turns right and starts to go down a steeper slope than might have been expected, considering how flat is the countryside around the town, as well as the approach to it. Now a man appears and crosses the road ahead of us, slantingly, as pedestrians do when they are confident that no approaching vehicle will trouble them. Dressed in shorts, a shirt and wellington boots, he has a plastic pail in each hand. On his head is a white handkerchief knotted at its corners. Our indispensable guide on this journey, Shlomo, has been told that 'the last Jew in Varniai' is a woman mathematics teacher, once married to a Lithuanian, who had taught in the local high school and is now widowed and retired. Her first name, his informant had said, was Vera; but her surname and address were not known to him. Seeing the bucket-carrying local, therefore, Shlomo leaps out of the car and a lively conversation ensues between them. It ends with much head-shaking on both sides.

Shlomo gets back into the car telling us not to worry, never mind, for sure he will find her. 'How many women maths teachers can there be in a place like this?' he says. It is an expression of scorn, not a question. He insists that we stay on this road, though Albertis makes a tentative dart to left or right at each crossing we come to. (There are few enough of them.) A car overtakes us and comes to a halt in response to Shlomo's frantic hand-waving through the open window. He gets out. More urgent conversation follows. Another failure.

In front of us now is a large white church. Its tower, decorated with tall, narrow, lancet-like windows, has an awkward appearance, like a man with elevated shoulders and a too-small head. In this case the head is a silver dome in the shape of an angular onion, if such a vegetable can be imagined. It is a common architectural motif in these parts. The building was formerly a 'cloister', I will be told later: by which I assume a monastery or convent is meant. It stands on a corner, just at the point where the downhill slope flattens out and the road begins to wind up once more. Albertis brings the car to a halt. My son spots a young couple emerging from one of the houses behind us. Shlomo immediately goes scrambling after them. He points enquiringly in one direction, they point in another. An adolescent boy with a bicycle joins in the debate. So does a dog. I get out of the car and take a road going off to the left, towards what I guess must be the centre of town.

197

A modest bridge carries me over a stream hitherto hidden behind trees and houses. Next to the bridge stands a smaller, red-roofed church, surmounted by a delicate cross. The two churches are a hundred yards apart, at most. There are wooden houses on both sides of the stream, with pathways and vegetable gardens going down in uneven steps from their back doors to the water. Upstream of the bridge a woman is doing her laundry on the river bank. Two little girls are paddling close by her, not venturing away from the rocks she stands on. They shout and giggle demonstratively, covering up their timidity with much noise. Downstream a middle-aged man in striped trunks is carefully wetting his torso before stepping into the water. Every handful of water he throws on himself shines briefly, like a necklace, in mid-air. It also produces a wide gaping of his mouth, but he is too far away for me to hear his gasps or cries. Behind him another man kneels to dig out weeds from a vegetable bed. Bells chime persistently from a church somewhere out of sight. Since both the churches I can see are closed and silent, I assume that a wedding is being celebrated elsewhere.

So this is the place.

I had wanted to be here physically, to become a part bodily of the locale in which my grandparents spent most of their adult lives; where my mother had passed her entire childhood. I had wanted to see, touch, smell, hear what had been to them as intimate, and as much taken for granted, as Kimberley had once been to me.

Here it is. This.

The river ran for them just where it runs now, over the same rocks, making the same noise and producing the same never-ceasing swirls and bubbles on its surface. The two churches stood then where they stand now. The wooden houses set unevenly on both sides of the slope, nearer or further from the stream, cannot be those my mother saw in her childhood—they are too new and neat—but I have no doubt they are built in the style of the ones they replaced. The vegetables and flowers of late June are the same now as they were then. So is the dark, turned-over earth of a bed that awaits planting. So are the clumps of grass in neglected corners, and the white-flowering bindweed clambering up walls and tree trunks wherever it is allowed to do so. The trees carry small green apples now just as they did then. Excited little girls have always cried out like these.

No one else has appeared on the road. No car comes down it. I become aware belatedly that the chimes have stopped. My son stands on the corner by the white-towered church, waving to me to come back.

Time now for me to turn directly to you, my dear grandfather, and to offer you my apologies. Not mockingly or self-abasingly, but out of the shame I feel at having lived so long and understood so little about us both. Which is to say: about the world given to us to live in but never to share.

Because of the decision you took to go back to Varniai, instead of settling in Cleveland, Ohio, I now know that the grudge I had held against you was even deeper than I had supposed. It sprang, obviously and irrationally, from your having 'chosen' to expose yourself, your wife and your children to the hideous death that would have been your lot and theirs, had you lived to enforce your will on the family. My mother among them, inevitably.

Yes, she too. She would have been just like all the other murdered women, the many tens of thousands of them in Lithuania, the millions of them elsewhere in Europe. They *were* just like her, precisely in each dear detail that made her different from the others, and every one of them different from her—her lambent brown eyes behind rimless glasses; her plump figure; her delicate calves and ankles; her large head; her puzzled brow and mouth; her curling, silky hair which she always wore short but could never control; her readiness to believe the best about people; her absent-mindedness and ineptitude with her hands; her vulnerability to spells of disabling depression; her incapacity to tell even the most harmless social untruth; her childish amusement at certain kinds of absurdity; the excessive devotion she displayed towards her younger siblings and the striking lack of devotion with which she responded to her husband's wishes and rages. Nothing of her, none of this, would have been mourned or remembered, since all likely mourners or rememberers would have suffered the same fate as herself. You and Menuchah among them; and her brothers and sisters and the children they would have had; and the unknown husband she would doubtless have had by then; and the children she would have loved as much as those she bore in South Africa.

Of course I knew that you would have sent your children to the furthest corner of the earth rather than let them be murdered; I knew you had no notion of what was going to happen to the Jews of Europe. Who did? Who could have foreseen a future so terrible that only a madman could envisage it and believe (rightly!) that he would find people ready to turn it into a reality for him?

That much was plain to me and had always been so. Yet something—reproach, blame, resentment—remained. I had to go to Lithuania to get rid of it. In some of the recesses of my own mind I had found it easier to reproach the helpless than to confront the real villains, the murderers who came from the west.

Your decision to return to Lithuania from the United States, and to remain there, was a principled one. You put your faith first. Of course the people who had asked you to join them in Cleveland wanted you there precisely because they needed your help in the task of preserving that faith. Yet the way of life you glimpsed in America seemed to you so repellent, you could not tolerate the thought of exposing yourself or your children to it. So you rejected the whole thing.

Should your descendants, then, not have honoured you for the earnestness with which you clung both to your beliefs and to the places that had sustained them for so many centuries?

Well, it did not work like that. How could it, when the stakes turned out to be so high? Along with all the others I had the advantage of knowing how suicidal your decision to remain in Lithuania was, or would have been, had you lived to carry it through. As a result the sense of reproach I felt did not confine itself to you alone; it spread from you to your religion. That too became irrevocably tainted in my eyes. On every account it was wrong, fatal, misguided. It was wrong factually, in being postulated on entities and events which did not exist: a purposive, intervening God, a history supposedly derived from his acts and wishes, and the prospect of a world-transforming, trans-historical

redemption (the coming of the Messiah) which was never going to
happen. More than that, it was morally culpable, too, in that it
had persuaded an entire people to keep themselves together,
separate from all others. To what end? Solely to experience the
endless nightmare of wandering and persecution assigned to them.
Culminating in a horror that was 'trans-historical' only in being
unlike anything else that history had yet witnessed.

So for heaven's sake, or for God's own sake, let go! Bring it
to an end. For how much longer should this grisly performance be
allowed to continue?

'The game was never worth the candle,' my uncle Leib once
said to me, apropos all Jewish history. And to my older brother
he said, 'What did the Jews think was going to happen to them, if
they carried on like that? Over there? They lay with their head in
the lion's mouth, and imagined that the lion would never close its
jaws on them. Well, it did.'

My mother spoke less reproachfully, but to similar effect.
'Whenever I hear people talking about "the Jewish contribution to
civilization",' she once said to me, 'I want to tell them that none
of it was worth the life of a single child the Nazis murdered.' To
this I responded, out of curiosity rather than out of a belief in
what I was saying: 'Perhaps people value the life of a child as
much as they do *because* of the Jewish contribution to
civilization.' 'Oh,' she said, with a tartness that was not really
characteristic of her, and a weary gesture of the wrist that was,
'Oh, they'd have discovered it without us.'

At least she was not postulating an 'alternative' history for
the Jews, as Leib had done, and as I had been trying to do, in
using the decisions you had taken, Heshel Melamed, to arraign
the religion and the peoplehood underwritten by it. In effect, what
I was asking of the Jews in eastern Europe was a complete
reconstruction of their history and the circumstances in which they
had found themselves. Which is an absurdity. In that part of the
world there had never been a neutral, secular, social space from
which they had chosen to exclude themselves. Most of those who
were lucky enough to leave Europe in the earlier decades of the
century did manage to find, and in some cases help to create,
more open societies in which they could live according to their

own inclinations. Those who remained in the 'ancestral' territories of the former pale, however, continued to be what they had always been: one among a multitude of competing groups—ethno-religions, I would call them, or once-and-future nations—gasping for life and breath under a variety of contested sovereignties. I might as well have scolded the Poles for choosing to be Catholic and to live between the hammer of the Germans and the anvil of the Russians; or the Armenians for choosing to speak their own language, to worship Christ according to their own rite, and to place themselves between Orthodox Russians on one side and Turkic Muslims on the other.

It is all nonsense of course. Yet I know what drove me towards it. To the murderers of the Jews, the perpetrators of the Final Solution, I had nothing to say. Not even an oath to utter. From them my imagination could only reel back in fear and despair. So once again I turned in unspoken reproach towards the victims—for no better reason than that they were available, they were weak, I knew them, I could so easily have been one of them.

☐

GRANTA

PIERRE CLASTRES
THE LIFE AND DEATH OF A
HOMOSEXUAL

Krembegi: 'A strange hunter, to say the least'

Pierre Clastres was a young French anthropologist whose book,
Chronique des indiens Guayaki, described the time he spent among
some of the stone-age tribes who then still lived in the jungles of
Paraguay and Venezuela. It was published in 1972 and among the
people intrigued by it was Paul Auster, who was living in Paris. After
Auster returned to the United States, he began to translate Clastres'
Chronicle and to exchange letters with the author. Eventually an
American publisher was found. Then Clastres died in a car accident.
The American publisher went bankrupt; and the manuscript, of which
Auster had no copy, was lost. There the matter stood for the next
fifteen years—a project consigned to oblivion—until in 1996 Auster
went to San Francisco to deliver a lecture. After the lecture was over,
a young man approached Auster and asked him to autograph a set of
bound galley proofs. The young man had bought them for five dollars
in a second-hand bookstore. Auster had never seen them before. They
were proofs of the long-lost *Chronicle of the Guayaki Indians*, from
which the following extract is taken.

There was no sweetness in the air that day: the corpse gave off a terrible stench. The man had been dead for only a little while, but the vultures had opened his belly, which accelerated the process of putrefaction, attracting numerous swarms of flies, and the flies had become drunk with everything oozing and flowing from the gashes. There were blood-splattered holes in the place of the eyes, which had been pecked out by the birds. The mouth was enlarged; the birds had forced their way through the teeth to get at the tongue. But even so we could recognize him: the length of his body left no doubt. It was a Stranger whose height had surprised me: he was four or five inches taller than the tallest hunter. And now he had become food for the vultures. The Atchei did not like to see this happen. He had left several days before, saying that he was going to meet up with two families who were hunting. He had been rather ill and had probably changed his mind on the way; but he had not been able to return to the camp at Arroyo Moroti. He had died all alone, and no doubt had seen the *briku* gather in the sky above and then swoop down on him one by one. The birds were motionless; bloody slivers of meat hung from their beaks. Hundreds of little yellow butterflies drily beat their wings around the corpse of Krembegi.

Unusual in many respects, he was immediately striking because of his exceptional height, which made him almost a giant compared to the little Atchei. But he was not proportionately more vigorous. He gave an overall impression of flabbiness. He had a broad, fat belly, whereas the bellies of the other men were hard and compact, even when relaxed. He was a strange hunter, to say the least.

But was this all? Krembegi came from one of the two small tribes of Atchei that belonged to the Guayaki 'nation'. Until recently, they had had no contact with one another, did not know one another, and even considered one another to be enemies. One tribe, the Atchei Gatu, knew the other tribe as the *Iroiangi*, meaning 'strangers'. Krembegi belonged to the Atchei Iroiangi or Strangers, and they did not like to talk about him, and when they did talk it was only with reticence. As for the Atchei Gatu, who were hardly more loquacious on the subject, their knowing looks and crafty smiles showed that even though they would not say anything, they had certainly devoted some thought to the matter. It seemed clear that Krembegi was not just anyone.

Because he wore his hair long like a woman (the men wore theirs short), I wanted to take his picture one day and asked him to hold his bow, which was standing nearby. He got up politely but refused to hold the weapon.

'Why?'

'It's not my bow.'

'Take it anyway.'

'I don't have a bow, I don't want to touch this bow.'

He spoke firmly and seemed disgusted, as if I had asked him to do something obscene. And then, to show that he did not feel any ill will, he pointed to something that I thought could not have been his.

'I'll hold my basket.'

This was the Atchei world turned upside down: a man with a basket and no bow! Who was Krembegi? As soon as I learned the secret of this man's strangeness, people were quite willing to talk to me about him. His story was told to me little by little, first by the Atchei Gatu, who were delighted to have another chance to show that they had good reasons for scorning the Strangers and that they would never allow someone like Krembegi to live among them. Later, the Iroiangi agreed with the portrait drawn by the Atchei Gatu and added details to it. But from the man himself I could get nothing. Timid and reserved, he would avoid talking to me. He died without having said anything.

The insistence of the Atchei tribes on instilling in their young men the idea of *bretete*, the great hunter, is the basis both of the groups' moral law and of individual honour; but it also arises from economic necessity. Since they are nomads in a forest that is rather limited in edible vegetation, the members of the two Guayaki tribes cannot subsist on gathering. Roots, berries, fruits, palm-hearts, honey and larvae unquestionably account for a considerable portion of their food: it is the women's responsibility to gather this hidden food, and all around their stopping places in the forest they are constantly foraging for it. But not all areas are rich in trees with edible fruit, and the forest is generous only during certain seasons. That is why the *kuja* sometimes return to the camp without their baskets pulling on their necks. There is very little to be found in the *naku*: a few larvae reserved for the children, especially the 'soft heads', because they are very nutritious, a rat, one or two frogs, and sometimes a snake, which is caught by the tail, quickly dashed against a tree before it can bite, and then roasted. Eating like this is all right once in a while, but if you make a steady diet of it you lose weight, and that is depressing.

The major portion of the food is produced by the men. In Guayaki society it is they who have the task of supplying the people with meat and fat, which are indispensable. *Bareka*, to hunt: this is their function; they identify themselves with it and define themselves by this activity. A man can think of himself only as a hunter, one cannot be a man and not a hunter at the same time. The entire symbolic space of masculinity unfolds in the act of *jyvo*, shooting an arrow, and from their earliest years the boys are prepared to enter their normal place, to fulfil their natural role. The long years of apprenticeship running along with their fathers through the woods, the initiation that confirms them as hunters, the women's preference for the best *bretete*, the night songs of the men loudly celebrating their exploits as archers—all these things combine to make the young men take on the collective will of the group as their own personal desire. They must become true hunters, for the survival of the tribe will depend on them. They know it, and in this knowledge lies their truth, their destiny as men: either one is a hunter or one does not exist. There is no choice.

Hunting is never considered a burden. Even though it is almost the exclusive occupation of the men, the most important thing they do every day, it is still practised as a 'sport'. There is work involved, of course, in endlessly tracking animals, in sitting still for hours watching the movements of a roebuck or a band of monkeys, in holding the bow poised for several minutes so that they will be ready for the brief instant when a bird or coati can be seen through the thickness of the foliage. They know that it is crouching in the branches above, but they can't see it: they have to wait until it shows itself, keeping their arrows at the ready. They must also dig holes for the tapir to fall into, and expand the armadillo's hole: the man digs, and the animal tries to escape by burrowing further into the tunnels. It is a race that the hunter usually wins, but only after considerable effort—sometimes he makes an excavation so big that he can disappear into it.

And then the hunters must keep replenishing the supply of arrows. The tips are made of very hard wood tempered by fire, but as they are used they wear out and break. They are often lost, either when a wounded animal gets away after being hit or when an arrow misses its mark and flies off into the vegetation and disappears. Whether the men are in the woods or resting in the camp, then, they are always involved with the work of hunting.

Hunting is always an adventure, sometimes a risky one, but constantly inspiring. Of course it is pleasant to take sweet-smelling honey from a hive or split a palm tree and find swarms of delicious *guchu* left behind by the scarabs. But everything is known in advance, there is no mystery, nothing unforeseen: it is absolutely routine.

Whereas tracking animals in the forest, proving that you are more clever than they are, approaching within arrow's range without revealing your presence, hearing the hum of the arrow in the air and then the dull thud as it strikes the animal—all these things are joys that have been experienced countless numbers of times, and yet they remain as fresh and exciting as they were on the first hunt. The Atchei do not grow weary of hunting. Nothing else is asked of them, and they love it more than anything else. Because of this they are at peace with themselves. They feel no internal division, no bitterness troubles their souls. They are what they do, their Self fearlessly achieves its fullness in doing what the group has always done since the beginning of time. One might say they are prisoners of fate. But from what point of view? The Atchei hunters themselves feel that they live in complete freedom.

To be a *bretete* requires strength, poise and agility: you have to reach a state in which the body and mind feel at ease, are sure of themselves. This is *pana. Pana: pané-at*, the opposite of *pané*. And *pané* is what frightens a man most. For once you have fallen victim to it, *bareka* is finished. Your arm has no strength, the arrow flies far from the target, useless and absurd. You can no longer kill anything. The return to camp is grim when your right shoulder is not straining under the weight of some animal. Instead of celebrating his catch with a sonorous chant, the empty-handed hunter sits in silence beside his fire. If *japa*—shooting wide of the mark—happens several times in a row, then measures must be taken, for *pané* has befallen the hunter. This is of course a painful humiliation, since it is an admission that he is incapable of being what he is: a hunter.

But it could be even more serious. A man never eats his own game: this is the law that provides for the distribution of food among the Atchei. A hunter kills an animal and his wife cuts it up, since he is forbidden to do it himself. She keeps a few pieces for herself and the children and the rest is given out, to relatives first, brothers and brothers-in-law, and then to the others. No one is forgotten, and if there is not much meat, then the shares are small, but each person gets something. In exchange the hunter receives a portion of the game brought back by the others. He feeds them with what he has killed, and they do the same for him. A hunter, then, spends his life hunting for others and eating what others have caught. His dependence is total, and the same is true of his companions. In this way things are equal, no one is ever wronged, because the men 'produce' equivalent quantities of meat. This is what is called *pepy*, exchange.

But if a man is *pané*, what can he give in return, how can he pay another man back for the game he has given him? You cannot receive without giving. It is impossible to be *pané* and to respect the law of reciprocity at the same time. In the end, your companions would grow weary of always giving without receiving anything in return. An old man who is too weak to hold a bow is given food. He deserves it, and a son never lets his father go hungry. If this parasitical existence goes on for too long, however, one day he will be left at the foot of a tree beside a fire. There he will wait patiently for death. But a strong male is not an old man. If he is *pané*, it is because he deserves it: he has certainly done something wrong. Every act against the order of things must be paid for, and this is how the imprudent man is punished. Why help a man who has been found guilty and condemned? It would not do any good.

Fortunately, long-term cases of *pané* are rare. Every man has his periods of bad luck, his hesitant arrow leaves too soon or too late, his hand does not draw back the bow with enough force. But this can be remedied. The young men's lips are pierced and their backs are scarred to confirm them in their condition of *pana*. If *pané* should occur, the operation is repeated. New scars are made, but much more superficial ones than the cruel stripes that were dug out of the skin before. They go around the biceps and criss-cross with the old cuts: some men cut their forearms, others their thighs. Very little blood flows, and once the wounds have been smeared with wood ashes and have closed up, the shallow scars have the effect of attractive embroidery on the skin. This treatment is almost always successful: the *pané* leaves you and once again you become *bretete*. And if you become *pané* again, you begin all over. The causes of this type of bad luck are mysterious. It can happen to anyone, and there is not a single Atchei hunter who does not have therapeutic tattoos in addition to the *jaycha* on his back.

If the cause of *pané* is unknown in some cases, in others it is very clear. One cause—and this would be so fatal that no one even dreams of attempting it—would be to eat your own game, to refuse to participate in the exchange. To insist on keeping the animals you have killed leads to a total and permanent separation from the world of animals, since the *pané* will prevent you from ever killing one again. When you do not want to mediate your relationship with food through your relationship with other people, you risk being completely cut off from the natural world and placed outside of it, just as you are pushed out of the social universe by refusing to share your goods. This is the foundation of all Atchei knowledge. It is based on the awareness that an underlying brotherhood binds the world and men together and that what happens among men is echoed in the world. A single order rules them, and it must not be disrupted.

The Atchei therefore avoid doing things that will attract *pané*. Young hunters, for example, never eat animal brain. Although it is a great delicacy, it also causes bad luck. For this reason it is reserved for the *chyvaete*, who hunt little or not at all and therefore run no risk. Some kinds of honey are also forbidden to the young men because they bring on *pané*, such as the honey from the *tei* bee. The honey of the *tare*, on the other hand, only prevents the *kybuchu* from growing pubic hair. But there is something else. For what does it mean to be a great hunter but to identify one's very existence with the bow? And doesn't *pané* separate a man from his bow so that it becomes exterior to him, as if it had rebelled against its master? The bow is the hunter himself: an initiate's first task is to make his first adult bow by himself. This weapon is much more than a tool. When its owner dies, it becomes *ove enda*, the dwelling place of the departed soul, as do the arrows. The bow and arrows have now become dangerous, and are discarded. The bow is the sign and symbol of the man, the proof that he exists and the means of his existing. When he dies, then, his bow disappears as well, for it is that part of the man which could not survive him. Conversely, if the bow abandons him when he is *pané*, then he is no longer a hunter, he is no longer anything.

The very strength of the bow makes it vulnerable. It is not difficult for *pané* to affect a hunter: it has only to affect his bow: he will immediately suffer from it and be *pané*. A bow is the essence of virility, the irrevocable metaphor of masculinity. Because of this, it is one of the things that must be protected from their opposites. How far does the hunter's space extend, what is the boundary of the masculine world? The boundary is the feminine world. An order presides over the lines of force in this geography and keeps the different regions separate. If some disorder causes them to interpenetrate, masculine space is contaminated, weakened and degraded by this contact with feminine space. In other words, if a woman touches a bow, *pané* befalls its owner. For this reason there is a severe taboo against women having any contact with a bow. They themselves run no risk, but for the men it can be fatal. Inversely, the equivalent of the bow for the *kuja* is the *naku*, the basket, which is the quintessence of a woman's femininity. After the ritual of seclusion and the scarring of her stomach, a young woman celebrates her entrance into the world of adults by weaving palms into her first basket. She knows how to do it because her mother has taught her; she made little ones when she was a girl. Now it is up to her to make it by herself, and until her death she will carry a basket. Just as the bow is the man, the basket is the woman. So that if a hunter touches a basket, or even thinks of carrying one—which would be even more absurd than comical—the result would be the same: *pané* would be his punishment for having contact with the basket.

It is always the men who suffer the consequences. The unwarranted overlapping of masculinity and femininity affects only the man. Of course the *kuja* will also suffer from the *pané* in the sense that the hunters will no longer have anything to give them to eat. But the women's power is so strong that it can be harmful to men. To be a hunter, that is to say a man, you must always be on your guard against women, even when they are not menstruating. You cannot be a man except by opposing yourself to women. When the distance separating men from women vanishes, when a man crosses the dividing line, a contagion is produced that makes him lose his worth, that wears away his masculinity: he finds himself within the sphere of women. Bowman, basket-woman, this is how people are divided up. What happens to a man without a bow? He becomes a basket person.

This is what had happened to Krembegi. He was not joking when he said 'my basket', because it really was his, made by his own hands with the help of one of the women. Why did he have a basket? Because he did not have a bow. And why didn't he have a bow? Because he was *pané*. But this had been the case for a long time; in fact, it had always been the case. He had never been able to kill an animal with a bow and arrow, and the matter became clear rather quickly: he was *pané* in the same way that the others were *bretete*. This was not an accident. It was his nature. But still, why, when circumstances had taken away his bow, did he provide himself with a basket? He could have had nothing at all, have remained, so to speak, between bow and basket. But is it possible to be neither a bow person nor a basket person?

Only in early childhood is there any space in which the difference between the sexes remains negligible. And Krembegi was a grown-up—he was no longer a *kromi*. He could no longer exist in this neuter universe. When one is an adult one is either a man or a woman, a bow or a basket: there is nothing in between, no third possibility. What, then, is a man without a bow? He is a non-man, and for this reason he becomes a basket-carrier.

There were two basket-carrying men at the camp at Arroyo Moroti where the tribes now lived, and both were Iroiangi. The second one was named Chachubutawachugi, the Great Wild Pig with the Long Beard. A very hairy beard covered his face. And since it often took him a long time to find a woman willing to shave him, his beard would grow quite prodigiously. I gave him a present of a mirror and some razor blades: he would put the blades in the middle of a split piece of bamboo and then fasten them tightly. In this way he could shave more often. In gratitude he gave me the name of *apaio*, father. Chachubutawachugi had a basket because he was *pané*. But unlike Krembegi he was very strong, and though he had not used a bow for several years because of the *pané*, he continued to hunt coatis by hand and to stalk armadillos in their burrows. He would distribute his catch and would receive presents from the other hunters in return. His shoulders, striped with thin black lines, attested to his efforts to overcome his bad luck with tattoos. But after repeated failures he had given up and resigned himself to his fate. One of his brothers' wives had made a basket for him. He lived with them, more tolerated than welcomed. When his sister-in-law was in a bad mood she wouldn't give him anything to eat. At those times he would cook for himself. No woman would have agreed to become the wife of a *pané* man; he therefore had to take on the feminine work himself. He had once been married, but his wife had died, leaving him alone. To judge by the evidence, Chachubutawachugi did not have the best of luck.

Krembegi, on the other hand, seemed comfortable with his situation. He did not say much, of course, but he looked serene. He lived with a family who accepted him completely. Cooking was not a question for him since he helped the wife in her daily household tasks. It was almost as if he was the co-wife of the man who lodged him. In the morning he would go off with the *kuja* to look for larvae, fruits and palm-hearts. His basket would be just as full as those of his companions when he came back. He would put it down, crouch on his heels, and diligently and efficiently begin to prepare the evening meal: husking berries, peeling roots, preparing *bruce*, a thick soup made of palm marrow mixed with larvae. He would fetch water and firewood.

When he had nothing to do he would rest or make necklaces with the teeth of the animals killed by his host. They were very pretty, far more attractive than those made by the women. The women were content to pierce the teeth of all the different animals killed by their husbands and to string them through with a thin cord. It amounted to little more than a collection of teeth of different sizes placed in the order in which the animals had been killed. These necklaces were sometimes very long, six feet or more, containing hundreds of teeth from monkeys, agoutis, and especially pacas—those from pigs and roebucks were not saved because they rattled against each other. When a woman is feeling happy she puts on her necklaces in several layers, glad to be able to wear the proof of her husband's prowess as a hunter. Then she puts them back in the bottom of her basket. Krembegi's necklaces showed more care. He would use only monkey canine teeth and only those that were more or less the same size. It is no small job to pierce all these tiny canines with nothing more than a paca tooth. But Krembegi had great patience.

No one in the camp paid any particular attention to him, he was like everyone else. He did only women's work, but this was known and taken for granted. Krembegi was no more or less anonymous than anyone else in the tribe, and he tranquilly filled the role destiny had given him. He lived with the women and did what they did; he did not cut his hair and carried a basket. He was at home in this role and could be himself. Why should he have been unhappy?

Chachubutawachugi was a different matter altogether. It was not at all assumed that he had found his niche, or that he was content with his lot. And the proof was that no one took him seriously. Whatever he said or did was greeted by the Atchei with condescension. They did not openly make fun of him, because that was not done, but they found him rather ridiculous and smiled behind his back. The men were somewhat wary of him and the women laughed into their hands when they saw him coming with his basket. The children, who were usually so respectful of their elders, forgot the rules of politeness and good conduct when they were with him. They ran wild, were insolent, and refused to obey him. Sometimes he would get angry and try to catch them, but they were always too fast; he would give up and sullenly take a walk in the woods or lie down somewhere off by himself. Everyone pretended to believe that he was stingy with what he brought back from the forest, while he was actually as generous as anyone else. For example, he had gone off in the morning one day saying that he was going to look for larvae. On his return he ran into a group of men. 'Well?' 'Nothing. No *guchu.*' And he walked on. When he was out of earshot one of the men said: 'Nothing? *U pa modo!* He ate everything up!' And they all burst out laughing. This was an unjust accusation.

Why were the Atchei so mean to poor Chachubutawachugi? It was true that they found him something of a clown, with his passion for adorning his neck and head with the most unexpected objects. If he saw a piece of metal, a cartridge case or a bottle, he couldn't resist; he would pick it up, attach it to a string and put it around his neck. He would walk around with his chest covered by a necklace made of a few dozen penicillin bottles, some sardine can keys, and formless pieces of scrap iron. He would wear it for a while, then abandon it and go to find other things. The *kybuchu* were once given a rubber ball. After a short time they had ruined it. For him it was a godsend. He cut it in two and made one of the pieces into a superb skullcap that covered his whole head down to the eyes. He was very happy with his idea. The Atchei, however, looked at the elegant fellow with an air of pity. 'Not at all surprising! That's his style, all right!' In other words, the victim of *pané* had found another way to call attention to himself through this rather awkward dandyism.

But there had to be another reason for the Atchei's ill will, for in the final analysis Chachubutawachugi's innocent faults were more than compensated for by his activity as a hunter of coatis and armadillos. This activity was of course somewhat limited; but it was by no means negligible. On the other hand, Krembegi, who never trapped animals, was not mistreated in the slightest way by the Atchei. This was why he was able to accept his fate with such placidity. What was the difference then, between these two *pané* men? What was the difference that made people adopt different

215

attitudes towards two negatively similar individuals—similar in that they were both excluded from the circle of hunters? As a rule, the Atchei would have had the same attitude towards both of them. But it was not at all the same. Therefore, the fact that both these men were *pané* did not make them identical. As it turned out, they were not.

Man=hunter=bow; woman=gatherer=basket: these two equations strictly determine the course of Atchei life. There is no third equation, no additional space to protect those who belong neither to the bow nor the basket. By ceasing to become a hunter, one loses one's very masculinity; metaphorically one becomes a woman. This is what Krembegi understood and accepted: his radical renunciation of what he was incapable of becoming—a hunter—automatically put him on the side of the women; he was one of them, he accepted himself as a woman. He carried his basket in the same way they did, with a carrying strap around his forehead.

And Chachubutawachugi? It was simple: he hadn't understood a thing. For he, the innocent one, thought that he could remain in the masculine universe even after he had lost the right to do so, so blind was he in his desire to remain a man—he who was no longer a hunter, who was no longer considered a hunter. *Esse est percipi.* What did the others see when they saw him? Perhaps this is not the right question. Because from a certain point of view Chachubutawachugi was invisible. Why? Because he did not live anywhere: neither among the men, because of the *pané*, nor among the women, for in spite of his basket, he refused to incorporate himself into their group, to inhabit their space. But the place he was obstinately trying to occupy, midway between the two, did not exist. And so he did not exist any more either; he was a pathetic inhabitant of an impossible place. This was what made him 'invisible'; he was elsewhere, he was nowhere, he was everywhere. Chachubutawachugi's existence was unthinkable.

And this was what annoyed the Atchei. What they reproached the *pané* man for without their even knowing it was his incomprehensible refusal to let himself be taken along by the logical movement of events, which should have put him in his new and real place, among the women. When you have a basket, it is because you are a *kuja*. But he did not want to be one, and this created disorder in the group and upset the ideas of the people—not to speak of the man himself. This was why he often seemed so nervous, so ill at ease. He had not chosen the most comfortable position for himself, and he had thrown things out of order.

You had only to see how Chachubutawachugi carried his basket. He did not do it as the women and Krembegi did, with the carrying strap around his forehead. In this position the women walked with their heads lowered, somewhat bent, looking at the ground. But he carried his *naku* differently, with the strap in front and slung over his shoulders. Whenever he slipped he would painfully squeeze his neck. But in this way he walked like a man.

As for Krembegi, his relations with the bow were the same as those of the women: he never touched a bow because this would attract bad luck to the owner of the weapon. Nothing set him apart from the *kuja*. That was why he refused when I asked him to hold a bow for the photograph, and had picked up his basket instead. But this was not all. Krembegi, who was separated from the bow and masculinity, had gone the full symbolic distance into the feminine world. This accounted for the Strangers' reticence and the hints made by the Atchei Gatu. What did the Atchei know about him? Why did the one group refuse to speak about him and the other group make only sarcastic remarks about him? It was because Krembegi was a *kyrypy-meno*, an anus-lovemaker, a homosexual.

The people of his tribe accepted it naturally, even though they were somewhat annoyed by it. But that was because of the Atchei Gatu, who were very disapproving. 'There are no *kyrypy-meno* among us! You have to be Iroiangi for that!' But everyone agreed that if Krembegi was what he was, it was because he was *pané*. The Atchei Gatu felt no contempt for him personally. For them it was rather comic that a man would accept the compliments of another man by offering him his *kyrypy*. They laughed about it and saw in this yet another proof of their superiority over the Strangers. They could not recall any similar cases among their group. They only told the story of Bujamiarangi. It had happened a long time ago, when Paivagi was still a young man. An Atchei went out hunting and had the good fortune to fall upon a *kware*, which was caught unawares and did not have time to escape into the thickets. The man did not even have to use an arrow; he beat the animal with his bow and broke its spine. The vegetation in this spot was very dense, the underbrush a tangle of creepers and climbing plants. The hunter left behind his still-dying prey and tried to open a hole in the vegetation by using his bow to knock down the plants and shrubs. He had progressed a few dozen yards when he came upon a more open space and then went back to get the anteater and put it on his back. He saw someone next to the animal. It was Bujamiarangi, a very young man, who had been following him. And what was he doing there? The hunter could not believe his eyes: Bujamiarangi was making *meno* with the dead anteater! He was so absorbed in taking his pleasure that he did not hear the man approach. The hunter did not hesitate for a second. Mad with rage over what the other man was doing with his game, he shot an arrow, and Bujamiarangi collapsed on to the cadaver of the *kware*. No one, concluded the Atchei, ever saw him again.

But as for *kyrypy-meno*, no, they didn't know anything about it. To be insensitive to the charms of women was something that surpassed the understanding of the Atchei Gatu. But then, to give in to the assaults of other men, that was too much! And all that because of *pané*. What did they say about Krembegi? First of all, of course, that he never 'went' to women. But why? Because his penis was very small, like the penis of a coati. It was freely compared to the little barbs put on the tips of arrows: it was really not much of anything, he could not use it. It could well have been that this was simply malicious gossip. But who were Krembegi's partners? Were the Strangers also different from the Atchei Gatu in that their hunters all enjoyed *kyrypy-meno*? For obviously Krembegi could not be a homosexual all by himself.

He did have partners. But not many, and not those one would have thought. It would be logical to assume that, to the extent that a man like Krembegi represents a certain disorder in the ethico-sexual world of the Atchei, a subversion of all accepted and respected values, the field of his sexual activity would not be governed by any rules, that he could pursue his own pleasure at will: in other words, that any man of the tribe, if he so desired, could make love with Krembegi. But this was not at all the case;

homosexual relations are not anarchic, they are governed by a very rigorous logic. Krembegi was the Atchei world upside down, but he was not its negation; he was part of another order, another group of rules which were the image—even though reversed—of the 'normal' order and rules.

The ultimate bases of Atchei social life are the alliances between family groups, relations which take form and are fulfilled in marriage exchanges, in the continual exchange of women. A woman exists in order to circulate, to become the wife of a man who is not her father, her brother or her son. It is in this manner that one makes *picha*, allies. But can a man, even one who exists as a woman, 'circulate'? How could the gift of Krembegi, for example, be paid back? This was not even imaginable, since he was not a woman, but a homosexual. The chief law of all societies is the prohibition against incest. Because he was *kyrypy-meno*, Krembegi was outside this social order. In his case the logic of the social system—or, what amounts to the same thing, the logic of its reversal—was worked out to its very end: *Krembegi's partners were his own brothers. 'Picha kybai* (meaning *kyrypy-meno*) *menoia*: a *kyrypy-meno* man does not make love with his allies.' This injunction is the exact opposite of the rules governing the relations between men and women. Homosexuality can only be 'incestuous'; the brother sodomizes his brother and in this metaphor of incest the certainty that there can never be any real incest (between a man and a woman) without destroying the social body is confirmed and reinforced.

That is why Krembegi's partners were so few in number. Of course now and then a man without family ties would solicit his favours—the dissolute Bykygi for example. But these things rarely leave the family, so to speak. Such was Krembegi's fate: *pané*, homosexual, a complete inversion of the sexual and social order. But still, he was not too unhappy with his lot.

But now it was all over. He had run into his last bit of bad luck, and the vultures were in the process of devouring him. It would not have been a good idea to let them go on. Krembegi was going to be buried. One of the men went back to the camp to give the news. He would bring back several women so that they could do the death *chenga-ruvara*. In the meantime the others would prepare the grave. With a few quick blows of the machete they cleared a small space in the woods at the centre of which a hole was dug. It was a sort of well that was more or less cylindrical, just wide enough for a human body, and more than three feet deep. The thick humus that covered the ground of the forest was not hard to dig, and the machetes went into it easily. The vultures were still waiting, not at all scared off by our activities. They did not try to get closer to the corpse. A man went off a little way under the trees to look for *chipo*, a fine creeper used as string.

The messenger came back, accompanied by three women. One was the wife of the chief, Karewachugi; she presided over all the tribe's rituals, she was always the first to intone the chants. The other two were Krembegi's sisters-in-law. Crouching on their heels, they burst forth in the *chenga-ruvara*. Their sobbing seemed even more lugubrious than it had the other times, because now it did not mingle with the quiet but constant noise of camp life. Silence, light, vultures. The men (among whom was a brother of the dead man) seemed indifferent. Krembegi's passing did not seem to affect them. Were the words they were speaking—so quickly that I could not understand them—an elegy to the dead man? I couldn't be sure, but I doubted it. When the farewell to Krembegi was finished, the men took over.

Working rapidly because of the stench, with almost brutal gestures they folded the legs high over the chest, having to force them a bit because rigor mortis had already set in. He was in the foetal position: as it is before birth, so it is after death. To keep the body in this position it was tied tightly with the creepers that had been gathered a little while before. The same process was repeated with the arms: they were folded in to the torso against the ribs, the forearms bent up to the shoulders, the elbows against the body. The head was last. The men pushed on the neck to lower it against the chest. The hands were then pushed against the temples with the fingers slightly separated and closed, like the claws of a bird of prey. The head was put between the hands and a solid knot of creepers fixed it in this position. Krembegi's large body now resembled a kind of ball caught in a net. It was ready for burial.

The Atchei always leave the area in which an adult is buried after destroying or burning his possessions: a woman's basket and mats, a hunter's bow and arrows. The bow is broken and thrown into the fire. The arrows are not burned, but shot off at random in all directions. Aren't they *ove enda*, the dwelling place of the soul? After a person's death nothing must remain that belonged to him during his life. Those things are too dangerous. As soon as Krembegi's death was known, therefore, his basket was thrown into the fire. □

'A good story is a hell of a gift.'

Geoffrey Wolff, 'The Great Santa', *Granta* 34

One reason to give a friend a *Granta* subscription this Christmas. Here are 1,026 more:

1. A subscription is excellent value: see the tear-out card in the middle of this issue for details on price.

2. It is a gift which *lasts*. The arrival of each issue will feel like getting—and *giving*—a gift again.

3-*1,026* That's how many pages a friend will receive with a one-year gift subscription: 1,024 pages, in four vivid issues, of:

'Essential reading.' *Observer*, 1997

'An oasis of good writing.' *New Statesman*, 1997

To place an order, use the tear-out card in the middle of this issue

JONATHAN LEVI
THE SCRIMSHAW VIOLIN

Madeleine Gordon was not much of a Jew. She was a Starbuck, the daughter of whalers, pirates and other not-so-genteel Semitophobes of Nantucket. But she had married David Gordon (who was the genuine article) and, in the innocence that calls itself love, had created her own cultural revolution, shocking not only her mother and several generations of Starbucks, but all the Jews of Nantucket by becoming more knowledgeable, more spiritual, more legalistic (and a better cook of gefilte fish—not to mention she caught her own pike) than any of the genetic Jewesses on the island. She hung a Chagall print above the headboard of her great-grandfather's four-poster, taught herself biblical Hebrew from CD-ROM, and read every word ever written by Elie Wiesel. She subscribed to the *Jerusalem Post* and the *Forward*, and had the *New York Times* delivered to the mansion on Orange Street, where she lived with David and her mother, scanning them religiously for the latest news on what it meant to be a Jew. And so it came to pass that Madeleine saw an op-ed by the Rabbi Doctor Alexander Abba Lincoln on the discovery of the Jew Gene—she was not entirely sure whether he was serious—and sent the invitation.

Sandy Lincoln was not much of a rabbi, at least not down in that secret place of superstition and fear that people call the soul. He had spent too much time in civil service, and worse yet, in the Talmudic details of forensics, to believe that humanity was much more than a hank of hair and a piece of bone.

But Sandy had discovered over the years—especially over the years after the communes and the jug bands and the solar-powered yurts, when the beads and batik gave way to a tight layer of fat around the belly and a halo of white hair around the jowls that made him seem perpetually open for business—that people, like Madeleine Gordon, flocked to him as if he were, God forbid, a practising rabbi. They wrote him letters, stopped him on the street, woke him at two o'clock in the morning. Every Friday night they invited him—a synagogue here, a Jewish community centre there—to speak to them, as a rabbi and a coroner, to instruct them on the Dahmer, the Anastasia, the O. J. of the day. And after the talks, in the hallway after the *kiddush*, by the swing set after the dinner, people sought him out, pressed his hand, looked into his eyes, not for his expert opinion on DNA or carbon dating (or even on their private concerns about stray hairs or semen stains), but for the kind of deep advice that only someone who knew both the Midrash and the Dead could provide. Within a $300 round-trip radius of New York, the word spread—Rabbi Sandy Lincoln, he's a *mensch*, he's got a soul.

Normally, Sandy would have scribbled a brief note to his assistant, Indira, to include a polite, but firm, apology to Madeleine, as he did with the many invitations he received that read more like the personal memoirs of the Chairwoman of the Speakers Committee of this synagogue or that JCC, lonely women in search of a little safe, spiritual recognition in the form of a travelling rabbi.

But Madeleine's invitation included a unique postscript. 'Rabbi,' it read, 'I hope you will find in my Nantucket what I have found in your religion.' Sandy was less moved by the chutzpah of the comparison, than by the mystery of what it was he might discover. Besides, the invitation arrived in the depression of February, when he was having trouble with Indira, and the Medical Examiner's Office was the warmest spot in Manhattan. Madeleine Gordon wanted him in the middle of July. There was the promise of a barbecue, the hint of a yacht. Sandy accepted.

Nevertheless, now that he was on the island, he found himself feeling less enthusiastic at half past seven than he'd expected. David Gordon, not Madeleine, had met the three-forty flight from LaGuardia in an open-sided Willys Jeep that made all conversation impossible on the way from the airport into town. He had deposited Sandy, without much more than a nod, at the entrance of the Unitarian sailors' chapel on Orange Street that served as a temple for the dozen sabbaths between Memorial Day and Labor, before disappearing with Sandy's overnighter.

The talk had gone well, that wasn't the problem. He had rambled around intermarriage (Madeleine had specifically requested the topic in her invitation) in mock forensic terms. He had dissected the current phobia—that the Jews were intermarrying themselves into extinction. The Jews of Nantucket sat at the edge of their Unitarian pews. Of course they were worried, all of them, no matter how many lobsters they allowed themselves between Shavuoth and Tisha b'Av. They worried that every time a David Gordon married a Madeleine Starbuck, he was finishing off what Hitler had begun. That ten years from now, you'd be more likely to run into a blue whale on Orange Street than a nice Jewish doctor for your daughter.

His advice had been greeted with the usual rush of applause by the seventy-five assorted Jews who had bought into the lighthouse baskets and lobster pants of the Gentiles but still wanted to maintain some semblance of Otherness. There had been the usual wilding afterwards by the local bridge ladies and their unmarried daughters. But Madeleine Gordon, if she was there, had failed to introduce herself. And while some might interpret her invisibility and the silence of her husband as a mystery, Sandy felt only annoyance and a need, despite the rush of the momentary celebrity, for air and a moment of tranquillity. He pleaded a weak bladder and stepped out the back door.

Orange was a one-way street of cobblestones. The Unitarian church was no larger, just more exposed than many of the white, clapboard mansions hidden behind generations of hedge and rose. To the right was the airport—Sandy guessed the town was in the other direction. There was to be a dinner at eight—that much David had communicated. With half an hour to regain some kind of enthusiasm, Sandy walked left.

The problem—if Sandy wanted to get to the root of it—had begun in the morning. The number three train had shut down between Twenty-third and Fourteenth Street for thirty minutes, and Indira was still out with a summer flu. Which meant that Sandy lacked the ten minutes' tranquillity at the beginning of the day, that moment with a cardboard cup of Colombian roast and two Danish, that can seal you against the daily pain. Selwyn, his other assistant, Selwyn of the hunched shoulders and nicotine hair, was in the office already, of course, as Sandy entered.

'What's in today?' The room was kept at forty-two degrees exactly. He missed his coffee.

'NYPD, Rabbi,' Selwyn said. He was standing at the examination table, waiting for Sandy, hunched over a police body bag. It smelled like smoke, even through the chill of the room and the polyurethane of the bag. 'Third Avenue, restaurant up in the eighties, kitchen fire. Owner says bad wires, Fire Department says arson. Some poor Jew found his Auschwitz.'

And so it began. All morning, as Sandy and Selwyn diluted powdered chemical, ran local tests and bagged parts for further analysis, Selwyn worked to keep the conversation within the perimeter of the death camps and the crematoria even as Sandy struggled to push it out. Selwyn was a survivor—his mother had died in Sobibor—and the Holocaust was never far from Selwyn's petri dishes and beakers. For Selwyn, this is what it meant to be a Jew. He wore his mother on his sleeve and the Holocaust around his neck like a Phi Beta Kappa key. All fire victims led to Auschwitz, all gold teeth to Switzerland.

Sandy felt great sympathy for Selwyn and had learned to accept this tic along with the shoulders and yellowed hair. For Sandy, the Holocaust, the fires, the teeth, the bones—these were human tragedies, human triumphs. There was nothing particularly Jewish about them. He was a Jew, he wouldn't deny it. But he was no more proud of being a Jew than he was proud of having two arms, a spleen, ten metatarsals and eighteen ribs. Sandy knew Selwyn, and Selwyn knew his boss. There was nothing new about this back and forth—Selwyn had worked for him for twelve years. Sandy wasn't going to jeopardize a good assistant by saying anything new.

It was after one when Sandy announced that he had finished whatever it was he could do with the polybag. 'Write out the report, Selwyn, will you?' He grabbed his overnighter. 'I've gotta run.'

'Rabbi,' Selwyn said, 'I've figured it out.'

'Yes, Selwyn?' Maybe his tone was patronizing, but Sandy was in a hurry to make his plane and would have to make do with whatever lunch he could find at LaGuardia. He had no time for more Jews.

'Rabbi,' Selwyn said, 'you have no soul.'

'Rabbi,' a voice called. Sandy looked up. For a moment, he felt the chill of the examination room. 'Rabbi,' the voice called again.

A woman was standing across the street. More exactly, she was standing on the raised portico of what looked, from Sandy's vantage, to be the grandest mansion on the block. Doric columns, iron lanterns, a curved driveway of crushed scallop shells. And this woman. Even at the distance of a couple of dozen cobblestones, Sandy guessed she was six feet tall. She wasn't beautiful in the breath-catching sense of the word. She was too tall, her blonde hair too frizzy and pulled back too tightly by a too colourful hair band. But Sandy recognized the confidence of her letter's postscript and allowed himself to be lured across the street.

'Mrs Gordon.'

'Madeleine.'

'Sandy.'

'I'm sorry,' Madeleine began, but Sandy waved her off, 'there was a last-minute hitch.' She stepped down from the portico. 'My mother—I wrote you.'

'Of course.' Sandy remembered the reference to old Mrs Starbuck who, if her late husband, in his wisdom and knowledge of inheritance law, hadn't bequeathed this mansion to his only daughter, would have shut the door on poor, silent David, Sandy, and the rest of their tribe.

'The talk?'

'Everyone was very kind.' Sandy looked down. Now that she was standing next to him, he began to feel an attraction, partially an awe—not just her height, but the straw of her hair, the pebbled beauty of her cheeks, the Nantucket she'd promised of sand and heath.

'Good,' she said, but Sandy felt she was looking down into his face in search of something else.

'I thought—'

'I'm sorry, Sandy.' Madeleine must have seen something in his face below the beard. 'You wanted to take a walk.' He stood there, realizing that some kind of response was expected of him. But something had caught Sandy as Madeleine spoke. It was a fragrance, something like wisteria, a breeze that came as much from the house as from Madeleine herself.

'No, no,' Sandy answered quickly, with a shy speed that convinced Madeleine of his sincerity.

'I'm glad,' she said, holding out her hand. 'Before the others come, I want to show you something.' The postscript, the promise of a discovery. Sandy forgot about his escape, forgot about Selwyn and the fire on Third Avenue. With the faint scent of wisteria in his nose, Sandy followed Madeleine across the threshold.

Inside, the Starbuck mansion was magnificent, a mid-nineteenth-century collage of exotic woods and veneers carefully chosen by homesick Starbucks on the distant shores of the whaling grounds. Although she seemed to have a specific destination in mind, there was a method to Madeleine's tour. She was determined to show Sandy every mahogany panel, every teak louvre, the priceless screens of bamboo and Javanese balsa. She led Sandy through the bedrooms, the dressing rooms, up into the attic, out on to the widow's walk where he could see the masts of the rich and famous 200 yards down the bluff in the marina. She led him back down again into the body of the house, linking each room to a tale of this captain or that shipowner who had left this piece of furniture or that bit of history. It was a treasury, a genealogy, each room a branch of a family tradition that fanned across the seas in search of another leviathan to bring home to this tiny island.

But Sandy found that, despite the melody of her voice, the obvious life she put into her description of these ancient histories, his mind had latched on to something else. It was that breeze again, that wisteria-laden breath, stronger in some rooms than in others, as if the house itself was teasing him with a secret. It came to him as the ebb and flow of a presence—he wasn't ready yet to call it anything more metaphysical.

He thought about asking Madeleine, but what would he ask her? Excuse me, but what is that perfume you're wearing? Sandy's greatest fear, almost a certainty, was that the presence he felt had little to do with smells, with something that Madeleine could recognize and share. It had to do with him. Maybe, despite Selwyn's barb, with his soul.

Was it love? It was a nonsense of a question, but one that he always felt compelled to ask himself—in a clinical way, of course—on these weekend road trips and these easy talks. Not that he was seeking a wife in the rabbinical sense of a woman to bear children and keep the accounts, nor was he looking for a fleshy bed-warmer, although both types were plentiful along the Friday-night circuit, and Indira, despite her summer flu and polytheism, was always a possibility.

One day, long ago—it was his last year in the seminary, but he'd long since forgotten who was teaching the seminar—he heard a story out of the *Pirke of Rabbi Eliezer*, or the *Alphabet of Ben Sira*, or some other lost fairy-tale, about the creation of the first woman. Early on the sixth day, the apocrypha ran, before the birth of Eve, God let Adam watch while he fashioned Woman. He began with a toe bone and then added a metatarsal, an ankle bone, one leg, then the other. Once he had the skeleton, God threaded it with muscle and sinew, vein and artery, organ and flesh. He covered the whole with a layer of the smoothest skin, topped it off with the richest head of the darkest hair. When God was finished, this first woman stood before Adam, this proto-Eve, more beautiful than her successor, more beautiful than any woman since. God smiled in delight at his own creation. He'd wanted Adam to understand completely, in the same way he did, just what it meant to be a woman.

But beautiful as this woman was, all Adam could see were the toe bones and the ligaments, the capillaries and the intestines. He clenched his eyes shut and then opened them. God saw he'd been wrong. Mystery was needed. To create the woman of Adam's dreams, God had to put Adam to sleep.

So what happened to the first woman?—Sandy remembered some bright fellow student's question. Did God send her away, did God destroy her? Did He dismantle her like a used car, recycle her liver and kidneys and corneas? Sandy knew, at least he knew now, after years in the morgues and the cutting rooms. She was there, before him, the first woman, on every table. She might be missing half her head from a gunshot wound, or bloated and peeling beyond mere formal recognition from a month or two in the East River, but there she was, nevertheless, the first woman, bones and stuff and nothing else.

What happened to Eve? That was the question, or maybe just the corner of the Talmud that Sandy was given to dissect. It was Eve who was missing, Eve, the woman God gave more than just a body, the woman God gave breath, gave a soul. Eve was the woman he'd never found no matter how many times he'd dragged the river. But this presence, this ebb and flow that he felt,

231

following Madeleine from room to room. Maybe here, Nantucket, this Eden, this Eve, leading him on, down some garden path, maybe here was the discovery Madeleine had promised in her invitation, far more confusing than love.

'Wait!' Madeleine stopped Sandy with a touch on his elbow. 'This is what I wanted you to see.' They were in a windowless ante-room, more of a passageway or a closet, with only a border of mirrored lozenges below the lowered ceiling to reflect the dim electric light. Had she felt something, too, Sandy wondered, a presence? She reached forward with two long arms to open a set of double doors concealed in the wall. 'Do you know about scrimshaw, Rabbi?'

At first, Sandy couldn't tell what he was looking at. He had expected that the double doors opened up into a glass case or a china cabinet of heirlooms, a shallow closet at the most, something flat, a recess in what he'd thought was the exterior wall of the house. Instead, he saw before him a hollow, ten, twenty feet deep, a cave lit at the roof and floor with tiny Christmas bulbs. The double doors must have opened into some hidden tower, a round space in the four-square symmetry of the Starbuck mansion, a secret grotto within the Quaker simplicity of Nantucket. The presence was so strong here, the feeling that this room was the *besomim* box, the censer, of the wisteria fragrance, that Sandy was unable, for a moment, to answer.

'Whalebone,' Madeleine said. 'One hundred and fifty years of whalebone.' She took his hand again, and he felt the pressure of her fingers as she led him into the room.

'A hundred and fifty years of Starbuck men going to sea, carving their lives on whalebone with knives and ink.' She pointed to the lights—not lights at all, but shining whale teeth, lit from below so that the India ink of their engravings, their whaling ships and sea monsters, glowed with an underwater incandescence. It wasn't just a blue grotto she had led him into, but the very jaw of a whale, fully open, the palate raised high enough for the tallest Jonah. The full skull, top and bottom, had been fitted into the cave, the room carved around it. Row upon row of teeth— Madeleine showed him each unique design and date, the signature and whereabouts of its Starbuck artist.

'A harpoon boat off Iceland,' she said. 'C. G. Starbuck, my grandfather's grandfather, 1843. Palm trees and hula girls,'—she pointed to another—'Pitcairn Island, T. Coffin Starbuck, his nephew, 1874.' Behind the teeth, along the curved wall of the room, a hanging garden of other artefacts—scrimshaw bowls, scrimshaw clocks, scrimshaw pipes—led down to the back of the throat.

Sandy followed the curve with Madeleine, her head bent as much in reverence as from the lowering ceiling. He was impressed—it would be a good story to file away for after-dinner conversation, maybe even insert into some other Friday night sermon, in an Iowa or an Illinois that knew not the whale. But this wasn't it, not yet. There was something else Madeleine wanted him to see. She led him deeper into the room, to the very gullet of the whale, where a thicket of walking sticks was wedged as a screen against future Jonahs.

Madeleine lifted her free hand. 'Here.' Very simply. Here. The fragrance was overwhelming, and Sandy understood. This is what she had meant in her postscript, this is what she wanted him to see. Here, in the centre of the thicket, its scrimshaw fingerboard shining like a ripe fruit, floated a violin.

Long before forensics and seminary, the violin—not *this* violin, but the violin as a way of life—had once been the cornerstone of Sandy's faith. In his thinner youth, with his bar mitzvah passed, when he spent every vacant minute with his hands wrapped around a violin, Sandy believed in a soul—not the human soul, perhaps, but the soul of the violin, a conjunction of fingers and wood and string that was greater than the sum of its parts. It was a transcendence that didn't add up, an experience he couldn't explain. It gave him a power over people very different from the one that later made the telephone ring in the small hours of the night. It frightened others and it frightened him, the soul of the violin. Even after it became clear that this soul would only take him as far as the first violin section of a third-rate orchestra and he began playing with long-haired guitarists and barefoot girls, Sandy continued to believe in that ineffable something called Music.

Then, in the doldrums of the Seventies, when it looked like disco was on its way to annihilating everything he found beautiful and potentially profitable about his way of playing music, Sandy

233

found himself slouching towards the seminary. While he had always gravitated towards displaced persons, he had never had much to do with Jews and Jewishness, at least not in the self-congratulatory, secret handshake kind of a way. But he found the seminary compatible, a distant, intellectual place that left him alone, by and large, and provided him with a free dorm room when he made the decision to seek his explanations of the world in the study of medicine over at the Mt. Sinai hospital.

He had planned on finishing his rabbinical courses and entering a graduate programme in medical research. But his Talmud classes gave him basic tools of investigation that seemed more suited to criminology than the study of origins, and the little bit of preaching he had to do to fulfil his rabbinical requirements gave him a view of the human heart that set him apart from the corpse-cutters in forensics. He found he had a gift of recognition, solving mysteries with a single bone the way dowsers find water with a single willow branch. So he switched to forensics, and he continued, albeit with the irregularity forced by circumstance, to play the violin.

He couldn't say when it happened, but with every autopsy, with every dissection into parts, his desire, his will to play the violin grew weaker and weaker. His fingers, once so adept at jumping positions, at finding the pitch, the exact timbre and vibrato for the music, grew more accustomed to weighing livers and reading femurs. First the violin, then music disappeared, leaving only the scattered ashes of notes.

'How?' Sandy began.

'It's my mother's,' Madeleine whispered. 'She brought it with her from France after the War.'

Sandy stepped closer, squatted down so that the bridge of the scrimshaw violin was level with his chin. It was a strange-looking beast, the violin, one of those freaks of nature, a calcium-white scrimshaw fingerboard—in place of the usual ebony—standing out like an albino against the varnished maple of the body. The carving on the fingerboard was exquisite. It was the figure of a mermaid, her hair spreading down from the scroll, her tail flowing down to the spumy sea, down where the rosin of the bow leaves white caps on the strings. In the distance, behind the mermaid's left shoulder, Leviathan spouted a carnivorous threat, a whale boat already protruding like an after-dinner toothpick—unrealistically if Sandy remembered his Melville—from his enormous jaws. It was a carving of a certain beauty, Sandy had enough intermediate aesthetics to recognize that. But there was a menace in the whale and, now that he looked more closely, in the mermaid too—not the next victim, but a co-conspirator, the lure, the bait that drew the men to the sea, into their boats and ultimately to their biblical deaths. Strange as it looked, the violin meant she knew. Madeleine knew about him and music and the violin, as if she, twenty years younger though she was, had been there at his own creation.

'It is the only scrimshaw violin in the world.' Sandy turned. The voice came full, with the husky depth of a Jeanne Moreau, from a tiny shadow in the far light of the hallway.

'Sandy,' Madeleine said, leading him over to the shadow, 'my mother, Françoise. Mama, Rabbi Lincoln.' Sandy followed Madeleine out of the mouth of the whale. The old lady was standing just far enough away from the light for a halo of shadow to blind him to her details.

'Mrs Starbuck,' he took the old lady's hand, 'I am overwhelmed.' He pointed into the grotto, and most specifically towards the deep distance where the violin floated like an extra rib in its own light.

'Yes,' she said, letting her hand go limp. 'My violin. A gift from a soldier.' Sandy tried to imagine old Mrs Starbuck dancing in the street of some French seaport—where would French whalers have sailed from? Brest?—with a laughing GI.

'Do you play?' Sandy asked. Looking down into her eyes for the first time, Sandy saw a deep yellow within the sockets that, despite the hatred that fired out from the pupils, spoke of a death imminent enough—the pulse, the general torpor of the palm he could feel in his practised hand, Sandy guessed a year, a little more, a little less—to excuse all behaviour.

'Once,' she said. 'My late husband, alas, he had no ear for music. But once I played.' She withdrew her hand and turned down the hallway. 'Like you.' Had she been able to read his eyes, his palm? 'But now it is time for dinner.'

There must have been fifty people in the ballroom. They stood and applauded Sandy as he entered between the two Starbuck women and took his seat at the head table. Candles, the dim light of the harbour filtering in through a full wall of French windows opening out into a garden, flowers—Sandy had been fêted by a number of congregations, but this was something well out of the ordinary. Even David smiled over to him from the second table, happy to be banished, Sandy guessed, to talk real estate.

Sandy felt—well, he had never been married, but he felt in the daze of a bridegroom being led to the altar. And why not? If intermarriage wasn't a sin, as he had explained in his talk, then why not this? Why not be celebrated by all these Jews, all these Jews whom he had taught, through the miracle of forensics, that morality, the commandment to treat all people as equal under the skin, was more important than survival? All these Jews whom he had forgiven for renting condos during the school vacations, for giving their children sailing lessons, for generally letting them sow their wild oats among alien corn and chowder?

What was it to be a Jew, after all? Wasn't the connection, the connection he'd felt once upon a time with the violin, the connection a violin now made between him and Madeleine, and, yes, even her tiny, French mother, wasn't all this beyond sects? Sandy felt—even as he blessed the wine and made the *motzi* over the sourdough challah—no more a Jew than old Mrs Starbuck. The joys of the Jewish people, their accomplishments, their Einsteins and Heifetzes and Hillels and Maimonideses, their Israels and their Sinais and their Holocausts with their bones and their teeth—Sandy didn't, he couldn't share these canine attachments. Teeth were teeth. And some teeth—he looked over to Madeleine, smiling at him about their secret scrimshaw upstairs—were works of art.

Wouldn't this be something, he thought—Madeleine's mezzo-soprano leading the grace after the meal, holier and faster and more lovely than the rest—to leave the laboratory and civil service and death and make a life up here on the island with this woman? Madeleine could stay with her silent David, have children with him, the whole nuptial package. He would counsel these people, why not, the bridge ladies, the debutantes, loosen his belt and listen to their issues over iced tea and Planter's Punch. Maybe he'd even find a violin. All Sandy wanted was the daily walk—he knew nothing of the island but he saw clearly the scrub forests, the heather-covered badlands, the bird sanctuary—the walk along the beach with Madeleine, the occasional pressure of fingers on palm. Anything, as long as he could get a daily fix of this breeze, this wisteria breath that made him believe, with the pure exultation of his barefoot youth, in the soul.

Sandy was deep in the fog of these ruminations, when a new sound came to him, the sound of bells, a lighthouse warning him away from the rocks. At the second table, David Gordon was leading a tinkling of forks against glasses.

'Rabbi.' Old Mrs Starbuck raised herself up with a difficulty more profound than disease. 'It has been an honour, indeed, to entertain you tonight.' Enthusiastic applause came from the four corners of the ballroom, as much for the old lady's capitulation as for the magnificence of the dinner. 'I know it is not polite to ask a guest to sing for his supper,'—there was a gaggle of titters over by the French windows—'but I was pleased to see that you admired my violin.'

Sandy became aware, first of the fragrance, and then of the movement off his port shoulder. One of the waiters was standing, a bow in one hand, a violin in the other.

'It's been fifteen, more, twenty years,' Sandy pleaded, knowing it would do no good.

'It has been twice as long, Rabbi,' Mrs Starbuck smiled, 'since my violin has been played. We are understanding people, we Starbucks, *n'est-ce pas?'*

'Hear, hear!' one of the voices by the French windows shouted out, and people who had wandered off to the bathroom or out into the garden for a smoke rushed back in to the murmur that the Rabbi was going to play old Mrs Starbuck's scrimshaw violin.

'Please, Sandy.' He hadn't seen her come about. Madeleine, herself, was urging him to his feet, her hand gripping his arm as if it were the neck of the violin. There was the mermaid, the whale, even more enticing out of the water of its glass case. He hadn't even held an instrument in the second half of his life. But the weight, the curves, the smell—he knew he couldn't resist, and he

237

knew equally well that he had been hoping for this from the moment he had seen the instrument. He took the fiddle.

The room had gone silent, the candles alone flickered among the last crumbs of dessert. They were all watching him. What should he play? 'Summertime' was his first thought, a little bit of dusky Gershwin, a cross-generational tune by a nice Jewish composer that he felt he could negotiate with dignity. But 'Summertime' was too light for the occasion and there was always the danger that the audience might insist that he follow it with another piece.

Bach—that's what the violin was saying to him—play some Bach on my vacant strings, play some Bach into my lonely belly. So Bach it was—the Vivace from Bach's 'G minor Sonata', a perpetual motion of a piece, cascading sixteenth-notes from beginning to end, a real Jewish God of Vengeance, Moby-Dick of a piece, quick and short enough for a Nantucket summer crowd. The Vivace in G minor, Sandy decided, with its triplet whitecaps, its perpetual unease—but easy enough that he'd had it memorized before he was old enough to *daven*. Sandy tucked the chin rest between his beard and shoulder, tuned the strings, and, with a bow to the Starbuck women, began.

The violin was brilliant—that was his first reaction. Who'd have suspected that an instrument exposed to the salt and fog of Nantucket could retain such vibrancy, such a confident voice as he passed easily through the personalities of the four strings. Still, there was something odd about the violin. It must be a top-heaviness due to the scrimshaw, Sandy thought, or the cloying smell of a violin that is polished more than it is played.

But gradually he heard, or rather, not heard, but felt a queasiness about the brilliance, felt it, not in his mind, but in the tips of his fingers as they pressed on the strings and met the scrimshaw of the fingerboard. He shook it off as a kind of craziness, thinking, now I have my first finger on the whale, now my third on the breast of the mermaid, no wonder I feel odd.

That wasn't it. There was another feeling, another sensitivity he had developed, even through the plastic gloves of forensics. It wasn't the design, but the fingerboard itself that was speaking to him every time his fingers pressed down on her surface. Had this violin belonged to some sad, young widow, who had memorialized the death of her whaling husband on this instrument of melancholy? Was the ghost—and being on Nantucket, Sandy permitted himself ghosts—of the widow, or maybe the ghosts of widow and husband together, watching over this violin, keeping it tuned, in tone, imbuing it with a despair that lived on long after their bodies had returned to the sea?

This fantasy—starring Madeleine as the bereaved young thing and Sandy himself as the waterlogged tar—inspired him through the first half of the Vivace. It added beauty to his playing, he thought. Surely, this was it, the connection with Madeleine, the presence that had gripped his hand the moment he stepped on to the portico of the Starbuck mansion.

With this confidence, he moved into the second half and allowed his eyes to lift from the violin to his audience. That's when it struck him. There were the men, sitting with their blazers and their Scotches, their hair long and loosened by the Starbuck feast and summer. But next to them, where once there had been women, sat lattice upon lattice of bones and sinew. Over by the French windows, the giggly young things had been reduced to cheekbones and marrow. Across the table—no longer an aged French lady with a yellow eye, but a rotting liver and badly stitched flesh.

Sandy blinked once, twice. There were the men, there was David, looking more than faintly bored and dreaming about who knew what. But blink as he might, he could no longer see the women, no longer see old Mrs Starbuck and the bridge ladies, the matrons and the debutantes, Jewish and otherwise. Worst of all, Madeleine had disappeared. The chair which moments before had supported the lanky bottom of his soulful Eve now held yards of intestines, kilometres of blood vessels, miles of hair, which wound through the room, around the legs of the tables, through the arms of the chandelier, delicate as lace, up to the inky strands that fell from the head of the mermaid on the scrimshaw fingerboard.

Sandy's music, the music of the violin, had scraped all sympathy, all humanity to the bone. He was back in the time before Eve, on the dissecting table of the sixth day, and blinking did no good. So he closed his eyes and kept playing, hoping that the dreams of Adam, the dreams that had grown a soul on to the

239

anatomy of Eve, that had blinded him to the clinical details, would clear the salt mist from his vision.

But he couldn't close his fingers. As he played on, the truth grabbed the calluses at the tips and rode the nerves up arm and neck to his slightly balding brain. It was the fingerboard. The fingerboard was not scrimshaw at all.

Madeleine had been mistaken. It wasn't whalebone that old Mrs Starbuck had brought with her from Europe after the War, this was no Nantucket ghost story—that was the message his fingers tapped out, had been tapping out from the first note. The fingerboard of this violin had once been a woman. This fingerboard had been meticulously carved from the humerus, the upper arm-bone, of a human woman, who, if not an Eve, had been, at least, a mature woman, a young mother, five feet three, his practised fingers told him, a mother who had known terrible agony at the end. And as the message filtered through to his ears and turned the Bach into a *nigun*, into a Polish melody, a kaddish, a song for the dead, he realized who this woman was. It wasn't Madeleine—it hadn't been her breath, as he had thought all evening—and it certainly wasn't old Mrs Starbuck. He didn't know the name of this woman, but he knew where she had died, what the music was that he had refused to hear for years. He heard the cry of this woman, of the nameless soul that had drained all the humanity from the women in the Starbuck ballroom, not in the voice of Selwyn's mother, but in a pitch and a timbre that sang directly and only to Sandy's ears, a song of history that all the forensics of the world could never explain.

And of course, because the fence he had built around his soul could only fall post by post, Sandy finished the Vivace. But the people who listened, and even those who were inclined to continue their conversations in whispers, remember a foggy chill as Rabbi Lincoln finished playing and, without a smile, or even a nod to his hostess, walked across the ballroom and through the French doors down to the harbour to give the scrimshaw violin a proper burial. Many of them said afterwards that it was months, even years, before they could listen to Bach again. As for Rabbi Doctor Alexander Abba Lincoln, there were no more trips to Nantucket, no more Friday nights. □

CLIVE SINCLAIR
A SOAP OPERA FROM HELL

Episode One

The facts of life. He learns them at Bournemouth, in the following order. (1) The body is a fragile thing. His brother, not yet four, trips over a beach ball and snaps his leg. He is in hospital for three months, while the fractured limb heals. (2) Life can be short. A pair of fledgling blue tits hop around the hotel swimming pool. All the bathers laugh. It is like watching a Disney cartoon. Until a tom-cat appears. He is not worried. In cartoons the predator always goes hungry. But this is a real cat, which eats the birds, one after the other. (3) Appearances can be deceptive. Sometimes the family visits the south coast in winter. He has a photograph of his brother, dressed as a pirate, shaking hands with a man disguised as Father Christmas. The former has just won first prize in the fancy dress competition. He comes nowhere, is zippered from head to toe in ersatz ursine fur. Not a very convincing bear. Not a very convincing boy either. 'You have a very pretty daughter,' say a couple to his parents. Had he really been a bear he would have devoured them on the spot, leaving only the bones. After the competition there is a tea party. He dips his spoon in a bowl, and delivers the contents to his mouth, only to experience temporary revulsion, rather than the anticipated delight. The stuff looks like chocolate ice cream, but isn't cold. On the contrary, it is warm and spongy; a shocking and horrid impostor. (4) Mind and body are not indivisible. Visiting Corfe Castle for the first time he sprints up the hill towards the picturesque ruins. Reaching the shattered portal he turns around and, confronted by the Isle of Purbeck far below, freezes on the spot. His head is not swimming. It is not vertigo. He has simply ceased to believe in gravity, does not trust his feet to stay earthed. Or perhaps it is the ground beneath that he doubts. Either way, he is stranded.

Episode Two

University. His parents deliver him in the Jag. On the return journey his father suffers a panic attack and is unable to drive in excess of twenty miles per hour. No explanation is ever offered for this uncharacteristic lapse. At the Freshers' Ball, that same night, he dances with the girl who is destined to be his wife. It is an unlikely destiny. She finds her partner physically repulsive, and accepts his invitation only because she is too kind to do otherwise. He asks her because he fancies her friend (already snapped up). The campus is equally ignorant of its future, being little more than a building site. Students are accommodated elsewhere; on a redundant airfield. The former dormitories have been partitioned with plywood, granting individual privacy, though the bathrooms remain communal. The tiled floors are stone cold throughout the winter. In spring the pollen count breaks all records. He never stops sneezing. At the end of his first academic year he is informed that he has been lucky, has been assigned a room on the campus, always assuming that Denys Lasdun's famous ziggurats will be habitable at the commencement of the winter term. He greets the news with indifference, since he does not expect to survive the summer.

Episode Three

War and Peace. 'You realize the dangers,' says the recruiting officer, when he volunteers to fly out to Israel on the eve of hostilities, 'it is possible that you will come under fire.' He shrugs his shoulders stoically. *Que sera sera.* Although his parents are passionate supporters of their endangered co-religionists they aren't too keen on donating their first-born to the cause. 'What's the problem?' he grumbles, looking at his father. 'You were prepared to sacrifice your life for the Spanish republic.' 'Up to a point,' he replies, 'the point being Waterloo Station.' Unfortunately they are arguing in his erstwhile bedroom, with its Lascaux-style wallpaper, and picture windows. These afford fine views of the mirror-image house across the garden. His mind wanders. He wonders if the buxom au pair is still as careless with her curtains. He acknowledges his disadvantage; this is hardly the place in which to feel a wholly autonomous unit, a grown-up. Nevertheless, he persists. He is determined to be a hero; heroic at least. The dispute is terminated by the arrival of Yves Montand, visible only to the eager young warrior. 'Let it be,' advises Yves, '*la guerre est finie.*' As it is, in six days.

Episode Four

The big question. He arrives, not as a volunteer, but as an ordinary tourist. Though the atmosphere is anything but ordinary. People watch newsreels in the cinema, and cheer whenever Moshe Dayan or Yitzhak Rabin appear. He stays on the coast, and shares his room with a convalescent soldier. After a few days he ascends to Jerusalem. Most pilgrims arrive with a hard question. Where do we come from? Why are we here? Where are we going? Does God exist? He is no exception. What he wants to know is this: Where is his friend Pamela? She has left London and enrolled at the Hebrew University. This is the limit of his knowledge. He has no address. What can he do? He searches the campus. But she is one among ten thousand, a needle in a haystack. It is hopeless. He admits defeat, and joins the other passengers-in-waiting outside the university gates. That's when he sees her, sitting in the back of a departing bus. She sees him too, waves, and disembarks at the next stop, where their friendship begins anew. Was their meeting simply a coincidence? Or was it another twist of fate in the city of crossed destinies?

Episode Five

Make love not war. After graduation our hero flies to America. Another university; the University of California at Santa Cruz. Alas, he misses the summer of love by a whisker. But is in time to demonstrate against the war in Vietnam. Joan Baez comes to the campus; not to sing, but to encourage new conscripts to tear up their draft cards. He meets Linda R. in Los Angeles. A friend of a friend, described by the latter as the most experienced virgin west of the Mississippi. She looks the part; Doris Day sans bleach. The must-see movie is *Z*. When Yves Montand is struck down by fascists in the first reel Linda R. grabs her date's hand. She continues to grip it throughout the movie. So he has great expectations when she agrees to return his visit the following weekend. Nixon, unfortunately, prefers armour to *amour*. He orders his air force to bomb Cambodia. More demonstrations. 'Apologies,' says Linda R., calling from UCLA, 'I'll have to take a rain check. We're organizing a big protest, and I need to be part of it.' She writes him a few passionate notes, but he never sees her again. He also receives letters from his future wife, doing voluntary service in St Vincent, and an invitation to Pamela's more imminent marriage in Jerusalem.

Episode Six

Two weddings. The first takes place at the King David Hotel, on a terrace overlooking the walls of the Old City. A few days after the ceremony he accompanies Pamela and her new husband to see *L'Aveu*. Yves Montand stars. He plays a character based upon Rudolf Slansky, sometime vice-premier of Czechoslovakia, who is falsely accused of being a traitor and—this awakens a flicker of interest in the restless cineasts—a Zionist. *L'Aveu* means 'the confession', and Montand's torturers do their best to extract one. Still trusting the party, the prisoner persuades himself that an error has occurred, but finally is forced to accept the dismal truth. He refuses to sign, thereby saving his soul, if not his neck. The struggle bores the audience, which emits a collective yawn. Individuals fidget in their iron-framed chairs. They place their empties on the cement floor, and watch the bottles roll down the slope towards the screen. They talk. They laugh. Unluckily two of the worst offenders are beside the happy couple and their friend from overseas. They treat Pamela's strictures with contempt. Their lack of respect—not for her, but for the tragedy re-enacted on the screen—drives her to distraction. And so, as they leave, she spits in their faces. The reaction is violent, and directed at her two male escorts (who retreat, con brio, and thereby preserve their skins). The wedding guest departs. His weapon is the biro, the poison pen. He writes a novel, and eventually marries Fran, the girl he asked to dance thirteen years before. The ceremony is performed at the registry office in Bury St Edmunds. It takes seven minutes.

Episode Seven

A normal life. He shouldn't complain; against all expectation it lasts for nineteen years. They live in Blackheath, Malmesbury, Bury St Edmunds, Santa Cruz (where their son is born), Uppsala (briefly), and St Albans. His wife teaches children with behavioural and learning difficulties. He writes books. At night he locks the doors, looks in on his sleeping son, slips into bed with his naked wife. He cannot believe his luck. Others begin their day with a jog around the block, in the confident expectation of averting the evil decree. He is not so ambitious. He merely hopes that his nerves will be sufficiently strong when the blow falls. To prepare them he fits in a daily session of light worrying. The first test comes on 12 July 1993, when his father makes the understatement of the year: 'We've got a problem.' His mother survives septicaemia, only to succumb to peritonitis (when her bowel is accidentally perforated in an attempt to uncover the source of the infection). She doesn't die at once. In fact she endures emergency surgery and several days in intensive care, where one of the drugs makes her crazy. She imagines she is in a hotel. She thinks it is breakfast, and the sheet a slice of bread. She holds the cotton between her fingers and nibbles an edge. Her son finds a doctor and explains that this behaviour is out of character. The drug is withdrawn, and his mother restored. She is also returned to a general ward, where another doctor assures the family: 'Mrs S. is not only stable, but recovering.' How little he knows her. When a nurse reveals the stoma bag for the first time she says, 'The operation was a mistake.' The following day, 24 August, she is feverish. A fan is placed beside the bed. In the afternoon she requests toast. A nurse brings a plate; two slices, cut diagonally, with a pot of Marmite and some pats of butter. His mother takes a few bites, then announces: 'I've had enough.' 'But you enjoyed it,' says his optimistic wife. Does his mother smile? Either way she dies three hours later. 'I've had enough,' are her

247

last words. His wife outlives her mother-in-law by less than a year. He remembers her last day of consciousness. How can he forget? The unassuageable terror apparent in her eyes. The fact that she too plucks at the sheet and puts it in her mouth.

Episode Eight

To the beach. He wants to get away. But he has inherited polycystic kidney disease from his mother, and is in end-stage renal failure himself. 'Can I risk a trip to Israel?' he asks his doctor. 'Go,' he is told, 'but be prepared for dialysis on your return.' In Tel Aviv he informs his thirteen-year-old son of his condition, and that he has a fifty per cent chance of passing it on. The boy absorbs the information. 'OK,' he says, 'now let's go to the beach.' They also fly to Egypt, hoping that the perfumes of Arabia will sweeten the bitter season. Pamela accompanies them, to protect the boy lest his father sickens. From Cairo they take the night train to Luxor, arriving before dawn. A guide leads them to the banks of the Nile, where they board the boat that will ferry them to the West Bank, the dominion of the dead. The full moon is descending, the sun warming up. As moonlight falls upon the still waters he unexpectedly recalls a sentence from a famous story by Anton Chekhov. Later, while parading in slow motion along the corniche at the blaze of noon, he feels that he has been transported to Yalta, and half expects to encounter the spectral presence of Anna Sergeyevna, the lady with the little dog. Instead he meets his new reality instructor; Lucy, the dialysis nurse. She teaches him how to inject himself with erythropoietin, to counteract his anaemia. He is on dialysis for eleven months, at which point he receives a transplant.

Episode Nine

Viva Zapata. The new modus vivendi lasts until 11 December 1996. That morning he awakes convinced that he has been very ill during the night, but can recall no nightmare, nor find any other evidence. He prepares breakfast. The telephone rings. It is still only seven-thirty. Will he accept a reverse-charges call from Mr S.? 'You'll never guess where I am,' says his father. It has to be one of two places; prison or hospital. He guesses correctly. He finds his father is sitting up in bed. His father has a good colour, but is in the coronary care unit. He explains that he had been playing bridge and was denouncing Netanyahu and his government, when he began to feel more and more unwell. He returned home and telephoned his doctor, who wouldn't come out. She told him to summon an ambulance if he was worried. He was. He did. But he didn't call either of his sons, lest they should worry too. By the afternoon he doesn't look so well. By the evening he is wearing an oxygen mask. 'Sleep well,' say son and grandson, as they depart. The following morning the former receives the 'come quickly' phone call all children dread. He collects his own son from school. They are greeted by a nurse at the reception desk. She smiles. Her teeth are tiny and exceptionally white. Could it have been a false alarm? She says, 'Let me show you to a family room, where a doctor will come to see you.' 'Are you telling me he's dead?' he asks. 'I'm afraid so,' she replies. His father has been placed in a side ward. They take their leave, watched by another nurse. Then they have lunch in a Mexican cantina across the road. After the meal he makes the funeral arrangements. His father is buried the following day, alongside his mother. In 1991 he cooked an alfresco meal to celebrate their golden wedding anniversary. Later he took some panoramic photographs of the family in the back garden. The scenery remains the same—the fig tree, the oak, and the spruce—but the figures in the foreground are sparse; his son, his brother, his two nephews. Gone are his mother (peritonitis, aged seventy-three), his father (heart attack, aged eighty-one), his wife (osteosarcoma, aged forty-six), his sister-in-law (breast cancer, aged forty-two). The house is on the market for less than a week. Relatives and friends are invited to see his mother's paintings in situ before the new owners take possession. Most hang in his old bedroom, long since redecorated. However, the well-remembered wallpaper remains inside the fitted wardrobes, the troglodytic testament of his ancestral self. The Last Picture Show is over.

Now he must remove the paintings from the hooks; luxuriant flowers and trees vanish in the blink of an eye, leaving a vacant space, a suburban desert. It reminds him of something. Of course! *The Cherry Orchard*, act four. Instead of a concluding 'twang', there's the owlish howl of the burglar alarm as he closes the front door. Shalom, finito, the end. Within days newcomers will change the code, turning him into a stranger, exiling him from his past.

Episode Ten

Dead is every word. He finds he can readily describe the externals, but lacks a vocabulary to explain his feelings. No. The vocabulary exists. What is missing is an internal dictionary to provide individual meanings. He is familiar with the word 'grief', but cannot be sure he has experienced it. How can he make such an assumption, if he has not shed a single tear? He has forgotten how to cry, which facial muscles to use. Therefore it comes as no surprise when an ophthalmist informs him that the tears he does produce—the consequence of various allergies—are deficient, poor-quality facsimiles of the real thing. The ophthalmist writes him a prescription, which he exchanges for a pot of artificial tears. Later he reads that genuine tears are life preservers. It seems they rid the body of harmful chemicals. The death rate among widowers who do not weep is alarmingly high. Serves me right, he thinks. When he was a student at the University of California he wrote a long paper entitled, 'Towards a Definition of Jewish-American Literature'. One of its major themes was contained in these lines from a Yiddish poem by Alter Esselin, 'Dead is every word./Would you say to a woman you really love,/'I love you'?/Unless with tears or a violin/The words no longer ring true.' He remains fascinated by the curse of self-consciousness, the impossibility of spontaneously translating feeling into language. The sad truth is that what the heart knows cannot be uttered; it emerges banal, inarticulate. Art is required to enable the hearer—or reader—to share the feeling. But by resorting to artifice the speaker—or writer—compromises the original impulse, subjects it to manipulation, works it up for the benefit of an audience. The writer finally has no choice; literature must always come before life. He writes a book called *The Lady with the Laptop*. It includes a description of his wife's death. His wife had an aunt who drowned herself. She left her niece a fur coat. A friend, seeing it for the first time, asked: 'What poor creature sacrificed itself to provide you with such a coat?' He couldn't help himself. 'Her aunt,' he said. His wife, not knowing whether to laugh or cry, did both. Now, if someone were to ask a similar question about his book, he would have to reply: 'My wife.' The book wins a literary prize. As a result its author is invited to the Jerusalem Book Fair.

Episode Eleven

Jorge Semprun. The highlight of the fair is the presentation of the Jerusalem Prize to Jorge Semprun. 'Have you heard of him?' he asks Pamela. She shakes her head. 'Me neither,' he replies. The ceremony is preceded by music. Mario Vargas Llosa supplies a passionate appreciation of the life and works. Semprun studied philosophy in Paris. But abandoned his studies when the Nazis occupied France. He joined the resistance, was betrayed, tortured, sent to Buchenwald. A finishing school, of sorts. Liberation arrived, but Semprun's struggles continued. He subdued the impulse to write. Instead he became a communist and dedicated his life to the defeat of Franco. The radical therapy failed. He was expelled from the party. In the end he had no choice, he had to write; novels, memoirs, film scripts. Mario Vargas Llosa names the movies. 'Ah,' thinks a listener, 'I know this man better than I thought.' He purchases a copy of Semprun's new book, *Literature or Life*. The title reminds him of his own abandoned thesis. The coincidence pleases him, as does the fact that he begins reading it on 11 April, the same day that Buchenwald was liberated. The book is a meditation upon Semprun's capture and incarceration there. It begins at the end, so to speak, with the liberation of the camp fifty-two years ago to the day. The coincidences multiply: ten years previously—11 April 1987—Semprun was working on a novel when he felt an unaccountable compulsion to compose

251

something other. So he recreated a strange encounter with three allied officers—two Britons and a Frenchman—which occurred on the day after liberation. Having recorded the scene to his satisfaction Semprun collected the accumulated pages and placed them in a file which he unhesitatingly marked, 'Literature or Death'. Only then did he learn that Primo Levi had taken his own life that very day. Semprun ascribes such curious linkages to 'a strategy of the unconscious mind'. It pleases his reader to believe that some similar force caused him to open the book exactly ten years later. There is the pathetic fallacy, in which an indifferent universe is supposed to reflect the prevailing emotional atmosphere, providing storms for troubled souls and sunshine for the contented. And there is biblio-fallacy, in which the reader believes that the author is speaking exclusively to him, or even—in more severe cases—for him. Both are a subspecies of paranoia.

Episode Twelve

Literature or life. He believes that he has found his internal dictionary, the book that can define his feelings. True he is merely acquainted with a cancerous force independent of human will, while Semprun had to contend with 'absolute evil'. Nevertheless, when he reads the following, he dares nod his head in agreement. 'I want only to forget, nothing else. I find it unjust, almost indecent, to have made it through eighteen months of Buchenwald without a single minute of anguish, without a single nightmare, carried along by constantly renewed curiosity, sustained by an insatiable appetite for life . . . having survived all that—only to find myself from then on the occasional prey of the most naked, the most intense despair, a despair nourished as much by life itself, by its serenity and joys, as by the memory of death.' Semprun now lives—or tries to live—'with the carefree immortality of the revenant'. He has experienced death, and feels that—unlike the rest of humanity—he is moving away from it, rather than towards it. A trajectory that is not reversed until he begins *Literature or Life* on the day that Primo Levi dies. His reader also rides the roller coaster of exhilaration and misery, with senses heightened, as if by a drug; all the while attended by an uncanny sense of untouchability (vanished since the death of his father—someone said it was an 'inevitable event'—the word 'inevitable' did it). He too has been spared insomnia or nightmares—at least until he dreamed his father's death. Like Semprun he remains curious, as well as stricken. 'It helps you to hang on in a way that is impossible to evaluate, of course,' he reads, 'but is surely decisive.' Semprun quotes Primo Levi: 'I felt a deep desire to understand, I was constantly filled with a curiosity that someone later described, in fact, as nothing less than cynical.' Suddenly his own cynicism seems more forgivable.

Episode Thirteen

The material of fiction. While still in the camp Semprun and other survivors initiated a discussion: how should they tell their stories, so that people would listen, and understand? We must tell the truth, insists one, with no fancy stuff. Semprun disagrees: 'Telling a story well, that means: so as to be understood. You can't manage it without a bit of artifice. Enough artifice to make it art!' Yes, says another; the essential truth of the experience can be imparted only through literature. Later Semprun describes the effect newsreel footage of Buchenwald had upon him. 'The grey, sometimes hazy images, filmed with the jerky motions of a hand-held camera, acquired an inordinate and overwhelming dimension of reality that my memories themselves could not attain.' It really happened; Buchenwald was no singular nightmare. Even so, says Semprun, the film, silent and unannotated, could do little more than turn the spectator into a sickened voyeur. In order to convey the reality of the experience itself, a writer would have 'to treat the documentary reality . . . like the material of fiction'. His reader breathes a little easier; perhaps he is not such a cold-hearted monster after all. Except . . . Semprun has a responsibility to history, and to the memory of the unnumbered dead, while he, on the other hand, has no imprimatur but his own loss. Just as an unknown woman donated her kidney to revitalize his body, so the beloved dead have revived his career. He recalls sitting on a log

253

with Dr R. outside the Cancer Ward, discussing the disposal of his dying wife's organs. In the event—given the systemic nature of cancer—only her corneas are taken. And her death, which he reserves for himself.

Episode Fourteen

The story of his life. Semprun may have favoured life, but literature was his *raison d'être*. When he finally returns to Ettersberg, which accommodated both Goethe and Buchenwald, the best and the worst, he is forced to acknowledge his dual inheritance. Like the Ancient Mariner he must tell and retell his story. His earlier visit to the museum where Goethe once lived took place in the first anarchistic days of liberty. He was accompanied by an American officer. They found the house in the charge of a curator with Nazi sympathies. So they locked him in a closet. This is the story that Semprun has to tell; of a civilization *sans pareil*, whose serenity is forever shaken by a Nazi hammering on the cupboard door. Let the beast out at your peril. Pamela, who has helped Semprun's new admirer keep hold of life, is driving the two of them—father and son—to the airport at Lod. All week he has been determined to utter the word love, preferably as the component of a comprehensible sentence. Now he has about thirty kilometres to say something. He counts the kilometres; twenty, ten, five. Still nothing. Finally, as they unload their bags, he manages: 'Take care of yourself, there are not many people in the world that I love.' Fuck, he thinks, as they wait to board their plane, that was nowhere near what I wanted to say. The story of his life.

Episode Fifteen

The answer. About a week before he flew to Israel for the Jerusalem Book Fair he stood in his attic contemplating the heavens. Hale-Bopp was unmissable, a spume of silver in the north-western quadrant. A picture-book comet, a fantasy from childhood made real. He could have happily watched it all night. No aliens contacted him, nor did he hear divine voices. Instead he was transported to the shores of the mighty Pacific, to the cliffs near Santa Cruz, from where he scanned the ocean for the salty exhalations of the grey whales. Whales are miraculous in their own right, fishy myths made flesh, but there is something equally marvellous about their presence in the sea, a secret life-force concealed beneath a blank sheet of water. Equivalents are the sculpture hidden in the stone, the words that wait to fill an empty book, the ancient treasure baked beneath a crust of earth, the secret bubbling up from the subconscious, the comet in the heavens—a celestial leviathan, snorting silver sequins. It gave him some comfort to observe that there was indeed something new under the sun. On the last afternoon of his wife's earthly existence—when she seemed entirely insensate—he suddenly became aware that she was expecting him to say something. 'Don't worry,' he said, without forethought, 'I'll keep in touch with your family.' His wife did not stir. Even so he was struck by a palpable wave of relief. So much so that he was moved to exclaim: 'It seems I've said the right thing.' He sought the comet night after night as it drifted by. The last people to witness it were the Ancient Egyptians. Now it was his turn. What was humanity to Hale-Bopp? Nothing but sentient plankton. □

Fran Sinclair 1947–1994

NOTES ON CONTRIBUTORS

AIMEE BENDER lives in Los Angeles; her first book of short stories, *The Girl in the Flammable Skirt*, will be published by Doubleday in August.

PIERRE CLASTRES lived with the Guayaki Indians in Paraguay from 1963–4. *The Chronicle of the Guayaki Indians* will be published in the UK by Faber in June 1998, and in the USA by Zone in March.

ARIEL DORFMAN is a Chilean expatriate who has made a second home in the United States. He is the author of the acclaimed play *Death and the Maiden*; his novels include *Konfidenz* and *Widows*. His memoir, *Heading South, Looking North*, will be published by Sceptre in the UK and Farrar, Straus and Giroux in the USA.

LINDA GRANT's first novel, *The Cast Iron Shore*, published in 1996, won the David Higham Fiction Prize and was shortlisted for the *Guardian* Fiction Prize. She writes a weekly column for the *Guardian*.

DAN JACOBSON's novels include *The Rape of Tamar* and *The God-Fearer*. His last book, *The Electronic Elephant*, described his travels along the 'missionary road' through southern Africa. *Heshel's Kingdom*, a family memoir, will be published by Hamish Hamilton early in 1998.

JONATHAN LEVI is the author of the novel *A Guide for the Perplexed*, published by Turtle Bay/Random House, and the recently completed *Blue Nude # 1*. He is a co-founder and former US Editor of *Granta*.

PETER MARLOW has been a member of Magnum Photos since 1981 and takes a special interest in photographing contemporary Britain. He decided to follow the Diana story when his local newsagent, who knew he was a photographer, refused to sell him a paper on the Sunday morning of her death.

JACK PICONE, a photographer with the Network agency, has covered eight wars in the past five years. His pictures have appeared in *Time*, the *Observer*, *Libération* and *Newsweek*. His documentation of the life of the Nuba is an ongoing project.

JOHN RYLE is a columnist for the *Guardian*. He visited the Nuba Mountains in 1995, and his first article about Sudan, 'The Road to Abyei', was published in *Granta* 26: Travel.

DEBORAH SCROGGINS lives in Atlanta, Georgia. A former editor and correspondent for the *Atlanta Journal and Constitution*, she is now a freelance writer.

CLIVE SINCLAIR lives in St Albans, Hertfordshire, with his teenage son. His book of essays, *A Soap Opera from Hell*, will be published by Picador in 1998. His previous book, *The Lady with the Laptop*, won both the PEN Silver Pen for fiction and the *Jewish Quarterly* award for fiction.